IT Esse

PC Hardware and

Labs and Study Guide, Third Edition

Patrick Regan

Cisco Press

800 East 96th Street

Indianapolis, Indiana 46240 USA

IT Essentials: PC Hardware and Software Labs and Study Guide, Third Edition

Patrick Regan

Copyright© 2008 Cisco Systems, Inc.

The CompTIA Authorized Quality Curriculum logo is a proprietary trademark of CompTIA. All rights reserved.

Published by:
Cisco Press
800 East 96th Street
Indianapolis, IN 46240 USA

Printed in the United States of America

Third Printing July 2009

Library of Congress Cataloging-in-Publication Data:
Regan, Patrick E.
  IT essentials : PC hardware and software labs and study guide/Patrick Regan. — 3rd ed.
    p. cm.
  ISBN-13: 978-1-58713-198-1 (pbk.)
  ISBN-10: 1-58713-198-6 (pbk.)
  1. Microcomputers. 2. Computer input-output equipment. 3. Operating systems (Computers) I. Title.
  TK7885.R38 2008
  004.16—dc22

                              2007049945

ISBN-13: 978-1-58713-198-1

ISBN-10: 1-58713-198-6

Publisher
Paul Boger

Associate Publisher
Dave Dusthimer

Cisco Representative
Anthony Wolfenden

Cisco Press Program Manager
Jeff Brady

Executive Editor
Mary Beth Ray

Managing Editor
Patrick Kanouse

Development Editor
Andrew Cupp

Senior Project Editor
Tonya Simpson

Copy Editor
Barbara Hacha

Technical Editors
Mayfield Fayose
Matt Newell

Editorial Assistant
Vanessa Evans

Book and Cover Designer
Louisa Adair

Composition
Louisa Adair

Proofreader
Williams Woods Publishing Services

Warning and Disclaimer

This book is designed to provide information about taking and passing the CompTIA A+ exam and about how to be a successful PC technician. Every effort has been made to make this book as complete and as accurate as possible, but no warranty or fitness is implied.

The information is provided on an "as is" basis. The authors, Cisco Press, and Cisco Systems, Inc. shall have neither liability nor responsibility to any person or entity with respect to any loss or damages arising from the information contained in this book or from the use of the discs or programs that may accompany it.

The opinions expressed in this book belong to the author and are not necessarily those of Cisco Systems, Inc.

Trademark Acknowledgments

All terms mentioned in this book that are known to be trademarks or service marks have been appropriately capitalized. Cisco Press or Cisco Systems, Inc., cannot attest to the accuracy of this information. Use of a term in this book should not be regarded as affecting the validity of any trademark or service mark.

Corporate and Government Sales

The publisher offers excellent discounts on this book when ordered in quantity for bulk purchases or special sales, which may include electronic versions and/or custom covers and content particular to your business, training goals, marketing focus, and branding interests. For more information, please contact: **U.S. Corporate and Government Sales**   1-800-382-3419   corpsales@pearsontechgroup.com

For sales outside the United States please contact: **International Sales**   international@pearsoned.com

Feedback Information

At Cisco Press, our goal is to create in-depth technical books of the highest quality and value. Each book is crafted with care and precision, undergoing rigorous development that involves the unique expertise of members from the professional technical community.

Readers' feedback is a natural continuation of this process. If you have any comments regarding how we could improve the quality of this book, or otherwise alter it to better suit your needs, you can contact us through e-mail at feedback@ciscopress.com. Please make sure to include the book title and ISBN in your message.

We greatly appreciate your assistance.

Americas Headquarters	Asia Pacific Headquarters	Europe Headquarters
Cisco Systems, Inc.	Cisco Systems, Inc.	Cisco Systems International BV
170 West Tasman Drive	168 Robinson Road	Haarlerbergpark
San Jose, CA 95134-1706	#28-01 Capital Tower	Haarlerbergweg 13-19
USA	Singapore 068912	1101 CH Amsterdam
www.cisco.com	www.cisco.com	The Netherlands
Tel: 408 526-4000	Tel: +65 6317 7777	www-europe.cisco.com
800 553-NETS (6387)	Fax: +65 6317 7799	Tel: +31 0 800 020 0791
Fax: 408 527-0883		Fax: +31 0 20 357 1100

Cisco has more than 200 offices worldwide. Addresses, phone numbers, and fax numbers are listed on the Cisco Website at **www.cisco.com/go/offices.**

©2007 Cisco Systems, Inc. All rights reserved. CCVP, the Cisco logo, and the Cisco Square Bridge logo are trademarks of Cisco Systems, Inc.; Changing the Way We Work, Live, Play, and Learn is a service mark of Cisco Systems, Inc.; and Access Registrar, Aironet, BPX, Catalyst, CCDA, CCDP, CCIE, CCIP, CCNA, CCNP, CCSP, Cisco, the Cisco Certified Internetwork Expert logo, Cisco IOS, Cisco Press, Cisco Systems, Cisco Systems Capital, the Cisco Systems logo, Cisco Unity, Enterprise/Solver, EtherChannel, EtherFast, EtherSwitch, Fast Step, Follow Me Browsing, FormShare, GigaDrive, GigaStack, HomeLink, Internet Quotient, IOS, IP/TV, iQ Expertise, the iQ logo, iQ Net Readiness Scorecard, iQuick Study, LightStream, Linksys, MeetingPlace, MGX, Networking Academy, Network Registrar, Packet, PIX, ProConnect, RateMUX, ScriptShare, SlideCast, SMARTnet, StackWise, The Fastest Way to Increase Your Internet Quotient, and TransPath are registered trademarks of Cisco Systems, Inc. and/or its affiliates in the United States and certain other countries.

All other trademarks mentioned in this document or Website are the property of their respective owners. The use of the word partner does not imply a partnership relationship between Cisco and any other company. (0609R)

About the Author

Patrick Regan has been a PC technician, network administrator/engineer, design architect, and security analyst for the past 16 years after graduating with a bachelor's degree in physics from the University of Akron. He has taught many computer and network classes at Sacramento local colleges (Heald College and MTI College) and has participated in and led many projects (Heald College, Intel Corporation, Miles Consulting Corporation, and Pacific Coast Companies). For his teaching accomplishments, he received the Teacher of the Year award from Heald College, and he has received several recognition awards from Intel. Previously, he worked as a product support engineer for the Intel Corporation Customer Service, a senior network engineer for Virtual Alert supporting the BioTerrorism Readiness suite, and as a senior design architect/engineer and training coordinator for Miles Consulting Corp (MCC), a premiere Microsoft Gold Certified Partner and consulting firm. He is currently a senior network engineer at Pacific Coast Companies, supporting a large enterprise network. He holds many certifications, including the Microsoft MCSE, MCSA, MCT; the CompTIA A+, Network+, Server+, Linux+, Security+, and CTT+; the Cisco CCNA; and the Novell CNE and CWNP Certified Wireless Network Administrator (CWNA).

Over the past several years, he has written several textbooks for Prentice Hall, including *Troubleshooting the PC*, *Networking with Windows 2000 and 2003*, *Linux*, *Local Area Networks*, *Wide Area Networks*, and the Acing series (*Acing the A+*, *Acing the Network+*, *Acing the Security+*, and *Acing the Linux+*). He also coauthored *Exam Cram 70-290 MCSA/MCSE Managing and Maintaining a Microsoft Windows Server 2003 Environment*, Second Edition.

About the Technical Reviewers

Mayfield Fayose has been teaching and working with computer technology since 1995 and has also been a consultant for large international corporations. He is currently working as a systems administrator and computer technology instructor. For the past eight years, Mayfield has been teaching A+ and Network+ certification programs, as well as MCP and CCNA classes. Mayfield has certifications in MCSE NT 4.0, CCNA, and A+.

Matt Newell has been with the Ohio CATC (TRECA) since 2000, serving as an IT instructor and systems administrator in its data center. At the Ohio CATC, Matt teaches instructor-level courses in IT Essentials, CCNA, Wireless, and PNIE. He has extensive experience with LAN/WAN hardware, structured cabling, and multiplatform server and desktop hardware. Over the years, Matt has gathered various IT certifications from Cisco, Microsoft, and CompTIA, and he is TRECA's technical contact for its Microsoft Certified Partner Program.

Dedications

To Jessica, my best friend and confidante. She is always there for me.

Contents at a Glance

Contents

Introduction

IT Essentials: PC Hardware and Software Labs and Study Guide is a supplemental book that helps the students in the Cisco Networking Academy course prepare to take and pass the CompTIA A+ exams (based on the 2006 objectives). The hands-on labs, worksheets, remote technician exercises, and class discussions from the course are also included within this book to practice performing tasks that will help you become a successful PC technician. By reading and completing this book, you have the opportunity to review all key concepts that the CompTIA exams cover, reinforce those concepts with hands-on exercises, and test that knowledge with review questions.

Who Should Read This Book?

This book is intended for students in the Cisco Networking Academy IT Essentials PC Hardware and Software version 4 course. This student typically is pursing a career in information technology (IT) or wants to have the working knowledge of how a computer works, how to assemble a computer, and how to troubleshoot hardware and software issues.

How This Book Is Organized

This course is divided into two main units. The first unit, covered in Chapters 1 through 10, covers the foundational knowledge that aligns with the CompTIA A+ Essentials exam (220-601). The second unit, covered in Chapters 11 through 16, explores more advanced concepts in greater depth and provides opportunities for practical application to prepare you for the specialized CompTIA A+ technician exams (220-602 for IT Technician, 220-603 for Remote Support Technician, and 220-604 for Bench Technician). You must pass both the CompTIA A+ Essentials and one of the technician exams to earn the CompTIA A+ certification.

The *Labs and Study Guide* is designed as a valuable teaching and learning tool for the Cisco Networking Academy curriculum, incorporating new features to improve your hands-on skills and reinforce the key topics of the course.

Each chapter includes a Study Guide portion and a Lab Exercises portion.

The Study Guide portion of each chapter focuses on certification exam preparation in context with the course objectives and assessments. The Study Guide section is designed to provide additional exercises and activities to reinforce your understanding of the course topics, preparing you for the course assessments and focusing on preparing for the associated certification exams.

The Lab Exercises portion of each chapter features the complete collection of the hands-on labs, worksheets, remote technician exercises, and class discussions specifically written for the IT Essentials course in the Cisco Networking Academy curriculum, reviewed by instructors and formatted and edited by Cisco Press. The labs are designed by Cisco to give students hands-on experience in a particular concept or technology.

The chapters cover the following topics:

- **Chapter 1, "Introduction to the Personal Computer"**: In this chapter you learn about IT industry certifications and then jump into identifying components of a computer system, including cases and power supplies, internal components, ports and cables, and input and output devices. The chapter also goes into system resources and their purpose.

- **Chapter 2, "Safe Lab Procedures and Tool Use"**: This chapter covers safe working conditions and procedures along with the tools and software used with personal computer components. You learn how to implement proper tool use.

- **Chapter 3, "Computer Assembly—Step by Step"**: In this step-by-step chapter you learn how to safely open the computer case, install the power supply, attach the components to the motherboard, and install the motherboard, internal drives, drives in external bays, and adapter cards. You connect all internal cables, reattach the side panels, and connect external cables to the computer. Then you boot the computer for the first time.

- **Chapter 4, "Basics of Preventive Maintenance and Troubleshooting"**: This chapter explains the purpose of preventive maintenance and helps you identify the elements of the troubleshooting process.

- **Chapter 5, "Fundamental Operating Systems"**: Covering the fundamentals of operating systems, this chapter explains the purpose of an operating system and compares the limitations and compatibilities of different systems. You learn how to determine the operating system based on customer needs, install an operating system, navigate a GUI, apply common preventive maintenance techniques, and troubleshoot.

- **Chapter 6, "Fundamental Laptops and Portable Devices"**: In this chapter, you learn how to identify external laptop components, comparing and contrasting desktop and laptop components. You also learn how to configure laptops, apply common preventive maintenance techniques and troubleshoot laptop and portable devices.

- **Chapter 7, "Fundamental Printers and Scanners"**: In this chapter you learn the types of printers and scanners currently available and how to install and configure them. You also learn how to apply common preventive maintenance techniques and troubleshoot.

- **Chapter 8, "Fundamental Networks"**: The principles of networking are explained in this chapter. You learn about the types of networks, basic networking concepts and technologies, and the physical components of a network. After completing this chapter, you will understand LAN topologies and architectures and can identify standards organizations and Ethernet standards. The OSI and TCP/IP data models are reviewed, and you configure a NIC and a modem. Additionally, you identify names, purposes, and characteristics of other technologies for establishing connectivity. Finally, you apply common preventive maintenance techniques for networks and troubleshoot the network.

- **Chapter 9, "Fundamental Security"**: You'll learn why security is so important in this chapter, which describes security threats and identifies security procedures, and learn common preventive maintenance techniques for security.

- **Chapter 10, "Communication Skills"**: To be a good PC technician, it is very important that you have good communication skills. This chapter thoroughly explains the relationship between communication and troubleshooting and describes good communication skills and professional behavior. You'll also learn some ethics and legal aspects of working with computer technology. The chapter provides a realistic description of the call-center environment and technician responsibilities.

- **Chapter 11, "Advanced Personal Computers"**: This chapter begins to move you into more tangible features of the job skills needed in this field. It gives an overview of field, remote, and bench technician jobs and underscores safe lab procedures and tool use. You'll be introduced to situations requiring replacement of computer components, upgrading and configuring personal computer components and peripherals, additional preventive maintenance techniques, and troubleshooting for personal computer components.

- **Chapter 12, "Advanced Operating Systems":** You learn how to select the appropriate operating system based on customer needs, and then how to install, configure, and optimize that operating system. The chapter describes how to upgrade operating systems and additional preventive maintenance and troubleshooting procedures for operating systems.

- **Chapter 13, "Advanced Laptops and Portable Devices":** Here you learn about the wireless communication methods for laptops and portable devices. You select laptop components and learn common repairs for laptops and portable devices along with advanced preventive maintenance and troubleshooting procedures for laptops.

- **Chapter 14, "Advanced Printers and Scanners":** This chapter describes potential safety hazards and safety procedures associated with printers and scanners. You'll cover more advanced topics in installing and configuring a local printer and scanner and how to share a printer and a scanner on a network. You'll also learn how to upgrade and configure printers and scanners as well as more preventive maintenance and troubleshooting techniques for printers and scanners.

- **Chapter 15, "Advanced Networks":** In this chapter you design a network based on the customer's needs, determining the components for your customer's network; then you learn how to implement and upgrade that network. The chapter also covers installation, configuration, and management of a simple mail server.

- **Chapter 16, "Advanced Security":** Going into greater depth, this chapter outlines the security requirements based on customer needs, and you can select security components to implement a customer's security plan.

 The logo of the CompTIA Authorized Quality Curriculum (CAQC) program and the status of this or other training material as "Authorized" under the CompTIA Authorized Quality Curriculum program signifies that, in CompTIA's opinion, such training material covers the content of CompTIA's related certification exam.

The contents of this training material were created for the CompTIA A+ exam covering CompTIA certification objectives that were current as of 2006.

CompTIA has not reviewed or approved the accuracy of the contents of this training material and specifically disclaims any warranties of merchantability or fitness for a particular purpose. CompTIA makes no guarantee concerning the success of persons using any such "Authorized" or other training material in order to prepare for any CompTIA certification exam.

How to Become CompTIA Certified

This training material can help you prepare for and pass a related CompTIA certification exam or exams. To achieve CompTIA certification, you must register for and pass a CompTIA certification exam or exams.

To become CompTIA certified, you must:

1. Select a certification exam provider. For more information please visit http://www.comptia.org/certification/general_information/exam_locations.aspx.

2. Register for and schedule a time to take the CompTIA certification exam(s) at a convenient location.

3. Read and sign the Candidate Agreement, which will be presented at the time of the exam(s). The text of the Candidate Agreement can be found at http://www.comptia.org/certification/general_information/candidate_agreement.aspx.

4. Take and pass the CompTIA certification exam(s).

For more information about CompTIA's certifications, such as its industry acceptance, benefits, or program news, please visit www.comptia.org/certification.

CompTIA is a not-for-profit information technology (IT) trade association. CompTIA's certifications are designed by subject matter experts from across the IT industry. Each CompTIA certification is vendor-neutral, covers multiple technologies, and requires demonstration of skills and knowledge widely sought after by the IT industry.

To contact CompTIA with any questions or comments, please call 1-630-678-8300 or e-mail questions@comptia.org.

Strategies for Exam Preparation

Although many websites offer information about what to study for a particular exam, few sites explain how you should study for an exam. The study process can be broken into various stages. However, key to all these stages is the ability to concentrate. Concentration, or the lack of, plays a big part in the study process.

To be able to concentrate, you must remove all distractions. Although you should plan for study breaks, it is the unplanned breaks caused by distractions that do not allow you to concentrate on what you need to learn. Therefore, first you need to create an environment that's conducive to studying or seek out an existing environment that meets these criteria, such as a library.

Do not study with the TV on, and do not have other people in the room. It is too easy for something on TV to grab your attention and break your concentration. Do not study with others in the room who might not share your dedication to passing this exam. Opinions differ on whether it is better to study with or without music playing. Some people need to have a little white noise in the background to study; if you choose to have music, keep the volume on a low level and listen to music without vocals.

After you find a place to study, you must schedule the time to study. Don't study on an empty stomach. You should also not study on a full stomach; a full stomach tends to make people drowsy. You may also consider having a glass of water nearby to sip. In addition, make sure that you are well rested so that you don't start dozing off. Find a position that is comfortable and use furniture that is also comfortable. Finally, make sure that your study area is well lit. Natural light is best for fighting fatigue.

The first thing that you should do when you begin to study is to clear your mind of distractions. So, take a minute or two, close your eyes, and empty your mind. When you prepare for an exam, the best place to start is to take the list of exam objectives and study the list carefully for its scope. The objectives can be downloaded from the CompTIA website (http://certification.comptia.org/a/). You can then organize your study with these objectives in mind, narrowing down your focus area to specific topics/subtopics. In addition, you need to understand and visualize the process as a whole, to help prepare you to address practical problems in a real environment and to deal with unexpected questions.

In a multiple-choice exam, you have one advantage: The answer or answers are already there, and you just have to choose the correct one(s). Because the answers are there, you can start eliminating the incorrect answers by using your knowledge and some logical thinking. One common mistake is to select the first obvious-looking answer without checking the other options. Don't fall into this trap. Always review all the options, think about them, and then choose the right answer. Of course, with multiple-choice questions, you have to be exact, and you should be able to differentiate among similar answers. This is one reason you need a peaceful place of study without distractions, so that you can read between the lines and don't miss key points.

Taking the Exam

The CompTIA A+ exam is explained in detail, including a list of the objectives, by visiting the following website:

http://certification.comptia.org/a/

When you are ready to take the exam, you must purchase and schedule your two CompTIA A+ exams. The necessary information to accomplish this can be found at the following website:

http://certification.comptia.org/resources/registration.aspx

Before you take an exam, eat something light, even if you have no appetite. If your stomach is actively upset, try mild foods such as toast or crackers. Plain saltine crackers are great for settling a cranky stomach. Keep your caffeine and nicotine consumption to a minimum; excessive stimulants aren't exactly conducive to reducing stress. Plan to take a bottle of water or some hard candies, such as lozenges or mints, with you to combat dry mouth.

When you take the exam, dress comfortably and arrive at the testing center early. If you have never been to the testing center before, make sure that you know where it is. You might even consider taking a test drive. If you arrive between 15 and 30 minutes early for any certification exam, it gives you the following:

- Ample time for whatever relaxes you: prayer, meditation, or deep breathing.

- Time to scan glossary terms and quickly access tables before taking the exam so that you can get the intellectual juices flowing and build a little confidence.

- Time to visit the washroom before you begin the exam.

However, don't arrive too early.

When you are escorted into the testing chamber, you will usually be given two sheets of paper (or laminated paper) with a pen (or wet-erase pen). As soon as you hear the door close behind you, immediately jot down on the paper information that you might need to quickly recall. For example, some of the things that you can jot down are the lengths for the various network cable types or speeds of the various wireless technology. Then, throughout the exam, you can refer to this information and not have to think about it. Instead, you can use this information as a reference and focus on answering the questions. Before you actually start the exam, close your eyes and take a deep breath to clear your mind of distractions. Then, throughout the test, you can jot down little notes that may be used in other questions or do some simple math, such as when you need to figure out how much available memory you have when you have a system that uses part of the memory for video memory.

Typically, the testing room is furnished with anywhere from one to six computers, and each workstation is separated from the others by dividers designed to keep anyone from seeing what's happening on someone else's computer screen. Most testing rooms feature a wall with a large picture window. This layout permits the exam coordinator to monitor the room, to prevent exam takers from talking to one another, and to observe anything out of the ordinary that might go on. The exam coordinator will have preloaded the appropriate CompTIA certification exam, and you are permitted to start as soon as you're seated in front of the computer.

All exams are completely closed book. In fact, you are not permitted to take anything with you into the testing area, but you receive a blank sheet of paper and a pen or, in some cases, an erasable plastic sheet and an erasable pen. Immediately write down on that sheet of paper all the information you've memorized for the test. You are given some time to compose yourself, record this information, and take a sample orientation exam before you begin the real thing. It's a good idea to take the orientation test before taking your first exam; but because all the certification exams are more or less identical in layout, behavior, and controls, you probably don't need to do so more than once.

All CompTIA certification exams allow a certain maximum amount of testing time (90 minutes). This time is indicated on the exam by an onscreen timer clock, so you can check the time remaining whenever you like. All CompTIA certification exams are computer generated, and the questions are multiple-choice questions.

CHAPTER 1

Introduction to the Personal Computer

The Study Guide portion of this chapter uses a combination of matching, identification, short-answer, and fill-in-the-blank questions to test your introductory knowledge of computers. This portion also includes multiple-choice study questions to help prepare you to take the A+ certification exams and to test your overall understanding of the material.

The Lab Exercises portion of this chapter includes all the online curriculum worksheets to further reinforce your mastery of the content.

Study Guide

Defining a Computer

A computer is a machine composed of electronic devices used to process data. Data is the raw facts, numbers, letters, or symbols that the computer processes into meaningful information. Examples of data include a letter to a company or a client, a report for your boss, a budget proposal for a large project, or an address book of your friends and business associates. After data is saved (or written to disk), it can be retrieved anytime, printed on paper, or sent to someone else using the Internet.

Computers can be classified into four main groups: personal computers, minicomputers, mainframe computers, and supercomputers. This book focuses on the personal computer, known as the PC. It is based on the Intel (or Intel-compatible) microprocessor. The microprocessor is the "brain" of the computer.

A personal computer is a computer that is meant to be used by one person at a time. It usually consists of a case that contains the essential electronic and mechanical parts of the computer, a monitor so that you can output (display) data, and a keyboard so that you can input (insert) data.

The case is the box that most of the computer components rest in, and it is designed to protect these components. It contains the power supply, motherboard, processors, RAM, floppy drives, hard drives, optical drives, and expansion cards.

Vocabulary Exercise: Matching

Match the definition on the left with a term on the right.

Definitions

a. Provides a stable area to mount internal components and provides an environment to keep the components cool.

b. Converts AC (alternating current) power from the wall outlet into the lower voltages of DC (direct current) power required to power all components of the computer.

c. Main printed circuit board that connects all the major components of a computer.

d. Long-term memory that retains instructions when the computer is shut down and that provides basic instructions to the computer.

e. Temporary memory that is used for the operating system, applications, and data.

f. Allows you to expand and customize the functionality of your computer by adding controllers and ports.

g. Brains of the computer where most calculations take place.

h. Main long-term storage device that holds the operating system, programs, and data using magnetic disks.

i. A storage device that stores files using removable magnetic disks.

j. A printed circuit board that you can insert into a computer to give it added capabilities.

k. A device or program that enables a computer to transmit data over, for example, telephone or cable lines.

l. An interface on a computer to which you can connect a device.

m. A storage device that stores files using removable disks that reads and writes using a laser.

n. Primary output device.

o. A device that prints text or illustrations on paper.

p. A number of integrated circuits that allow the processor to communicate with other components within the computer.

q. A specialized interface for display adapters.

r. Most common type of expansion slots.

Terms

_j_ adapter card

_q_ AGP

_a_ case

_f_ expansion slot

_i_ floppy disk drive

_h_ hard drive

_k_ modem

_n_ monitor

_c_ motherboard

_m_ optical drive

_r_ PCI

_b_ power supply

_o_ printer

_e_ RAM

_d_ ROM

_g_ CPU

_p_ chipset

_l_ port

Processors

The computer is built around an integrated circuit called the *processor* (also known as microprocessor and central processing unit [CPU]). It is considered the "brain" of the computer because all the instructions it performs are mathematical calculations and logical comparisons. The processor is the central component of the computer. It is plugged into a large circuit board called the *motherboard* (sometimes referred to as system board).

Vocabulary Exercise: Completion

Fill in the blanks with the appropriate terms about processors.

Pentium II and older Pentium III processors plug into a Slot *1 or SC242 connector*

Later Pentium III processors connect using a *370*-pin connector.

Early Pentium 4 processors use a *423*-pin connector. Newer Pentium 4 processors use a *775*-pin connector.

Socket T, also known as a *LGA 775*, is Intel's socket used by today's modern Intel processors.

Slot A is used for AMD processors ranging from the AMD Athlon K7 to the AMD Athlon XP 3200+, and AMD budget processors. It uses a *242*-pin connector.

Socket AM2, produced by AMD, has *940* contacts

Intel Pentium MMX consists of 57 instructions that improve the performance of multimedia tasks.

Hyperthreading, used in newer Intel processors, allows the processor to act like two processors (logical processors) so that it can utilize the processor resources more efficiently and improve performance. Hyper-Threading can be enabled or disabled in the system _____ program.

To keep a processor cool, it must use a *heat sink* (with thermal paste or tape) and *fan* or some other cooling system.

Some motherboards with dual processor sockets require having a special terminator or _____ _____ in the empty processor slot or socket when both processors are not installed.

Motherboards

The motherboard allows the processor to branch out and communicate with all the computer components. It can be considered the nervous system of the PC.

Motherboards are often described by their form factors (physical dimensions, sizes, and layout). Older motherboards are based on the Baby AT. Newer form factors include ATX (including mini-ATX, Micro-ATX, and Flex-ATX), NXL, and BTX. Different from the Baby AT form factor, the ATX motherboards have the expansion slots parallel to the short side of the board, which allows more space for other components. The processor and RAM are next to the power supply so that heat generated by the CPU and RAM are immediately drawn out of the casing to reduce the amount of heat trapped inside the casing. In addition, the processor and memory modules can be replaced or upgraded without removing any of the expansion cards.

The BTX form factor is designed to balance size, performance, features, and cost. To improve heat dissipation and acoustics, the board has been redesigned to improve airflow through the system;

moving the processor to the "front" of the case allows it to be right next to the intake fan, giving it the coolest air of any component in the system. The airflow is also channeled over the chipset, graphics card, and memory chips.

Read-only memory (ROM) chips contain instructions and data that the processor accesses directly. Unlike the contents of the RAM, the contents of the ROM are permanent. They cannot be changed or erased by normal means and are maintained when power is off.

ROM chips (including flash memory) are used within the PC to provide instructions and data to the processor. The chips and software (programs and data) that have been written onto these chips are called *firmware*.

The ROM chip contains the basic input/output system (BIOS) that provides instructions and data to the processor. BIOS is the built-in software that determines what a computer can do without accessing programs from a disk. Therefore, you can think of these ROM chips as the instincts of the computer. They contain all the code required to control the boot process, and they control many hardware devices, including the keyboard, display, screen, disk drives, serial communications, and others.

The system BIOS, which is located on the motherboard, directs the boot up and allows basic control of the majority of the hardware. The BIOS chips are typically made from flash memory, which is computer memory that can be electrically erased and reprogrammed, typically by a flash program. Updating the system ROM BIOS (also known as flashing the BIOS) can correct a wide range of problems and will allow the system to work with components that did not exist at the time the motherboard was manufactured.

The motherboard configuration is stored in the complementary metal–oxide–semiconductor (CMOS) memory. Like normal RAM, if the CMOS memory loses power, the content of the CMOS memory is lost. Therefore, the CMOS memory and a real-time clock (to keep track of the date and time) are powered by a CMOS battery.

One essential, yet inexpensive, part of the PC is the motherboard chipset. A chipset consists of the chips and other components on the motherboard that allow different PC components, including the processor, to communicate with each other. It consists of the bus controllers, peripheral controllers, memory controllers, cache controllers, clocks, and timers. The chipset used in a motherboard design greatly influences the performance and limitations of the PC. It defines how much RAM a mother-board can use and what type of RAM chips it will accommodate, as well as cache size, processor types and speed, and the types of expansion slots.

Most of Intel's earlier chipsets and many non-Intel chipsets are broken into a multi-tiered architecture incorporating North and South Bridge components.

Intel's newer chipsets are based on the Intel Hub Architecture (IHA). Like the older chipsets, IHA has two parts: the graphics and AGP memory controller hub (GMCH) and the I/O controller hub (ICH). The GMCH communicates with the processor over the system bus and acts as a controller for memory and AGP. It sometimes comes with integrated video. Unlike the North Bridge, the GMCH does not come with a PCI controller. ICH provides a connection to a PCI bus, ATA disk interface, a USB controller, and the firmware hub. The firmware hub stores system and video BIOS and includes a hardware-based random number generator.

When working within a PC, you must be able to identify the different parts of the motherboard, including the processor, expansion slots, drive connectors, and power connectors. You should also be able to look at the layout to determine its form factor.

Concept Questions

Answer the following questions about motherboards:

Describe what the North Bridge component holds.

controls access to RAM, video card

Describe what the South Bridge component holds.

Hard Drives, sound card, USB Ports

Identify the following in Figure 1-1:

- CPU socket ✓
- Expansion slots ✓
- Memory sockets ✓
- Chipset ✓
- Ports ✓
- Battery
- Drive connectors ✓
- Power connector ✓

Figure 1-1   Motherboard Components

RAM

RAM is the computer's short-term memory. Program instructions and data are stored on the RAM chips, which the processor accesses directly. The more RAM you have, the more instructions and data you can load. The amount of RAM greatly affects the performance of the PC. However, if power is discontinued to the RAM, as when you shut off your PC, the contents of the RAM disappear. This is why disks are used for long-term storage.

Vocabulary Exercise: Completion

Fill in the blanks with the appropriate terms about RAM.

RAM stands for ___Random Access Memory___

___Insufficient___ RAM can cause the computer to run slower.

RAM chips are volatile, meaning that they immediately lose their data when the computer is ___switched off___.

_____ SDRAM operates at 100 MHz and requires 10 ns DRAM chips, but requires 8 ns DRAM chips that are capable of running at 125 MHz.

_____ SDRAM operates at 133 MHz and requires 7.5 ns DRAM chips.

The DDR in DDR DRAM is short for ___Double Data Rate___ DDR chips that run at 400 MHz are known as _____. DDR chips that run at 677 MHz are known as _____.

SIMM is short for ___Single Inline Memory Module___.

DIMM is short for ___Dual Inline Memory Module___.

RIMM is short for ___RAM Bus Inline Memory Module___

72-pin SIMMs are _____ wide and can be installed _____.

_____ supports 64-bit pathways, whereas _____ is the only memory module that is 16-bits wide.

DIMMs are available in _____-pin and _____-pin sticks.

DDR DIMMS use ___184___-pin connectors, whereas DDR2 DIMMS use 240-pin connectors.

RIMM is available in ___184___-pin version.

VRAM and SGRAM is a specialized memory used on _____.

Ports

A port is an interface on a computer to which you can connect a device. Most ports are located at the back of the computer. Some ports are physically part of the motherboard or are connected directly to the motherboard, whereas other ports are physically part of or connected directly to expansion cards. To identify the capabilities of the system and to identify an expansion card, you will need to identify the port by sight.

PC 99 is a specification for PCs jointly developed by Microsoft and Intel in 1998. Its aim was to encourage the standardization of PC hardware to aid Windows compatibility. The PC 99 specification set out the color code for the various standard types of plugs and connectors used on PCs. Because many of the connectors look very similar, particular to a novice PC user, the color scheme made it far easier for people to connect peripherals to the correct ports on a PC. This color code was gradually adopted by almost all PC, motherboard, and peripheral manufacturers.

Serial ports and parallel ports are traditional ports found on PCs, and newer ports that offer more functionality include USB and IEEE 1394 (FireWire). As a PC technician, you need to know the characteristics of these ports.

Identify Ports and Connectors

In the following table, identify the port, the type of connector, and its purpose.

Image	Port	Type of Connector	Purpose
	SCSI	25 pin female	
	Serial Port	DB-9 Male	To connect mouse on older motherboards
	Game Port/ Midi		
	PS2 Port		mouse + keyboard
	VGA Video Graphics	3-Row 15 pin Female connector	Analogue output to monitor
	S-Video in port		
	Parallel Port	36 pin centronics	To connect printer
	Digital Video Interface	24 pin female connector	
	Fire Wire Port	Nine Pin Connector	connects peripheral Devices
	Fire Wire Port	Four Pin Connector	
	USB	USB	To connect camera, scanners, storage devices

Identify the colors typically used for the following ports:

- Keyboard: _____Purple_____
- PS/2 Mouse: _Green_____
- Parallel Port: _____
- VGA: _Blue_____
- Digital Monitor: _____
- Speakers (Main): _____
- Microphone (input): _____

Identify the following as serial port or parallel port:

- Also known as IEEE 1284: _Parallel_____
- Also known as RS-232: ____Serial_____
- Connects external peripheral devices such as modems and mice: _serial_____
- Maximum length of cable is 10 feet (3 m): _Parallel_____
- Maximum length of cable is 50 feet (15.2 m): _Serial cable_____
- Transmits data, multiple bits at a time: _Parallel_____
- Transmits data, one bit at a time: _serial Port_____
- Used primarily to connect printers: _Parallel_____

Identify the following as USB 1.1, USB 2.0, or IEEE 1394:

- Also known as FireWire: _IFFE 1394____
- The maximum data transfer rate speed is 12 Mbps: _USB_____
- The maximum data transfer rate speed of is 480 Mbps: _USB 2_____
- Has a data transfer rate of 400 Mbps and supports up to 63 devices: _IEEE 1394_____
- Supports up to 127 devices: _USB_____

Expansion Slots and Boards

The expansion slot, also known as the input/output (I/O) bus, extends the reach of the processor so it can communicate with peripheral devices. Expansion slots are so named because they allow the system to be expanded by the insertion of circuit boards, called expansion cards (also known as daughter boards). They are essential to the computer because a basic system cannot satisfy everyone's needs, and they allow the system to use new technology as it becomes available. Expansion slots consist of connectors and metal traces that carry signals from the expansion card to the rest of the computer, specifically the RAM and processor. These connections are used for power, data, addressing, and control lines.

Throughout the years, several types of expansion slots have been developed. The original IBM PC used the 8-bit PC slot, and the IBM AT used the 16-bit ISA slot. Today's desktop computers include PCI slots and their derivatives (AGP, PCI-X, and PCI Express). As a PC technician, you will need to know the commonly used expansion slots and their characteristics.

Vocabulary Exercise: Completion

Fill in the blanks with the appropriate terms about expansion slots.

PCI is short for <u>Peripheral component interconnect</u>. PCI runs at either <u>33</u> MHz or ____ MHz.

AGP is short for <u>Advanced Graphics Port</u>. AGP is made exclusively for <u>video Adapters</u>

The original specification for AGP (AGPx1) has a clock speed of 66 MHz and has a maximum bandwidth of 266 Mbps.

AGPx2 has a clock speed of <u>66 MHz</u> and has a maximum bandwidth of <u>528 MBps</u>

AGPx4 has a clock speed of <u>66 MHz</u> and has a maximum bandwidth of <u>2112 MBps</u>

AGPx8 has a clock speed of <u>66 MHz</u> and has a maximum bandwidth of <u>4224 MBps</u>

PCI Express is a much faster interface to replace PCI, PCI-X, and AGP interfaces for computer expansion cards and graphics cards.

Whereas PCI, PCI-X, and AGP are based on a parallel interface, PCI Express is based on a <u>point to point</u> <u>serial</u> interface.

Cases

The case of the PC is a metal or plastic box designed to hold and protect the motherboard, the drives, and the power supplies. Like motherboards and processors, cases come in many configurations, which are characterized by the orientation of the box, the number of drives and expansion slots it can hold, and the size of the expansion cards it can take. The computer case should be durable, easy to service, and have enough room for expansion.

Concept Questions

Answer the following question about cases:

List and describe the factors in choosing the computer case:

- <u>Needs to match motherboard   ie ATX, BTX</u>
- <u>is there room for expansion</u>
- <u>is there room for sufficient air flow</u>
- <u>Is it to sit on desk top</u>
- <u>Colour</u>
- _____

Power Supplies

Electricity is the blood of the computer and comes through the power supply. The power supply converts AC into clean DC power. Like cases and motherboards, power supplies come in many sizes and shapes. The most common are the Baby AT power supplies and ATX power supplies.

Power supplies are rated in what unit?

_____watts_____

In the United States, what voltage does the power supply run on?

_____115 v_____

Hard Drive

Disks are half-electronic, half-mechanical devices that store magnetic fields on rotating platters. The magnetic fields represent the data. They are considered long-term storage devices because they do not "forget" their information when power is disconnected. They are also considered the primary mass storage system because they hold all the programs and data files that are fed into RAM. Hard drives are sometimes referred to as fixed disks because they are usually not removed from the PC easily, like a floppy disk or optical disk. This term does not describe all hard drives because there are external hard drives (disks that rest outside of the case) and removable hard drives.

Hard drives communicate with the rest of the computer by means of a cable connected to a controller card or interface, which is either an expansion card or built in to the motherboard. All hard drives consist of the following components: rotating platters, read/write heads, and head actuators.

Today, the common hard drive types include integrated drive electronics (usually referred to as IDE) and small computer system interface (usually referred to as SCSI; pronounced "skuzzy"). IDE hard drives follow the AT attachment (ATA) specification, which has been expanded throughout the years. The SCSI interface, typically found on high-end computers and servers, supports multiple devices in and out of the computer.

Concept Questions

Answer the following question about hard drives:

Define the following hard drive terms:

- Disk platters: Disks which contain magnetically stored information

  _____

- Read/write heads: float over the HDD platters & read information from them
- Head actuators: Are the arms that move the heads over the platters
- Spindle: _____

Vocabulary Exercise: Completion

Fill in the blanks with the appropriate terms about hard drives.

The most popular hard drive interface is _ATA_. There are two main types of IDE interfaces. They are _PATA_ and _SATA_. Of the two main types of IDE interfaces, _SATA_ is faster than _PATA_. The _PATA_ interface uses a 40-pin ribbon cable. The _SATA_ interface uses a two-cable connector (a _7_-pin data connector and a _15_-pin power connector).

The transfer rate of _PATA_ is up to 133 Mbps. The transfer rate of _SATA_ begins at 150 Mbps.

The _SCSI_ interface is used for high-end computers.

The older SCSI-1 interfaces supported up to _7_ SCSI devices (_8_ if you include the host adapter), whereas newer SCSI interfaces, including Wide SCSI, support up to _15_ devices (_16_ if you include the host adapter).

Different from the IDE interface, the two ends of the SCSI chain must be _terminated_. Each SCSI device, including the adapter/controller card, is numbered with a _unique identifier_ from 0 to 7 or 0 to 15. Narrow SCSI cables use _50_-pin connectors, whereas wide SCSI uses _68_-pin connectors. Ultra SCSI interfaces can have a maximum cable length of _6 metres_. Although traditional SCSI interfaces used a single-ended (SE) signaling method, most SCSI devices use the _high-voltage differential_ signaling method.

Video Systems

The video system includes the monitor and the video card/adapter. The monitor is a device similar to a television, which is the computer's main output device.

Video Graphics Array (VGA) is an analog computer display standard that has been technologically outdated in the PC market for some time. However, VGA (with a resolution of 640×480 and 16 colors) was the most recent graphical standard that the majority of manufacturers conformed to, making it the lowest common denominator that all PC graphics hardware supports before a device-specific driver is loaded into the computer. For example, the Microsoft Windows splash screen appears while the machine is still operating in VGA mode, which is the reason that this screen always appears in reduced resolution and color depth. Today, computers use a higher resolution and more colors.

The number of pixels (colored dots) that can be displayed on the screen at one time is called the *resolution* of the screen. The resolution consists of two numbers, the number of pixels going from left to right and the number of pixels going from top to bottom. When you use a higher resolution, you will need additional video memory for the video system to store the additional pixels and more processing by the computer.

Color depth, or bit depth, is the amount of information that determines the color of a pixel. The more colors each pixel can show, the more colors the screen can show and the more shades of the same color, which can produce a more realistic, detailed picture. However, the higher number of bits required to give each pixel a higher color depth requires more video memory for the video system to store the pixel's information and more processing by the computer.

Vocabulary Exercise: Matching

Match the definition on the left with a term on the right.

Definitions

Terms

✓**a.** Distance between the dots.

✓**b.** How often per second the image is rebuilt, measured in hertz.

✓**c.** High-definition multimedia interface.

d. Made primarily for consumer market: CAMCORDERS, VCRs, DVD.

e. Analog signal that offers excellent quality.

✓**f.** An analog computer display standard that offers a resolution of 640×480 and 16 colors.

✓**g.** The number of pixels that can be displayed on the screen at one time, usually expressed as the number of dots going across and down the screen.

✓**h.** The dots used in a display to generate text, lines, and pictures.

✓**i.** The amount of information that determines the color of a pixel.

✓**j.** Older type of monitor that tends to be heavy and bulky.

✓**k.** A thin, flat display device made up of any number of color or monochrome pixels arrayed in front of a light source or reflector.

✓**l.** Connector/interface that usually passes digital video signals.

_g_ resolution

_j_ CRT

_a_ dot pitch

_c_ HDMI

_k_ LCD

_b_ refresh rate

_h_ pixel

_d_ RGB

_e_ S-video

_i_ color depth

_f_ VGA

_l_ DVI

Concept Questions

Answer the following question about video systems.

Complete the following table:

Common Name	Color Depth	Number of Displayed Colors
16 colors (VGA)	4 bits	16
256 colors	8 bits	256
High color	16 bits	64K
True color	24 bits	16.7 million

Study Questions

Choose the best answer for each of the questions that follow.

1. Which of the following SCSI interfaces allow up to 16 devices, including the adapter, to be connected on a single shared cable? (Choose all that apply.)

   A. Ultra Wide SCSI ✓

   B. Fast SCSI ✗

   C. Ultra SCSI ✗

   D. Fast Wide SCSI ✓

   E. Ultra2 Wide SCSI ✓

   F. Ultra 2 SCSI ✗

2. The part that moves the read/write heads back and forth within a hard drive or optical drive is called what?

   A. Stepper motor

   B. Spindle

   C. Head actuator

   D. Magnetic coupler

3. When you purchase a power supply, the output power supply is measured in which units?

   A. Ohms

   B. Watts

   C. Hertz

   D. Mbps

   E. Amps

4. Which of the following must be installed in pairs?

   A. 72-pin SIMMs

   B. 168-pin DIMMs

   C. 184-pin DIMMs

   D. 184-pin RIMMs

5. You have a 3-row, 15-pin female connector on an expansion card. What kind of expansion card is it?

   A. EGA display adapter

   B. Serial port adapter

   C. VGA display adapter

   D. Game port adapter

   E. Modem adapter

6. What is the SCSI ID number commonly assigned to the boot device in a PC?

    A. 0

    B. 15

    C. 7

    D. 8

7. When you upgrade the BIOS, you are _____.

    A. Replacing the BIOS

    B. Flashing the BIOS

    C. Replacing the CMOS chip

    D. Resetting the CMOS settings

8. Which of the following has 184 pins and is 16 bits wide?

    A. SIMMs

    B. DIMMs

    C. RIMMs

    D. SODIMMs

9. Which two of the following describe the number of pins normally associated with dual in-line memory modules (DIMMs)?

    A. 30

    B. 72

    C. 144

    D. 168

    E. 184

10. Which of the following is 64 bits wide? (Select all that apply.)

    A. 72-pin SIMM

    B. 168-pin DIMM

    C. 184-pin DIMM

    D. 184-pin RIM

11. The size of the monitor is measured in __Inches__.

    A. Inches diagonally across the screen

    B. Square inches of the screen

    C. Dots going across and dots going down

    D. Pounds

12. Which of the following produces an image that has a resolution of 640×480 and 16 colors?

    A. EGA

    B. VGA

    C. Super VGA

    D. Ultra Super VGA

13. If the display adapter is set to 8-bit color, how many colors can it show at one time?

    A. 256 colors

    B. 65,536 colors

    C. 16 million colors

    D. 4 billion colors

14. Which is the latest type of printer interface?

    A. Serial

    B. DVI

    C. USB

    D. Parallel

Lab Exercises

Worksheet 1.1.2: Job Opportunities

In this worksheet, you will use the Internet, magazines, or a local newspaper to gather information for jobs in the computer service and repair field. Be prepared to discuss your research in class.

1. Research three computer-related jobs. For each job, write the company name and the job title in the column on the left. Write the job details that are most important to you as well as the job qualifications in the column on the right. An example has been provided for you.

Company Name and Job Title	Details and Qualifications
Gentronics Flexible Solutions/ Field Service Representative	Company offers continuing education. Work with hardware and software. Work directly with customers. Local travel.
	■ A+ certification preferred
	■ One year installation or repair experience of computer hardware and software required
	■ Requires a valid driver's license
	■ Must have reliable personal transportation
	■ Mileage reimbursement
	■ Ability to lift and carry up to 50 lbs

2. Based on your research, which job would you prefer? Be prepared to discuss your answer in class.

_____

_____

_____

_____

_____

Worksheet 1.4.7: Research Computer Components

In this worksheet, you will use the Internet, a newspaper, or a local store to gather information about the components you will need to complete your customer's computer. Be prepared to discuss your selections.

Your customer already owns the case described in the table that follows.

Brand and Model Number	Features	Cost
Cooler Master	ATX Mid Tower	
CAC-T05-UW	ATX, Micro ATX compatible form factor	
	2 External 5.25" drive bays	
	2 External 3.5" drive bay	
	2 Internal 5.25" drive bays	
	7 expansion slots	
	USB, FireWire, audio ports	

Search the Internet, a newspaper, or a local store to research a power supply compatible with the components that your customer owns. Enter the specifications in the table that follows:

Brand and Model Number	Features	Cost

Your customer already owns the motherboard described in the table that follows:

Brand and Model Number	Features	Cost
GIGABYTE GA-965P-DS3	LGA 775 DDR2 800 PCI Express X16 SATA 3.0 Gbps interface 1.8V–2.4V RAM voltage 1066/800/533 MHz front side bus 4 memory slots Dual-channel memory supported ATA100 connector RAID 0/1 4 USB 2.0 ports ATX form factor	

Search the Internet, a newspaper, or a local store to research a CPU compatible with the components that your customer owns. Enter the specifications in the table that follows:

Brand and Model Number	Features	Cost

Search the Internet, a newspaper, or a local store to research a cooling device compatible with the components that your customer owns. Enter the specifications in the table that follows:

Brand and Model Number	Features	Cost

Search the Internet, a newspaper, or a local store to research RAM compatible with the components that your customer owns. Enter the specifications in the table that follows:

Brand and Model Number	Features	Cost

Your customer already owns the hard disk drive described in the table that follows:

Brand and Model Number	Features	Cost
Seagate	400 GB	$119.99
ST3400620AS	7200 RPM	
	16 MB Cache	
	SATA 3.0 Gbps interface	

Search the Internet, a newspaper, or a local store to research a video adapter card compatible with the components that your customer owns. Enter the specifications in the table that follows:

Brand and Model Number	Features	Cost

1. List three components that must have the same or compatible form factor:

2. List three components that must conform to the same socket type:

3. List two components that must use the same front side bus speed:

4. List three considerations when you choose memory:

_____

_____

5. What component must be compatible with every other component of the computer?

_____

CHAPTER 2

Safe Lab Procedures and Tool Use

The Study Guide portion of this chapter uses a combination of fill-in-the-blank, matching, and open-ended questions to test your knowledge of safe lab procedures and tool use. This portion also includes multiple-choice study questions to help prepare you to take the A+ certification exams and to test your overall understanding of the material.

The Lab Exercises portion of this chapter includes all the online curriculum labs and worksheets to further reinforce your mastery of safe lab procedures and tool use.

Study Guide

Electrostatic Discharge

While fixing a computer and handling electronic components, you must be careful that you do not cause any damage to the computer and its components. Therefore, it is essential that you do not cause damage from electrostatic discharge.

Concept Questions

Answer the following electrostatic discharge questions:

How is electrostatic electricity generated?

Static electricity is the build up of an electrical charge resting on a surface. The build up and sudden release is called electrostatic discharge

How many volts must be built up before you feel the ESD?

3,000 v

How many volts can damage an electronic component?

30 v

What are the four ESD protection recommendations for preventing ESD?

1. *Antistatic bags*

2. *Antistatic wrist strap*

3. *Antistatic mats on work bench & floor areas*

4. *Avoid working in carpeted areas*

How does humidity affect ESD?

Low humidity increases ESD

To reduce further risk of ESD, what type of clothing should you not wear?

Polyester, nylon

Why should the metal on the back of the wrist strap remain in contact with the skin at all times?

To conduct the electricity to the equipment & equalise the charge

What should you do with sleeves and neckties when working with electronic components?

Roll up sleeves & remove ties

PC Maintenance

To keep a computer running well and to extend its life, you need to perform regular maintenance. Part of the maintenance is to keep the computer clean inside and outside.

Concept Questions

Answer the following PC maintenance questions:

What can happen if a computer has an excess buildup of dirt and dust?

It restricts the airflow around the computer causing overheating & possible damage

Describe the best method to clean the following components:

1. Keyboard

   A small hand held vacuum or compressed air

2. LCD monitor

   Very dilute washing up liquid & cloth

3. CRT monitor

   Glass cleaner spray & cloth

4. Mouse

   Glass cleaner & cloth

5. Contacts on a PCI expansion card

   Isopropyl alcohol & Q-tips

6. Removing dust and dirt from inside the computer

   compressed air

Power Fluctuations

Computers are designed to run off of clean DC power. Therefore, when your system experiences power fluctuations, these power fluctuations can affect the reliability and functionality of your computer.

Vocabulary Exercise: Matching

Match the definition on the left with a term on the right.

Definitions

a. Complete loss of AC power. A blown fuse, damaged transformer, or downed power line can cause this.

b. Reduced voltage level of AC power that lasts for a period of time. These occur when the power line voltage drops below 80% of the normal voltage level. Overloading electrical circuits can cause this.

c. Interference from generators and lightning. This results in unclean power, which can cause errors in a computer system.

d. Sudden increase in voltage that lasts for a very short period (less than a second) and exceeds 100% of the normal voltage on a line. These can be caused by lightning strikes but can also occur when the electrical system comes back on after a blackout.

e. Dramatic increase in voltage above 110% of the normal voltage that lasts for a few seconds.

Terms

_e_ Power surge

_c_ Noise

_a_ Blackout

_b_ Brownout

_d_ Spike

Concept Questions

Answer the following questions about power fluctuations.

Which type of computer protection device will protect against spikes and surges?

Surge Protector

Which type of computer protection device will protect against brownouts and blackouts?

Back-up power supply eg battery

Fires and Fire Extinguishers

Computers are half mechanical, half electronic devices. As with any mechanical or electronic device, there is always a chance that a computer can catch fire. Therefore, you need to know how to handle a fire if it does occur.

Concept Questions

Answer the following questions about fires and fire extinguishers:

What are the four steps in using a fire extinguisher?

Step 1. _Remove Pin_

Step 2. _Aim at base of fire_

Step 3. _Squeeze lever_

Step 4. _Sweep nozzle side to side_

Identify the usage of fire extinguisher classifications.

- _A_ _wood & paper_
- _B_ _Chemical_
- _C_ _Electrical & mechanical_
- _D_ _Combustible metals._

If your computer catches on fire, which classification of fire extinguisher should you use?

Material Safety and Data Sheets and Component Disposal

Some components and the supplies that you use to maintain computers have or are considered hazardous material. Therefore, special safety and environmental considerations exist for handling and disposing of these components and materials.

Vocabulary Exercise: Completion

Fill in the blanks with the appropriate terms about safety and disposal.

A _material safety & data sheet_ is a fact sheet that summarizes information about material identification, including hazardous ingredients that can affect personal health, fire hazards, and first aid requirements. The MSDS sheet contains chemical reactivity and incompatibilities information that includes _spill_, _leak_, and _disposal_ procedures. It also includes _protective_ measures for the safe handling and storage of materials. To determine whether a material used in computer repairs or preventive maintenance is classified as hazardous, consult the _manufacturer's MSDS_.

Concept Questions

Answer the following questions about MSDS and component disposal:

What valuable information can be found within the MSDS?

- name of material
- physical properties of material
- Hazardous ingredients
- Reactivity data eg fire & explosion
- Procedure for spills & leaks
- Special precautions
- Health Hazards
- Special Protection requirements

Why do batteries need to be properly disposed of?

Because they contain rare earth materials which can be damaging to the environment

Why do monitors need to be properly disposed of?

They can contain rare earth materials which can be damaging to environment

What guidelines should you follow when you are disposing of batteries, monitors, and toner cartridges?

local environment guidelines

Maintenance Safety

Because computers use electricity to operate, a danger always exists when you are fixing a computer. Therefore, you need to take certain steps to make sure that you don't get hurt and that you don't damage the computer and its components.

Concept Questions

Answer the following questions about safety:

What should you do before cleaning any device or repairing a computer?

switch off from mains, remove from socket, remove battery

Which two devices contain such very high voltages that you should not wear antistatic wrist straps when repairing them?

- *Power supplies*

- *monitors*

Tools of the Trade

Because computers are complicated devices that use ever-changing technology, you are not going to know everything about computers. There will be times when you need help to fix a problem. However, knowing where to get this help will greatly enhance your ability as a PC technician.

Concept Questions

Answer the following question about tools of the trade:

You just purchased a fax modem. Unfortunately, it does not include the CD or manuals. Where can you go to find the drivers and manuals?

Manufacturer's website

Study Questions

Choose the best answer for each of the questions that follow.

1. What is the correct procedure to dispose of a monitor?

    A. Incineration.

    B. Dispose in local landfill.

    C. Consult local guidelines for disposing of hazardous material.

    D. Dispose in a trash can or dumpster.

2. As a computer technician, you notice a leak in the server room. What should you do?

    A. Place a bucket under the leak.

    B. Call the local water department.

    C. Notify building maintenance and the system administrator who is responsible for the servers.

    D. Phone the janitor to clean up the water.

3. Which of the following rating of fire extinguisher should you use on a PC on fire? (Choose all that apply.)

   A. Class A

   B. Class B

   C. Class C

   D. Class ABC

4. You are going to replace faulty memory within a computer. You shut down the computer. What should you *not* do to avoid ESD?

   A. Use an ESD mat.

   B. Use an ESD strap.

   C. Touch the ground of the workshop or building.

   D. Touch the metal case of the power supply that is plugged in to a properly grounded outlet.

5. Wrist straps will be useful only if

   A. They are plugged in to the wrist strap jack.

   B. They are clean and make good skin contact.

   C. The cord has not been damaged.

   D. All of the above.

6. Before opening a static-shielding container or bag that contains an electronic device, you should

   A. Look inside to see whether it is really sensitive.

   B. Check for paperwork inside the container.

   C. Ground yourself in an ESD-protected area.

   D. Call the manufacturer for operating instructions.

7. Before transporting an ESD-sensitive device, it must be

   A. Enclosed in a static-shielding container or bag

   B. Put into a cardboard box

   C. Thoroughly cleaned

   D. Wrapped in newspaper

8. To prevent ESD, humidity should be kept to at least _____ when working on a computer.

   A. 10%

   B. 25%

   C. 50%

   D. 75%

9. How should you apply the cleaning solution to a CRT monitor?

   A. A soft brush

   B. A lint-free cloth

   C. A damp sponge

   D. A dripping wet cloth

10. To remove dust from inside a laptop, which of the options should the technician use? (Select two answers.)

   A. Use alcohol swabs.

   B. Use compressed air.

   C. Gently blow the dust out.

   D. Vacuum the dust out of the system with a special antistatic vacuum cleaner.

   E. Use a wet cloth.

Lab Exercises

Worksheet 2.2.2: Diagnostic Software

In this activity, you will use the Internet, a newspaper, or a local store to gather information about a manufacturer's hard drive diagnostic program. Be prepared to discuss the diagnostic software you researched.

Based on your research, list at least two different hard drive manufacturers.

_____

Choose a hard drive manufacturer from question one. Does this manufacturer offer hard drive diagnostic software to go with its products? If so, list the name and the features of the diagnostic software.

_____

Manufacturer: _____

Software Name: _____

File Name: _____

File Size: _____

Version: _____

Publish Date: _____

Description: _____.

_____

_____

 ## Lab 2.3.4: Computer Disassembly

In this lab you will disassemble a computer using safe lab procedures and the proper tools. Use extreme care and follow all safety procedures. Familiarize yourself with the tools you will be using in this lab.

Note: If you cannot locate or remove the correct component, ask your instructor for help.

The following are the recommended tools for this lab:

- Safety glasses or goggles
- Antistatic wrist strap
- Antistatic mat
- Flat-head screwdrivers
- Phillips-head screwdrivers

- Torx screwdrivers

- Hex driver

- Wire cutters

- Plastic

- Part retriever (or tweezers or needle-nose pliers)

- Thermal compound

- Electronics cleaning solution

- Can of compressed air

- Cable ties

- Parts organizer

- Computer with hard drive installed

- Plastic tub for storing computer parts

- Antistatic bags for electronic parts

Step 1

Turn off and disconnect the power to your computer.

Step 2

Locate all the screws that secure the side panels to the back of the computer. Use the proper size and type of screwdriver to remove the side panel screws. Do not remove the screws that secure the power supply to the case. Put all these screws in one place, such as a cup or a compartment in a parts organizer. Label the cup or compartment with a piece of masking tape on which you have written "side panel screws." Remove the side panels from the case.

What type of screwdriver did you use to remove the screws?

_____

_____

How many screws secured the case cover to the chassis?

_____

_____

Step 3

Put on an antistatic wrist strap. One end of the conductor should be connected to the wrist strap. Clip the other end of the conductor to an unpainted metal part of the case.

If you have an antistatic mat, place it on the work surface and put the computer case on top of it. Ground the antistatic mat to an unpainted metal part of the case.

Step 4

Locate the hard drive. Carefully disconnect the power and data cable from the back of the hard drive.

Which type of data cable did you disconnect?

_____

Step 5

Locate all the screws that hold the hard drive in place. Use the proper size and type of screwdriver to remove the hard drive screws. Put all these screws in one place and label them.

_____

Caution: Do *not* remove the screws for the hard drive enclosure.

_____

What type of screws secured the hard drive to the case?

_____

How many screws held the hard drive to the case?

_____

Is the hard drive connected to a mounting bracket? If so, what type of screws secure the hard drive to the mounting bracket?

_____

Step 6

Gently remove the hard drive (touching only the sides) from the case. Place the hard drive into an antistatic bag.

Look at the jumper settings on the hard drive. Is a jumper installed?

_____

Look for a jumper reference chart on the hard drive. If a jumper is installed on the hard drive, use the jumper reference chart to see whether the hard drive is set for a Master, Slave, or Cable Select (CS) drive.

_____

Step 7

Locate the floppy disk drive. Carefully disconnect the power and data cable.

Step 8

Locate all the screws that secure the floppy drive to the case. Use the proper size and type of screwdriver to remove the floppy drive screws. Put all these screws in one place and label them.

Place the floppy drive into an antistatic bag.

How many screws secured the floppy drive to the case?

_____

Step 9

Locate the optical drive (CD-ROM, DVD, and the like). Carefully disconnect the power and data cable from the optical drive. Remove the audio cable from the optical drive.

What kind of data cable did you disconnect?

Is there a jumper on the optical drive? What is the jumper setting?

Step 10

Locate all the screws that secure the optical drive to the case. Use the proper size and type of screwdriver to remove the optical drive screws. Put all these screws in one place and label them.

Place the optical drive into an antistatic bag.

How many screws secured the optical drive to the case?

Step 11

Locate the power supply. Find the power connection(s) to the motherboard.

Gently remove the power connection(s) from the motherboard. How many pins are in the motherboard connector?

Does the power supply provide power to a CPU fan or case fan? If so, disconnect the power cable.

Does the power supply provide auxiliary power to the video card in the PCI, AGP or PCI-E slot? If so, disconnect the power cable.

Step 12

Locate all the screws that secure the power supply to the case. Use the proper size and type of screwdriver to remove the power supply screws. Put all these screws in one place and label them.

How many screws secure the power supply to the case?

Carefully remove the power supply from the case. Place the power supply with the other computer components.

Step 13

Locate any adapter cards that are installed in the computer, such as a video card, NIC, or modem adapter.

Locate the screw that secures the adapter card to the case. Use the proper size and type of screwdriver to remove the adapter card screw. Repeat this process for all adapter cards that are installed in the computer. Put the adapter card screws in one place and label them.

Carefully remove the adapter card from the slot. Be sure to hold the adapter card by the mounting bracket or by the edges. Place the adapter card in an antistatic bag.

Repeat this process for all the adapter cards. Place each card in an antistatic bag.

List the adapter cards and the slot types in the following table.

Adapter Card	Slot Type

Step 14

Locate the memory modules on the motherboard.

What type of memory modules are installed on the motherboard?

How many memory modules are installed on the motherboard?

Remove the memory modules from the motherboard. Be sure to release any locking tabs that may be securing the memory module. Hold the memory module by the edges and gently lift it out of the slot. Put the memory modules into an antistatic bag.

Step 15

Remove all data cables from the motherboard. Make sure to note the connection location of any cable you unplug.

What types of cables were disconnected?

At this point, the computer case should contain the motherboard, the CPU, and any cooling devices. Please ask your instructor for help in removing any additional components.

CHAPTER 3

Computer Assembly—Step by Step

The Study Guide portion of this chapter uses a combination of fill-in-the-blank and open-ended questions to test your knowledge of computer assembly. This portion also includes multiple-choice study questions to help prepare you to take the A+ certification exams and to test your overall understanding of the material.

The Lab Exercises portion of this chapter includes all the online curriculum hands-on labs to further reinforce your mastery of computer assembly.

Study Guide

Installing a Processor

Now that you can identify the various parts of a computer, can follow ESD prevention procedures, and are familiar with the safety issues, you are ready to learn the various steps to build a PC. Because the processor is considered the brain of the computer, you will eventually need to install the processor and its thermal solution onto the motherboard.

When installing a processor, the chip must be oriented properly on the motherboard. If a processor is off by 90 degrees or inserted backward, it may damage the processor or the motherboard.

Pin A1 on the processor is often used to identify one corner of the processor and to help you properly insert the processor into the motherboard. These are designated by a slightly clipped corner, a small dot or triangle on one corner, or a missing pin on one or two of its corners.

Concept Questions

Answer the following questions about installing a processor:

Before installing a motherboard, processor, RAM, or expansion card, you should be wearing what?

An antistatic wrist strap

When installing a processor, how do you know how to insert the processor so that is not off 90 degrees or inserted backward?

Align connection 1 to pin 1

When you insert the processor, the processor does not slide into the socket. What should you do?

Place it into socket

Close the CPU load plate

After the processor is installed onto the motherboard, what is the next component or components that you should install?

Heat sink

Before you install the heat sink, what should you apply directly on the processor?

Thermal compound

Fill in the following table.

Socket Type	Number of Pins	Processors Used in Socket
Socket 370	370 pins	Pentium III and Celeron processors
Socket 423	423 pins	Pentium 4
Socket 478	478 pins	Pentium 4
Socket T	775 pins	Pentium 4, Celeron D,
Socket A		Athlon and Duron
Socket 754	754 pins	AMD Athlon 64, Sempron, Turion 64
Socket 939	939 pins	Athlon 64 and Athlon64 FX
Socket 940	940 pins	AMD Athlon 64x & Opteron.

Installing RAM

After the processor is installed, you are ready to install RAM onto the motherboard. Much like the processor, you must make sure that you follow the same ESD prevention and safety procedures that you follow for the installation of the processor.

Concept Questions

Answer the following questions about installing RAM:

Describe the basic steps in inserting DIMMs or RIMMs onto the motherboard.

Align notches on RAM module to keys in the slot
Make sure side tabs have locked the RAM module

Describe the basic steps in removing a DIMM or RIMM.

Unlock side tabs, lift out RAM module

Installing the Motherboard

After the processor and RAM are installed onto the motherboard, you are ready to slide the motherboard into the case. Again, be sure to follow basic ESD prevention and safety procedures.

Concept Questions

Answer the following questions about installing the motherboard:

What is used to physically separate the motherboard so that metal contacts do not make contact with the metal case?

Standoffs

What are the basic steps when installing a motherboard?

Step 1. _Install standoffs in computer case_

_____

_____

Step 2. _Align I/O connectors on back of motherboard with openings_
Step 3. _Align screw holes on motherboard with standoffs_   _in case_

_____

_____

Step 4. _Insert all motherboard screws_

_____

Step 5. _Tighten all motherboard screws_

_____

Step 6. _____

_____

What type of power connector does an ATX motherboard use, and how many pins does the main connector have?

ATX main power connector — 20 or 24 pins

Installing a Power Supply

Because the power supply contains a fan to help cool the entire system, the power supply is a half electronic, half mechanical component. Because it is partly mechanical, it is a high failure item. (Mechanical components fail more often then electronic components.) If a power supply fails, it is best to replace it because the power supply contains high voltage; a repair will take an electronics technician instead of a PC technician, and the cost of labor will usually exceed the cost of the power supply.

Concept Questions

Answer the following power supply questions:

Is the power supply a high failure item in a computer? If it is, why is it considered a high failure item?

Because it is half electronic, half mechanical as it
contains a fan. Mechanical components fail more
often than electronic

When you remove the power supply from the case, how many screws usually hold the power supply in the case?

_3 or 4_

Installing Optical Drives

Just about every system today has an optical drive. Therefore, you will eventually have to install or replace one. Like other computer components, be sure to follow basic ESD prevention and safety procedures.

Concept Questions

Answer the following questions about installing optical drives:

What are the main steps in physically installing an optical drive?

Position optical drive so that it aligns with 5.25 inch bay
Insert into bay so that screw holes align with those in case
Secure with screws

If the optical drive is using a parallel IDE interface, how should you configure the optical drive?

Installing Floppy Disk Drives

Although many newer systems do not have a floppy disk drive, a large number of older systems do. Therefore, you might need to install or replace one. Like other computer components, be sure to follow basic ESD prevention and safety procedures.

Concept Questions

Answer the following questions about installing floppy disk drives:

What are the main steps in physically installing a floppy disk drive?

Position FDD so that it aligns with 3.5inch bay
Insert FDD so that screw holes align
Secure using screws

If you insert the floppy drive cable incorrectly, what would happen?

The activity light will display continuously

To help you insert the ribbon cable properly, how do you know which pin on the cable is pin 1?

Pin 1 on floppy data cable needs to be aligned with pin 1

As a general rule concerning the power connector, where should the red line be when connecting the floppy with the ribbon cable?

Installing a Hard Drive

Today, every system has at least one hard drive. Therefore, you will eventually have to install or replace one. Like other computer components, be sure to follow basic ESD prevention and safety procedures.

Vocabulary Exercise: Completion

Fill in the blanks with the appropriate terms about installing a hard drive.

IDE ribbon cables have a colored line on one side of the ribbon that indicates which edge of the cable connects to _pin 1_ on the socket.

Modern IDE ribbons are _keyed_ so that they can be inserted only one way on the motherboard and IDE drive.

Each IDE ribbon cable can support up to _2_ devices.

An EIDE controller supports up to _2_ devices.

When you have one device connected to the ribbon cable, it is configured as a _primary_ device or _secondary_ device if the standalone option is not available.

When you have two devices connected to the ribbon cable, one is configured as the _master_ and the other is configured as the _slave_ .

To configure a drive to be a master, a slave, or a standalone drive, you use _jumpers_ .

The original _____ ribbon cable could not handle the faster data rates (66 MB/s or higher). Therefore, starting with DMA/66, a ___ -pin conductor with ___ wire ribbon cable was introduced.

The serial ATA data connector uses ___ pins.

The older SCSI interfaces (including SCSI-1) supported up to _8_ SCSI devices (including the host adapter) connected to the host adapter, whereas newer SCSI interfaces (including Wide SCSI) support up to _16_ devices (including the host adapter) connected to the host adapter.

Different from the IDE interface, the two ends of the SCSI chain must be _terminated_ .

Each SCSI device, including the adapter/controller card, is numbered with a _SCSI ID_ from 0 to 7 or 0 to 15.

Although SCSI devices can be configured to use any free SCSI ID number, ID ___ is usually set aside for the floppy drive; it is recommended that optical drives such as CD and DVD drives are set to ID ___.

The SCSI adapter is usually set to _15_ , and the primary SCSI hard drive or any other boot device is set to _0_ .

To configure the SCSI ID numbers for SCSI hard drives, you typically use _jumpers_ .

BIOS and the BIOS Setup Program

The BIOS setup program is stored in the system ROM chip. It varies greatly from computer to computer. Today's BIOS setup programs include many options. To organize them, they are often grouped together. Most BIOS setup programs are menu based, including standard CMOS setup, advanced chipset setup, power management, PCI configuration, and peripheral configuration.

The standard CMOS setup includes the information for the date, time, floppy drives, hard drives, keyboard, and video card. The advanced chipset is used to fine-tune the hardware setup of the system, such as fine-tuning the processor (including enabling or disabling Hyper-Threading), cache system, memory system, or I/O system. The peripherals setup options include onboard floppy disk drives, parallel ports, and serial ports that can be disabled or configured using the BIOS setup program. Power management includes several options to extend the battery life of notebook computers and to conserve power on desktop computers.

Concept Questions

Answer the following questions about BIOS and the BIOS setup:

What is POST short for?

Power On Self Test

Define what the POST does.

The POST program checks out the system every time the computer boots. It sends out a standard command to all the devices to run their own internal diagnostic. It then conveys that information in a series of beep codes & messages.

What is the problem when you hear a single beep?

There is usually no problem - a single beep denotes that a computer is functioning properly.

How do you enter the BIOS setup program?

The proper key or key sequence must be pressed during POST. It is often the delete key

Study Questions

Choose the best answer for each of the questions that follow.

1. If an IDE ribbon cable is not keyed, how do you know how to connect the cable?

   A. Pin 1 of the cable will be indicated with a red or blue stripe. Connect the red or blue stripe lining up to pin 1.

   B. Attach the cable any way that fits.

   C. Purchase a new cable.

   D. Purchase a new drive.

2. You have an IDE hard drive and an IDE DVD drive on the same ribbon cable. What do you need to do so that both drives will function properly?

   A. Select the hard drive to be the master and the DVD drive to be the slave.

   B. Connect the hard drive at the end of the cable and the DVD drive into the middle connector. Be sure that the ribbon cable has a twist in it.

   C. Select the hard drive and the DVD drive to be the master so that you can get the best performance.

   D. Select the hard drive to IDE #1 and the DVD drive to IDE #2.

3. Which of the following determines master or slave on an IDE ribbon cable?

   A. A twist in the cable

   B. Which device was installed first

   C. The jumper settings

   D. The BIOS

4. If you connect a new IDE hard drive and the drive is not recognized, what should you check first?

   A. The cable

   B. The jumper settings

   C. The BIOS

   D. The drive

5. You just installed a second hard drive onto the ribbon cable that hosts the first hard drive. The second hard drive is not being recognized. You therefore verify that the ribbon cable is connected properly and that the jumper settings are configured properly. What else should you do?

   A. Make sure that the hard drive has been partitioned and formatted.

   B. Run the FDISK /MBR to repair the master boot record.

   C. Verify that the partition is active.

   D. Verify that the BIOS has been configured to detect a second hard drive.

6. Which of the following is a task that you have to perform when installing SCSI devices? (Choose two answers.)

    A. Set the jumpers for master/slave.

    B. Perform a low-level format on the SCSI drive.

    C. Assign each SCSI device a unique ID number.

    D. Set the drive type in the CMOS setup.

    E. Make sure that the two ends on the SCSI chain are terminated.

7. If a power supply fails, what should you do?

    A. Send it to an electrical technician.

    B. Try to fix it yourself.

    C. Replace the power supply.

    D. Replace the computer.

8. When installing a new processor, what should you apply directly to the processor?

    A. Cooling liquid

    B. Thermal compound

    C. A heat sink

    D. A fan

9. When connecting a floppy drive ribbon cable, how should the ribbon cable be connected?

    A. Attach cable any way that fits.

    B. Typically, the red or blue line should be farthest from the power connection.

    C. Typically, the red or blue line should be closest to the power connection.

    D. If the cable does not have a red or blue line, you are using the wrong cable, so it has to be replaced.

10. On an AT power supply, how should you connect the P8 and P9 power connectors?

    A. The green wires have to be together.

    B. The white wires have to be together.

    C. The brown wires have to be together.

    D. The black wires have to be together.

11. How do I know if I have an ATX power supply instead of an AT power supply?

    A. An AT power supply will have two power connectors that connect to the motherboard. The ATX power supply will have either a 20- or 24-pin power connector that connects to the motherboard.

    B. An ATX power supply will have two power connectors that connect to the motherboard. The AT power supply will have either a 20- or 24-pin power connector that connects to the motherboard.

    C. The AT power supply will have eight power connectors for drives and other devices.

    D. The ATX power supply will have eight power connectors for drives and other devices.

12. Which of the following sockets are used for a 3.8 GHz Pentium 4 processor?

    A. Socket 423
    B. Socket 426
    C. Socket 478
    D. Socket 754
    E. Socket A

13. You are looking at a processor socket that has 462 pins. Which processors can be inserted into it?

    A. Intel Pentium 4 processor
    B. AMD Athlon processor
    C. AMD Athlon 64 processor
    D. Intel Core2 processor

14. If you wanted to disable Hyper-Threading on a 3.6 MHz Pentium 4 system, what would you use?

    A. Windows Device Manager.
    B. Jumpers on the motherboard.
    C. The BIOS setup program.
    D. The Pentium 4 running at 3.6 MHz does not support Hyper-Threading.

Lab Exercises

Lab 3.2.0: Install the Power Supply

In this lab, you will install a power supply in a computer case.

The following is the recommended equipment for this lab:

- Power supply with the same form factor as the computer case
- Computer case
- Tool kit
- Power supply screws

Step 1

Remove the screws that hold the side panels in place.

Remove the side panels.

Step 2

Align the screw holes in the power supply with the screw holes in the case.

Secure the power supply to the case using the proper screws.

Step 3

If the power supply has a voltage selection switch, set this switch to match the voltage in your area.

What is the voltage in your area?

_____

How many screws hold the power supply in place?

_____

What is the total wattage of the power supply?

_____

Lab 3.3.3: Install the Motherboard

In this lab, you will install a CPU, a heat sink/fan assembly, and a RAM module on the motherboard. You will then install the motherboard in the computer case.

The following is the recommended equipment for this lab:

- Computer case with power supply installed
- Motherboard
- CPU

- Heat sink/fan assembly

- Thermal compound

- RAM module(s)

- Motherboard standoffs and screws

- Antistatic wrist strap and antistatic mat

- Tool kit

- Motherboard manual

Step 1

Place the motherboard, CPU, RAM, and the heat sink/fan assembly on the antistatic mat.

Step 2

Put on your antistatic wrist strap and attach the grounding cable to the antistatic mat.

Locate pin 1 on the CPU. Locate pin 1 on the socket.

Note: The CPU may be damaged if it is installed incorrectly.

Align pin 1 on the CPU with pin 1 on the socket.

Place the CPU into the CPU socket.

Close the CPU load plate and secure it in place by closing the load lever and moving it under the load lever retention tab.

Step 3

Apply a small amount of thermal compound to the CPU, and then spread it evenly.

Note: Thermal compound is necessary only when not factory applied on the heat sink assembly. Follow all instructions provided by the manufacturer for specific application details.

Step 4

Align the heat sink/fan assembly retainers with the holes on the motherboard around the CPU socket.

Place the heat sink/fan assembly onto the CPU and the retainers through the holes on the motherboard.

Tighten the heat sink/fan assembly retainers to secure it.

Plug the fan connector into the motherboard. Refer to the motherboard manual to determine which set of fan header pins to use.

Step 5

Locate the RAM slots on the motherboard.

In what type of slot(s) will the RAM module(s) be installed?

_____

How many notches are found on the bottom edge of the RAM module?

_____

Align the notch(es) on the bottom edge of the RAM module to the notches in the slot.

Press down until the side tabs secure the RAM module.

Ensure that none of the RAM module contacts are visible. Reseat the RAM module if necessary.

Check the latches to verify that the RAM module is secure.

Install any additional RAM modules using the same procedures.

Step 6

Install the motherboard standoffs.

Align the connectors on the back of the motherboard with the openings in the back of the computer case.

Place the motherboard into the case and align the holes for the screws and the standoffs. You may need to adjust the motherboard to line up the holes for the screws.

Attach the motherboard to the case using the appropriate screws.

Step 7

Connect the wires from the case link lights and buttons to the motherboard connectors.

 # Lab 3.5.2: Install the Drives

In this lab, you will install the hard disk drive, the optical drive, and the floppy drive.

The following is the recommended equipment for this lab:

- Computer case with power supply and motherboard installed
- Antistatic wrist strap and antistatic mat
- Tool kit
- Hard disk drive
- Hard disk drive screws
- Floppy drive
- Floppy drive screws
- Optical drive

- Optical drive screws
- Motherboard manual

Step 1

Align the hard disk drive with the 3.5-inch drive bay.

Slide the hard disk drive into the bay from the inside of the case until the screw holes line up with the holes in the 3.5-inch drive bay.

Secure the hard disk drive to the case using the proper screws.

Step 2

Note: Remove the 5.25-inch cover from one of the 5.25-inch external drive bays if necessary.

Align the optical drive with the 5.25-inch drive bay.

Insert the optical drive into the drive bay from the front of the case until the screw holes line up with the holes in the 5.25-inch drive bay and the front of the optical drive is flush with the front of the case.

Secure the optical drive to the case using the proper screws.

Step 3

Note: Remove the 3.5-inch cover from one of the 3.5-inch external drive bays if necessary.

Align the floppy drive with the 3.5-inch drive bay.

Insert the floppy drive into the drive bay from the front of the case until the screw holes line up with the holes in the 3.5-inch drive bay and the front of the floppy drive is flush with the front of the case.

Secure the floppy drive to the case using the proper screws.

 # Lab 3.6.3: Install Adapter Cards

In this lab, you will install a NIC, a wireless NIC, and a video adapter card.

The following is the recommended equipment for this lab:

- Computer with power supply, motherboard, and drives installed
- NIC
- Wireless NIC
- Video adapter card
- Adapter card screws
- Antistatic wrist strap and antistatic mat
- Tool kit
- Motherboard manual

Step 1

What type of expansion slot is compatible with the NIC?

_____

Locate a compatible expansion slot for the NIC on the motherboard.

Remove the slot cover from the back of the case, if necessary.

Align the NIC to the expansion slot.

Press down gently on the NIC until the card is fully seated.

Secure the NIC by attaching the PC mounting bracket to the case with a screw.

Step 2

What type of expansion slot is compatible with the wireless NIC?

_____

Locate a compatible expansion slot for the wireless NIC on the motherboard.

Remove the slot cover from the back of the case, if necessary.

Align the wireless NIC to the expansion slot.

Press down gently on the wireless NIC until the card is fully seated.

Secure the wireless NIC by attaching the PC mounting bracket to the case with a screw.

Step 3

What type of expansion slot is compatible with the video adapter card?

_____

Locate a compatible expansion slot for the video adapter card on the motherboard.

Remove the slot cover from the back of the case, if necessary.

Align the video adapter card to the expansion slot.

Press down gently on the video adapter card until the card is fully seated.

Secure the video adapter card by attaching the PC mounting bracket to the case with a screw.

 # Lab 3.7.2: Install Internal Cables

In this lab, install the internal power and data cables in the computer.

The following is the recommended equipment for this lab:

- Computer with power supply, motherboard, drives, and adapter cards installed
- Hard disk drive data cable

- Optical drive data cable
- Floppy drive data cable
- Antistatic wrist strap and antistatic mat
- Tool kit
- Motherboard manual

Step 1

Align the motherboard power supply connector to the socket on the motherboard.

Gently press down on the connector until the clip clicks into place.

Step 2

Note: This step is necessary only if your computer has an auxiliary power connector.

Align the auxiliary power connector to the auxiliary power socket on the motherboard.

Gently press down on the connector until the clip clicks into place.

Step 3

Plug a power connector into the hard disk drive, optical drive, and floppy drive. Ensure that the floppy drive power connector is inserted right side up.

Step 4

Note: This step is necessary only if your computer has a fan power connector.

Connect the fan power connector into the appropriate fan header on the motherboard.

Step 5

Note: Pin 1 on a PATA cable must align with Pin 1 on the motherboard connector and the hard disk drive connector.

Align and plug the hard disk drive data cable into the motherboard connector.

Align and plug the other end of the hard disk drive data cable into the hard disk drive connector.

Step 6

Note: Pin 1 on a PATA cable must align with Pin 1 on the motherboard connector and the optical drive connector.

Align and plug the optical drive data cable into the motherboard connector.

Align and plug the other end of the optical drive data cable into the optical drive connector.

Step 7

Note: Pin 1 on a floppy drive cable must align with Pin 1 on the motherboard connector and the floppy drive connector.

Align and plug the floppy drive data cable into the motherboard connector.

Align and plug the other end of the floppy drive data cable into the floppy drive connector.

Lab 3.8.2: Complete the Computer Assembly

In this lab, you will install the side panels and the external cables on the computer.

The following is the recommended equipment for this lab:

- Computer with power supply, motherboard, drives, and adapter cards installed and internal cables connected
- Monitor cable (DVI or VGA)
- Keyboard
- Mouse
- USB cable for the USB hub
- USB cable for the USB printer
- Network cable
- Wireless antenna
- Power cable
- Tool kit
- Motherboard manual

Step 1

Attach the side panels to the computer case.

Secure the side panels to the computer using the panel screws.

Step 2

Attach the monitor cable to the video port.

Secure the cable by tightening the screws on the connector.

Step 3

Plug the keyboard cable into the PS/2 keyboard port.

Step 4

Plug the mouse cable into the PS/2 mouse port.

Step 5

Plug the hub USB cable into any USB port.

Step 6

Plug the printer USB cable into a USB port in the hub.

Step 7

Plug the Ethernet cable into the Ethernet port.

Step 8

Connect the wireless antenna to the antenna connector.

Step 9

Plug the power cable into the power socket of the power supply.

 ## Lab 3.9.2: Boot the Computer

In this lab, you will boot the computer for the first time, explore the BIOS setup program, and change the boot order sequence.

The following is the recommended equipment for this lab:

- Assembled computer without an operating system installed
- Motherboard manual

Step 1

Plug the power supply cable into an AC wall outlet.

Turn on the computer.

Note: If the computer beeps more than once, or if the power does not come on, notify your instructor.

Step 2

During POST, press the BIOS setup key or key combination.

The BIOS setup program screen will appear.

What is the key or combination of keys used to enter the BIOS setup program?

Who manufactures the BIOS for your computer?

What is the BIOS version?

_____

What menu options are available?

_____

Step 3

Navigate through each screen to find the boot order sequence.

What is the first boot device in the boot order sequence?

_____

How many additional devices can be assigned in the boot order sequence?

_____

Step 4

Ensure that the first boot order device is the optical drive.

Ensure that the second boot order device is the hard disk drive.

Why would you change the first boot device to the optical drive?

_____

What happens when the computer boots and the optical drive does not contain bootable media?

_____

Step 5

Navigate through each screen to find the power management setup screen, or ACPI screen.

What power management settings are available?

_____

Step 6

Navigate through each screen to find the PnP settings.

What PnP settings are available?

_____

Step 7

Save the new BIOS settings and exit the BIOS setup program.

Step 8

The computer will restart.

An operating system can be installed at this time.

CHAPTER 4

Basics of Preventive Maintenance and Troubleshooting

The Study Guide portion of this chapter uses a combination of multiple-choice and open-ended questions to test your knowledge of maintaining and troubleshooting computers. This portion also includes multiple-choice study questions to help prepare you to take the A+ certification exams and to test your overall understanding of the material.

There are no online curriculum items for this chapter.

Study Guide

Preventive Maintenance

You might have heard the old saying, "An ounce of prevention is worth a pound of cure." In computers, this expression is very true because a little preventive maintenance can prevent some major problems down the road. However, no matter how much preventive maintenance you perform, problems will eventually occur if you wait long enough. Therefore, you will need to know how to troubleshoot these problems using a systematic approach.

Concept Questions

Answer the following preventive maintenance question:

Why is it important to perform periodic maintenance?

Periodic maintenance can prevent problems occurring in the future. It increases data protection, extends the life of components, increases equipment stability, reduces repair costs, & reduced the number of equipment failure

Troubleshooting

When encountering a computer problem, you should follow certain guidelines. First, you must be clear and rested. You must be able to concentrate on the problem. You must not panic. Don't get frustrated, and be sure to allow enough time to do the job correctly. And you must keep an open mind because the problems can be caused by hardware failure, compatibility problems, an improper configuration, a software glitch, an environmental factor, or a user error. Finally, you need to be systematic when trying to isolate the problem.

Concept Questions

Answer the following troubleshooting questions:

Why is it important to follow a troubleshooting model?

A logical approach allows you to eliminate variables in a systematic order

What are the six main steps in troubleshooting a PC?

Step 1. Gather data from the customer

Step 2. Verify the obvious

Step 3. Try quick or less intensive solutions first

Step 4.   _Gather data from the computer_

Step 5.   _Evaluate the problem & impliment the solution_

Step 6.   _Close with the customer_

What should you do before you do any type of repair or modification?

Protect data. Verify with the customer the date of the last backup, contents of the backup, data integrity of the backup & availability of all backup media for a data restore.

Why is it important to check the obvious when troubleshooting?

Even though the customer might think there is major problem it is more efficient to start with the obvious issues before moving to more complex diagnosis

Explain the importance of closing with the customer.

It is important that the customer verifies that the problem has been solved.

Troubleshooting Example

Follow through this troubleshooting example to gain a better understanding of the details involved in the troubleshooting process.

Problem: You get a call saying that a computer will not boot.

Step 1.   Gather data from the customer.

When you get to the office, you confirm that the computer has not booted. So you ask the customer the following:

Has it ever worked?

When was the last time it worked?

Have any changes been done to the system?

Has any maintenance been done on the system?

Are there any lights on or is the fan running?

If lights are on or the fans are on, it is most likely not a power problem.

Steps 2 and 3.   Verify the obvious issues and try quick solutions first.

To check the obvious first, you decide to make sure that the computer is turned on and is plugged in. You make sure that you do have power from the AC outlet. Make sure that the AC outlet is not connected to an on-off switch on the wall with the switch off. If the computer is connected to a surge protector, make sure that the surge protector is on. Also check for any damaged power cables. If any item has been changed or if maintenance has been recently done, check to see what was done and verify that the work was done properly.

Step 4.   Gather data from the computer.

Make sure that there are no lights and the fans are not running. If lights are on or the fans are on, it is most likely not a power problem. If the computer does not turn on, there is not much more data that you can gather from the computer itself.

Step 5.   Evaluate the problem and implement the solution.

Try the following to evaluate and isolate the problem:

- Verify that the AC outlet is supplying the correct power.

- Make sure that the power connections are properly connected to the motherboard.

- Make sure all other cables are connected properly.

- Make sure the processor and RAM are installed properly.

After checking the easy items, you may have to dig deeper because you suspect a faulty component. Faulty components that would cause a system not to boot and not to have any lights or fans include the following:

- Processor

- Motherboard

- Power supply

- Power cord

To figure out which item is faulty, you will need to swap each of these items one by one until you find the faulty component. You can also test each component in a known-good system to see whether the component is working or faulty.

Step 6.   Close with the customer.

After the problem has been solved, close with the customer to show that the computer is fixed and is working properly. Also verify with the customer that no other problems exist with the system. You also need to make sure that you document the steps that you took in identifying the problem and implementing the solution.

Study Questions

Choose the best answer for each of the questions that follow.

1. You need to add a second hard drive and add more memory to a computer. What should you do first?

   A. Back up all the data.

   B. Determine the amount of RAM that is in the system.

   C. Run scandisk on the current hard drive.

   D. Flash the BIOS with the newest version.

2. You decide to do some preventive maintenance on a computer system, including blowing out dust and dirt. When you perform the preventive maintenance, what should you also be doing? (Choose all that apply.)

   A. Make sure the system has the newest security patches.

   B. Replace all the cables.

   C. Check for visual defects.

D. Replace the CMOS battery.

E. Check the conditions of the environment, such as space around the case for air flow and dripping water.

3. When the memory test is completed onscreen, you get one short beep. What is the problem?

A. There is a memory failure.

B. There is a video card failure.

C. There is a loose cable.

D. There is no problem.

4. You have a system that has one short beep with nothing on the screen. What is most likely the problem?

A. There is a faulty processor.

B. There is a video card failure.

C. There is a loose cable.

D. There is no problem.

5. You have been called to an office where a computer is not functioning properly. After they tell you the problem, what is the first thing you should do in troubleshooting the problem?

A. Gather data from the customer.

B. Verify the obvious issues.

C. Isolate the problem.

D. Eliminate possibilities.

E. Document your findings and solutions.

6. When you gather information, what are some of the best questions to ask? (Choose all that apply.)

A. Can you show me the problem?

B. Is the computer still under warranty?

C. Has any new software been installed recently?

D. Where did you buy your computer?

E. Have any other changes been made to the computer recently?

F. Was the system running fine before?

7. After you gather information from the customer, what are the next two things you should try?

A. Verify the obvious issues.

B. Gather information from the computer.

C. Evaluate the problem and implement the solution.

D. Test the solution.

E. Try quick solutions.

8. What should you use to gather information from the computer? (Choose all that apply.)

A. Windows Event Viewer.

B. Device Manager.

C. Listen for beep codes or look for error messages on the screen.

D. Run diagnostic software.

E. Connect to the Internet and look for problems concerning the make and model of the computer in question.

9. You are troubleshooting a computer problem but cannot figure out the cause. How can you reduce the possibility of redundant effort by another technician?

   A. Isolate the problem.

   B. Verify the problem and solution.

   C. Document activities and outcomes of the repair steps.

   D. Verify the obvious issues.

10. You are called into an office where the user complains that the monitor is blank. Of these answers, which of the following will you not do?

   A. Determine whether the monitor is on.

   B. Determine whether the computer is on.

   C. Determine whether the contrast and brightness is turned down.

   D. Determine the type of computer it is.

   E. Determine whether there is a light on the monitor to indicate if it is on.

11. You have a computer that has been turned on, but the monitor is blank and none of the fans are spinning. What is the most likely cause of the problem?

   A. The computer is unplugged.

   B. The monitor is off.

   C. The power supply is bad.

   D. The processor is bad.

12. Which of the following can cause a computer to reboot often? (Choose all that apply.)

   A. An overheating processor

   B. A power outage

   C. Bad AC power

   D. A software upgrade

   E. A RAM upgrade

13. You have a client that often shows the incorrect date and time when the computer is first turned on. Which of the following should fix the problem?

   A. Replace the BIOS chip.

   B. Replace the CMOS battery.

   C. Replace the hard drive.

   D. Reinstall Windows.

14. You connected to a Cisco device using a cable that connects to your serial port. When you go into Windows Device Manager, you do not see the serial port. What is most likely the problem?

   A. You have a faulty serial cable.

   B. You need to enable the serial port in the BIOS setup program.

   C. You need to reboot the Cisco device.

   D. You need to detect hardware devices in Windows.

   E. You need to reinstall Windows.

CHAPTER 5

Fundamental Operating Systems

The Study Guide portion of this chapter uses a combination of matching, fill-in-the-blank, and open-ended questions to test your knowledge of operating systems. This portion also includes multiple-choice study questions to help prepare you to take the A+ certification exams and to test your overall understanding of the material.

The Lab Exercises portion of this chapter includes all the online curriculum hands-on labs and worksheets to further reinforce your mastery of operating systems.

Study Guide

Introduction to Operating Systems

The operating system (OS) is the computer's most important software. It coordinates the actions of the hardware, the software, and the user so that they can work as one. During bootup, the operating system is loaded from the boot disk (typically the hard disk) to RAM. It provides an interface to the user so that he or she can start other programs by entering a command at the keyboard or by using the mouse to perform an action. Then, depending on the actions of the user and instructions specified in the software, the operating system directs the computer's hardware. When the user saves a file to disk, the OS automatically records the location so that the user can find and access the file in the future and so that the operating system will not accidentally write over it with another file.

Concept Questions

Answer the following questions about operating systems:

What are the four main roles of an operating system?

1. Control Hardware Access
2. Manage Files & Folders
3. Provide a user interface
4. Manage Applications

List and describe the two types of operating system interfaces:

Command-Line Interface (CLI) user types commands at a prompt.

Graphical user Interface (GUI) user interacts with menus & icons

List at least two command-line operating systems:

DOS

List at least four GUI operating systems made by Microsoft:

Windows 2000   Windows Vista

Windows XP   Windows 2007

Installing Windows

As a desktop technician, you need to know how to install the various Windows operating systems. You also need to make sure that you know the minimum requirements to install the operating system and what resources the operating system can utilize.

Vocabulary Exercise: Completion

Fill in the blanks with the appropriate terms about installing Windows.

Windows 2000 Professional and Windows XP support up to _____ of memory.

Windows XP Home Edition supports up to ____ processor(s), whereas Windows 2000 Professional and Windows XP Professional support up to ____ processor(s).

Concept Questions

Answer the following questions about installing Windows.

Fill in the blanks in the following table.

	Windows 2000 Professional	Windows XP Professional
Processor	Pentium processor running at 133 MHz	
RAM		64 MB
Free Disk Space	650 MB	

What is the importance of using hardware that is on the hardware compatibility list (HCL)?

To ensure that the hardware is compatible with the installed operating system.

If you are trying to boot from a Windows installation CD, such as a Windows 2000 or Windows XP installation CD, and the system appears not to boot from the CD, what do you need to do?

Check that the BIOS is configured to boot system from a CD/DVD

When installing Windows 95, Windows 98, or Windows Millennium, what is the executable that starts the installation process, and where can it be found?

When you install Windows 98, list and describe the four types of Windows setups.

Windows 2000 and Windows XP can use one of two executable files to install Windows. What are the names of the two executable files?

File Allocation Table 32-bit (FAT 32) & New Technology File System NTFS

If you wanted to upgrade Windows 2000 Professional to Windows XP, which executable would you use to perform the upgrade?

After Windows is installed, you should visit the Microsoft update website and install what?

The latest OS updates

Vocabulary Exercise: Matching

Match the definition on the left with a term on the right.

Definitions

a. The process of assigning part or all of the drive for use by the computer.

b. A central information database for Windows 2000 and Windows XP organized into a structured hierarchical database to hold hardware, operating system, and application settings and configuration.

c. Allows a user to manage files and directories from a single graphical interface.

d. Normally installed on a server, it has much of the same functionality as a desktop operating system but contains additional components and features that enable the computer to control network functions such as sharing resources.

e. The partition used by the operating system to boot the computer.

f. Prepares a file system in a partition for files to be stored.

g. A method for storing and organizing computer files and the data they contain to make it easy to find and access them.

h. A collection of fixes and patches bundled as a single upgrade.

i. A configuration file that contains configuration data (that is, idiom terms) for Microsoft Windows-based applications.

Terms

_e_ Active partition

_g_ File system

_f_ Formatting

_i_ Initialization files

_d_ Network Operating System (NOS)

_a_ Partitioning

_b_ Registry

_h_ Service pack

_c_ Windows Explorer

Registry

The Registry is a central, secure database in which Windows 2000 and Windows XP stores all hardware configuration information, software configuration information, and system security policies. Components that use the Registry include the Windows kernel, device drivers, setup programs, NTDETECT.COM, hardware profiles, and user profiles.

The Registry is organized in a hierarchical structure. The Registry is first divided into five subtrees. Subtrees have names that begin with the string HKEY, which stands for Handle to a Key, often referred to as *hive key*. A subtree is similar to a root directory of a disk.

The Registry stores most of its information in sets of files called *hives*. A hive is a discrete body of keys, subkeys, and values. Each hive has a corresponding Registry file and LOG file located in the *%systemroot%*\SYSTEM32\CONFIG folder. When you back up and restore the Registry, you are working with hives.

Concept Questions

Answer the following questions about registries:

Identify the following Windows Registry subtrees:

- HKEY_CLASSES_ROOT: _Info about which file extensions map to a particular application_
- HKEY_CURRENT_USER: _Info eg. desktop settings & history related to the current user of a PC_
- HKEY_USERS: _Info about all users who have logged onto a system_
- HKEY_LOCAL_MACHINE: _Info relating to hardware & software_
- HKEY_CURRENT_CONFIG: _Info relation to all active devices on a system_

What utility do you use to make changes directly to the Registry?

REGEDIT

Windows 98 Boot Sequence

You need to be familiar with the Windows 98 boot sequence. It is different from other versions of Windows.

Concept Questions

Answer the following questions about the Windows 98 boot sequence.

Which system boot files are required for Windows 98 to boot?

Which boot files initiate the Windows 9x protected load phase and read the file system?

What is the first configuration file processed by the IO.SYS file?

Which system files are required for boot for Windows 95, Windows 98, and Windows Millennium?

Which files initiate the Windows 9x protected load phase?

Windows 2000/XP Boot Sequence

You also need to be familiar with the Windows 2000/XP boot sequence.

Concept Questions

Answer the following questions about the Windows 2000/XP boot sequence.

Which file is the first file read when booting Windows 2000 or Windows XP?

Master Boot Record (MBR)

Which file reads the Registry files, chooses a hardware profile, and loads device drivers?

NTLDR

Which file gets information about installed hardware?

ntdetect.com

Which file contains the Boot Loader Operating System Selection menu and specifies the path to find the boot partition?

boot.ini

Which two files make up the core of Windows 2000 and Windows XP?

ntoskrnl.exe and hal.dll

Which file is used for SCSI devices during bootup?

ntbootdd.sys

What file is used in a dual-boot configuration to keep a copy of the DOS-based operating system's boot sector so that the DOS-based operating system environment can be restored and loaded as needed?

Master Boot Record (MBR)

Which core file provides and handles the interaction between software and hardware via the Hardware Abstraction Layer and is necessary for the Windows NT-based operating system to boot and function?

NTLDR

If you get the Kernel File Is Missing from the Disk error message, what is the cause of the problem and how would you correct the problem?

What generates a Non-System Disk or Disk Error?

non bootable media in the floppy drive during computer boot up

If you get a Non-System Disk or Disk Error, what is the first thing you should check?

That there are no disks left in drives.

Windows 2000 and Windows XP Advanced Boot Menu

When you have problems with Windows starting, you have several tools available to help troubleshoot and fix these problems. Most of these tools are available under the Advanced boot menu.

Concept Questions

Answer the following questions about the boot menu:

Which key do you press while the Windows boot menu is listed to display the Advanced boot menu?

_F8_

Which mode starts the computer using only the basic drivers and files needed including the mouse, VGA monitor, keyboard, hard drive, and default system services?

Safe Mode

If you have a faulty driver that does not allow Windows to boot properly, what would you use to remove the faulty driver or roll back a driver that has been upgraded?

Boot into Safe Mode   then use Device Driver to locate problem.

Which mode loads the basic VGA driver (with a resolution of 640×480 and 16 colors) instead of any other video driver?

'Enable VGA Mode'

Which mode starts the computer by using the configuration that was saved the last time the computer started properly?

'Last known Good Configuration'

Which mode would you use to start basic drivers and files needed to boot with network connections?

'Safe Mode with Networking'

Windows File Systems

To become a successful computer technician, you must be familiar with the various file systems available to the various versions of Windows. You also need to know the characteristics of each of the file systems and the advantages and disadvantages of each.

Concept Questions

Answer the following questions about Windows file systems.

Which file system is used by DOS and can be accessed by all Microsoft Windows versions?

FAT

Which file system is used by Windows 95B, Windows 98 and Windows Millennium, Windows 2000, and Windows XP?

FAT 32

Which file system is the most secure and reliable file system used by Windows 2000 and Windows XP and supports disk quotas, disk compression, and encryption?

NTFS

In Windows XP, which file system supports only up to 32 GB volumes?

Which file system supports up to 2 TB?

FAT 32

File Management

When you work with Windows, you will have to work with files. In Windows, file management is done with Windows Explorer, which allows you to copy, move, and delete files. Therefore, as a computer technician, you will need to know how to manage these files.

Concept Questions

Answer the following questions about file management:

At the command prompt, how do you copy multiple files and folders?

Type `CD\Docs` to prompt to Docs, Type `copy` & a space Type *. [File Extension] space the destination.

When using Windows Explorer, how do you select several files at the same time so that you can copy them to the D: drive?

Hold CTRL key & left click mouse for each file to be copied. When all files selected right click mouse & select copy. Click in destination folder. Right click mouse & select paste.

How do you create a folder using Windows Explorer?

Left click on `File` to get drop down menu. Click `New` then folder

How do you display the directory listing at the command prompt?

Type CD\ followed by directory name

Control Panel

The Control Panel is a graphical tool used to configure the Windows environment and hardware devices. The most commonly used applets are the System applet, the Display applet, the Add/Remove Programs applet, and the Add New Hardware applet.

Concept Questions

Answer the following questions about the Control Panel:

How do you open the Device Manager in Windows?

(1) Start > Control Panel Double click System icon. This brings up Systems Properties dialog box. Select Hardware tab & then click Device Manager button.

(2) Right-click 'My Computer' & select 'Manage' This opens window called 'Computer Management' where 'Device Manager is listed on left side of screen under 'System Tools'

If you want to add hardware drivers for a new device, which Control Panel applet would you use?

'Add Hardware'

To keep your system loaded exclusively with drivers from the compatibility list so that there is less chance for system instability, Microsoft introduced what?

Driver Signing

To specify which screen saver your system uses, which Control Panel applet would you use?

'Display'

How do you create a bootable system disk using Windows 95/98?

What utility would you use to roll back a driver?

Open Device Manager, access properties for device you want to adjust. On drivers tab there is a rollback driver button.

Troubleshooting Tools

You need to be able to troubleshoot operating systems to be a successful computer technician.

Concept Questions

Answer the following questions about troubleshooting:

Which utility will allow you to see which applications are using too much system resources?

Task Manager

Which utility scans the Registry and checks for errors and allows you to back up the Registry files?

What utility looks for corrupt file problems and disk errors such as cross-linked files?

CHKDSK

* (3) Open Administrative Tools applet in Control Panel then select Computer Management

Study Questions

Choose the best answer for each of the questions that follow.

1. To make a startup disk using a Windows 98 machine, you would do what?

   A. Open a command prompt and execute the SYS A: command.

   B. In the Add/Remove Program applet, click the Windows Setup tab and click the System disk button.

   C. In the Add/Remove Program applet, click the Startup Disk and create the disk.

   D. Create the disk using the System Disk applet.

2. Which of the following support NTFS? (Choose all that apply.)

   A. Windows 98

   B. Windows Millennium

   C. Windows 2000

   D. Windows XP

3. Which of the Registry subtrees specifies which file extensions are associated with which programs?

   A. HKEY_CURRENT_USER

   B. HKEY_USERS

   C. HKEY_LOCAL_MACHINE

   D. HKEY_CLASSES_ROOT

4. Which files are needed to boot Windows 98?

   A. IO.SYS

   B. MSDOS.SYS

   C. Command.com

   D. WIN.Com

   E. BOOT.INI

5. In Windows XP, how do you lock the computer?

   A. Windows key-L shortcut

   B. Ctrl key-L shortcut

   C. Windows key-K shortcut

   D. Ctrl key-K shortcut

6. For the Windows operating system, where is the primary configuration information stored?

   A. System Registry

   B. NTLDR

   C. SYSTEM RESTORE

   D. NTDETECT.COM

7. What command do you use to copy multiple files and directories?

   A. Copy

   B. Xcopy.exe

   C. Diskcopy.exe

   D. Smartdrv.exe

8. Which of the following is a characteristic of the NTFS file system? (Choose all that apply.)

   A. Supports compression, encryption, disk quotas, and file ownership.

   B. Allows for file-level security to protect system resources.

   C. Can be accessed by DOS and Windows 9x operating systems.

   D. Can be easily converted back to FAT.

9. Which utility allows you to manage files and folders using a graphical interface in Windows 2000/XP?

   A. Command prompt

   B. Windows Explorer

   C. Internet Explorer

   D. Computer Management

10. When you install Windows 98, what does the Compact installation install?

    A. Components generally needed for a compact or mobile computer.

    B. Selected components and options.

    C. General set of components that are used by most users.

    D. A minimum set of components and options.

11. Which file is used to display the boot menu in Windows XP?

    A. SYSTEM.INI

    B. BOOT.INI

    C. NTDETECT.COM

    D. NTOSKRNL.EXE

    E. BOOTSECT.DOS

12. A user has Windows 2000, which needs to be upgraded to Windows XP. Which of the following should you do?

    A. Boot the system with the Windows XP CD.

    B. Start the Windows XP program from within the operating system.

    C. Copy Windows XP to the C: drive and restart the computer.

    D. Format the C: drive and copy the Windows XP to the C: drive.

13. Which program is used to install Windows 98?

    A. WINNT.EXE

    B. WINNT32.EXE

    C. SETUP.EXE

    D. INSTALL.EXE

14. Which programs are used to install Windows XP? (Choose two.)

    A. WINNT.EXE

    B. WINNT32.EXE

    C. SETUP.EXE

    D. INSTALL.EXE

15. What is the minimum recommended free disk space to install Windows XP Professional edition?

    A. 320 MB

    B. 1 GB

    C. 2 GB

    D. 1.5 GB

16. Which of the following drivers are most likely compatible with Windows 2000?

    A. Windows NT drivers

    B. Windows 95 drivers

    C. Windows 98 drivers

    D. Windows XP drivers

17. Windows XP Professional supports up to _____ processors and _____ GB of RAM.

    A. 1, 1

    B. 1, 2

    C. 1, 4

    D. 2, 2

    E. 2, 4

18. To make sure that drivers are tested, you should install only what kind of drivers on a Windows XP machine?

    A. Unsigned drivers

    B. Signed drivers

    C. Windows 2000 drivers

    D. Drivers from the manufacturer's website

19. You upgraded a driver in Windows XP. Unfortunately, your machine does not boot. How do you fix it?

    A. Boot with a Windows XP CD, access the Device Manager, and find out more about the issue.

    B. Boot to safe mode, access the Device Manager, and roll back the driver.

    C. Start Windows in safe mode and remove the problematic driver.

    D. Boot into VGA mode and roll back the driver.

20. Which two utilities can you use to identify problems in Windows XP?

    A. Task Manager

    B. Control Panel

    C. Event Viewer

    D. System Restore

21. You installed a program and now Windows will not boot. What should you do?

    A. Try booting to VGA mode.

    B. Boot to the last known good configuration.

    C. Boot to safe mode with networking.

    D. Boot to debugging mode.

22. Which startup mode loads only the basic files and drivers needed to boot Windows?

    A. VGA mode.

    B. Boot to the last known good configuration.

    C. Safe mode with networking.

    D. Safe mode.

23. How do you determine whether a program is using too much memory?

    A. Use the Task Manager.

    B. Use the Computer Management Console.

    C. Use the **MEM /C** command.

    D. Use the Device Manager.

24. What is the first file loaded when Windows XP starts?

    A. NTLDR

    B. BOOT.INI

    C. NTBOOTDD.SYS

    D. NTDETECT.COM

25. What do you use to check the integrity of the hard drive file system in Windows XP and to attempt to repair the problems found?

    A. SCANREG

    B. SCANDISK

    C. CHKDSK

    D. DISKSCAN

Lab Exercises

Worksheet 5.2.2: Search NOS Jobs

In this worksheet, you will use the Internet, a newspaper, or magazines to gather information about network operating system certifications and jobs that require these certifications.

Use the Internet to research three different network operating system certifications. Based on your research, complete the table that follows:

	Network Operating System(s) Covered	Certification(s) Title	Courses/Training Required for Certification

Use the Internet, a newspaper, or a magazine to find at least two network jobs available in your area. Describe the network jobs and the required certifications needed for the position.

_____

_____

_____

_____

_____

_____

_____

_____

_____

_____

_____

Which job would you prefer? List reasons for your selection.

_____

_____

_____

Worksheet 5.3.2: Upgrade Hardware Components

In this worksheet, you will use the Internet, a newspaper, or a local store to gather information about hardware components. Your customer's computer currently has 1 module of 256 MB of RAM, a 40-GB hard disk drive, and an AGP video adapter card with 32 MB of RAM. Your customer wants to be able to play advanced video games.

Shop around, and in the following table list the brand, model number, features, and cost for two different 1 GB modules of DDR400 (PC3200).

Brand and Model Number	Features	Cost

Based on your research, which RAM would you select? Be prepared to discuss your decisions regarding the RAM you select.

Shop around, and in the following table list the brand, model number, features, and cost for two different 500 GB 5400 rpm IDE hard disk drives.

Brand and Model Number	Features	Cost

Based on your research, which hard disk drive would you select? Be prepared to discuss your decisions regarding the hard disk drive you select.

Shop around, and in the following table list the brand, model number, features, and cost for two different 8x AGP video adapter cards with 256 MB RAM.

Brand and Model Number	Features	Cost

Based on your research, which video adapter card would you select? Be prepared to discuss your decisions regarding the video adapter card you select.

_____

_____

_____

Lab 5.4.2: Install Windows XP

In this lab, you will install the Windows XP Professional operating system.

The following is the recommended equipment for this lab:

- A computer with a blank hard disk drive
- Windows XP Professional installation CD

Step 1

Insert the Windows XP installation CD into the CD-ROM drive.

When the system starts up, watch for the message Press Any Key to Boot from CD (see Figure 5-1).

If the message appears, press any key on the keyboard to boot the system from the CD. The system will now begin inspecting the hardware configuration. If the message does not appear, the hard drive is empty and the system will now begin inspecting the hardware configuration.

Figure 5-1   Booting from a Computer with a Bootable CD

Step 2

The Windows XP Professional Setup screen appears (see Figure 5-2). During this part of setup, the mouse will not work, so you must use the keyboard. On the Welcome to Setup page, press Enter to continue.

Figure 5-2   Welcome Screen During the Windows XP Installation

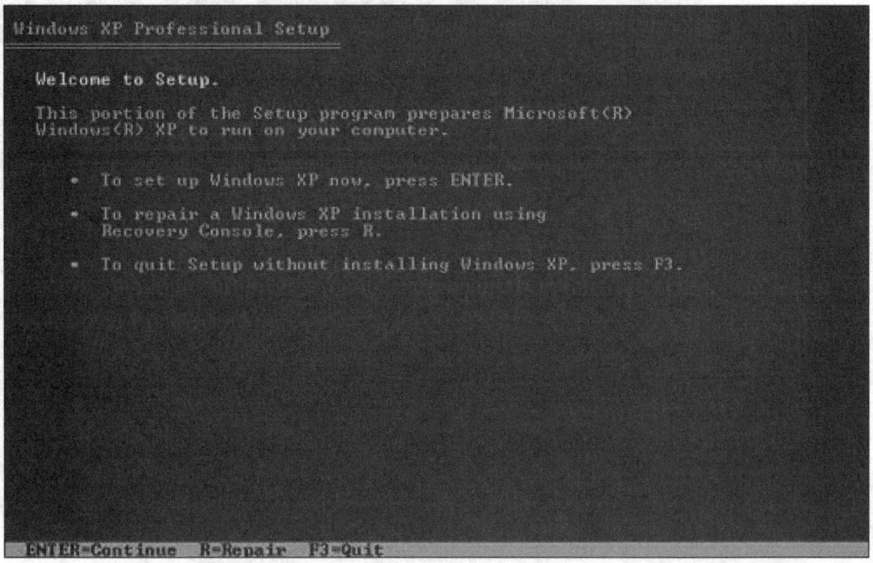

Step 3

The Windows XP Licensing Agreement page appears (see Figure 5-3). Press the Page Down key to scroll to the bottom of the license agreement. Press the F8 key to agree to the license.

Figure 5-3   The Windows XP Licensing Agreement

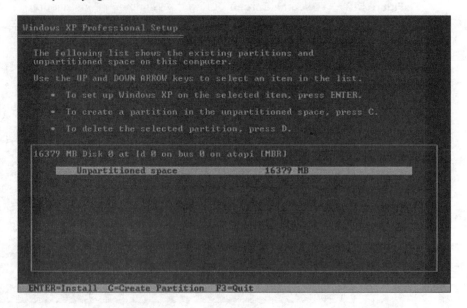

Step 4

Select the hard drive or partition on which Windows XP will be installed.

Press Enter to select Unpartitioned Space, which is the default setting (see Figure 5-4).

Figure 5-4   Specifying the Partition on Which to Install Windows XP

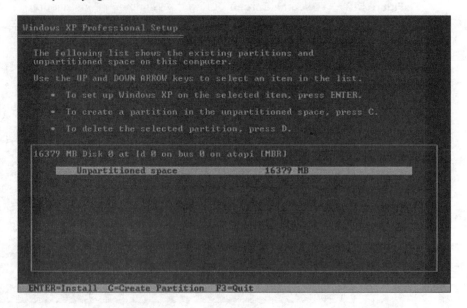

Step 5

Press Enter again to select Format the Partition Using the NTFS File System, which is the default setting (see Figure 5-5).

Figure 5-5   Choosing to Format the Partition Before You Install Windows XP

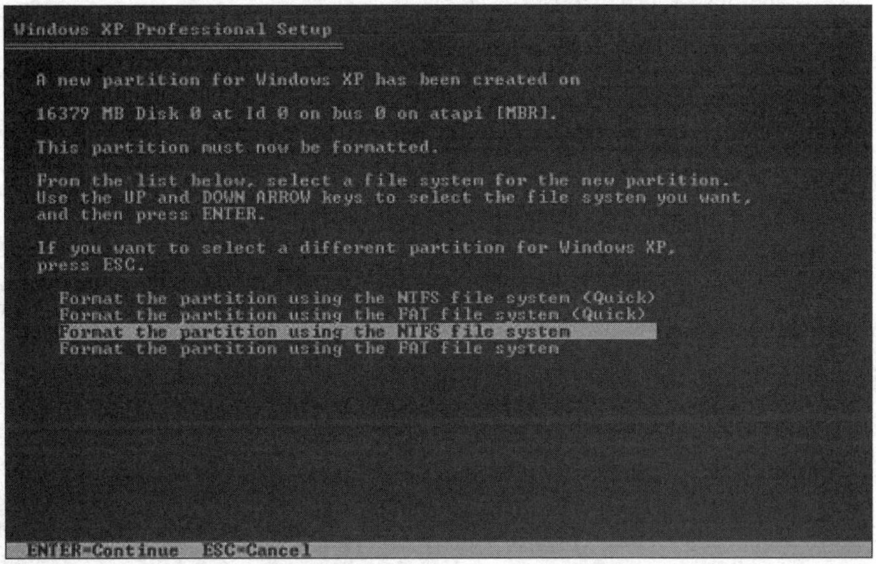

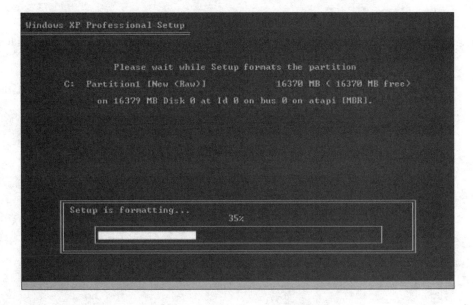

Windows XP Professional Setup erases the hard disk drive, formats the hard disk drive (see Figure 5-6), and copies the setup files from the installation CD to the hard disk drive. This process should take between 20 and 30 minutes to complete.

Figure 5-6   Formatting of the Partition During the Windows XP Installation

Step 6

After the formatting and copying processes, Windows XP restarts and continues with the installation process. At this point, the mouse can be used to make selections. The Regional and Language Options page appears. Click Next to accept the default settings. Regional and language options can be configured after setup is complete.

The Personalize Your Software page appears. Type the name and the organization name provided by your instructor. Click Next (see Figure 5-7).

Figure 5-7   Specifying the Name and Organization During Windows XP Installation

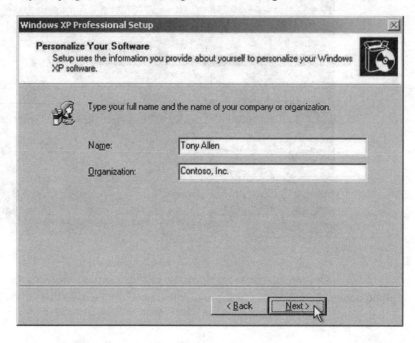

Step 7

The Your Product Key page appears. On this page, type your product key as it appears on your Windows XP CD case. Click Next (see Figure 5-8).

Figure 5-8   Entering the Product Key During the Windows XP Installation

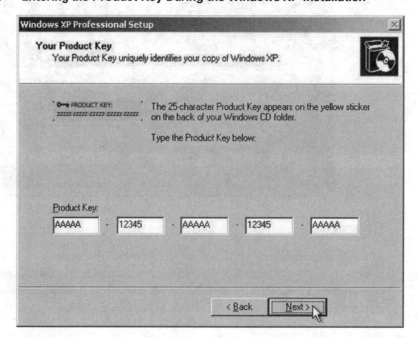

On the Computer Name and Administrator Password screen, type the computer name provided by your instructor. Type the Administrator password provided by your instructor, and retype it in the Confirm Password section. Click Next (see Figure 5-9).

Figure 5-9   Specifying the Computer Name and Administrator Password

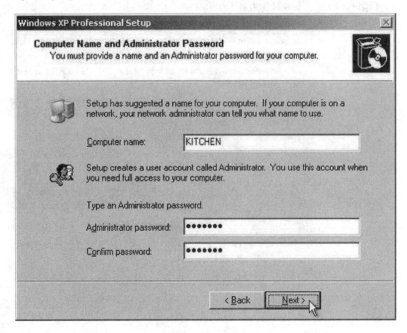

Step 8

On the Date and Time Settings screen, configure the computer clock to match your local date, time, and time zone. Click Next (see Figure 5-10).

Figure 5-10   Specifying the Date and Time During the Windows XP Installation

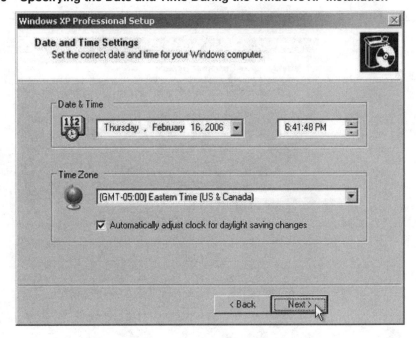

Step 9

On the Networking Settings page, click Next to accept Typical Settings. Custom Settings can be configured after setup is complete (see Figure 5-11).

Figure 5-11   Selecting a Typical or Custom Installation

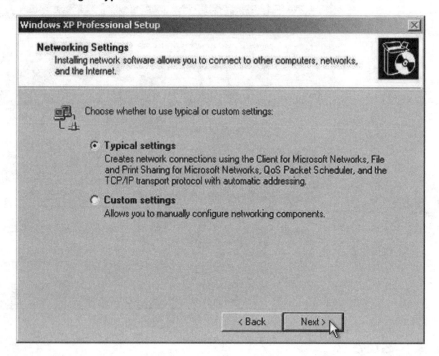

Step 10

On the Workgroup or Computer Domain page, accept the default settings and click Next (see Figure 5-12).

Figure 5-12   Specifying a Workgroup or Joining the System to a Domain

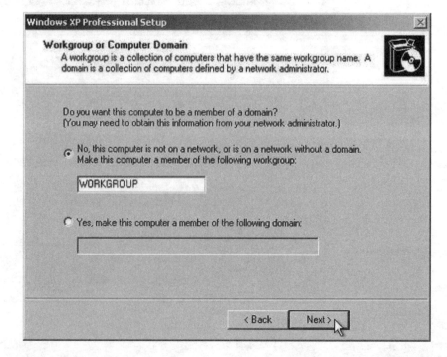

Step 11

Windows XP Professional Setup may take about 25 minutes to configure your computer. Your computer will automatically restart when the setup program is complete. When the Display Settings dialog box appears, click OK (see Figure 5-13).

Figure 5-13   Automatic Improvement of Display

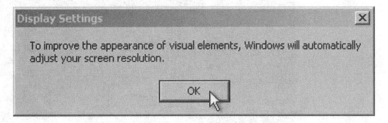

Step 12

When the Monitor Settings dialog box appears, click OK (see Figure 5-14).

Figure 5-14   Monitor Adjustment Check

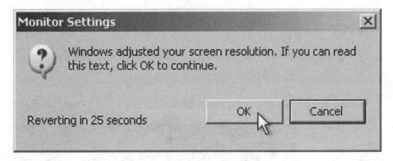

Step 13

The final phase of Windows XP Professional Setup begins. On the Welcome to Microsoft Windows page, click Next (see Figure 5-15).

Figure 5-15   Windows XP Welcome Screen

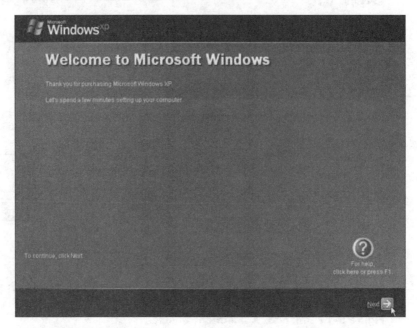

Step 14

On the Help Protect Your PC screen, select Help Protect My PC by Turning On Automatic Updates Now. Click Next (see Figure 5-16).

Figure 5-16   Configuring Automatic Updates for Windows XP

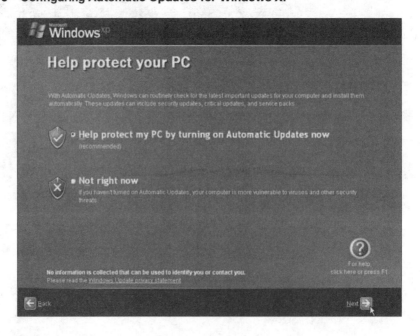

Step 15

Windows XP will now check to make sure that you are connected to the Internet. If you are already connected to the Internet, select the choice that represents your network connection. If you are unsure of the connection type, accept the default selection and click Next (see Figure 5-17).

Figure 5-17   Configuring Your Internet Connection

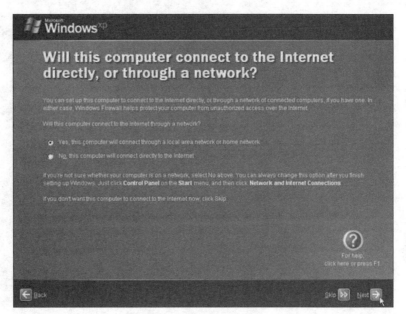

Step 16

If you use dial-up Internet access, or if Windows XP Professional Setup cannot connect to the Internet, you can connect to the Internet after setup is complete. Click Skip to continue (see Figure 5-18).

Figure 5-18   Selecting a DSL/Cable Connection or Specifying a Network Connection

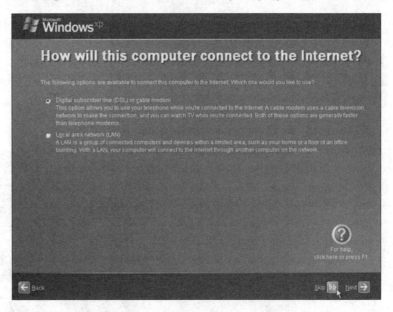

Step 17

Windows XP Professional Setup displays the Ready to Activate Windows? screen (see Figure 5-19).

Figure 5-19   Activating Windows XP

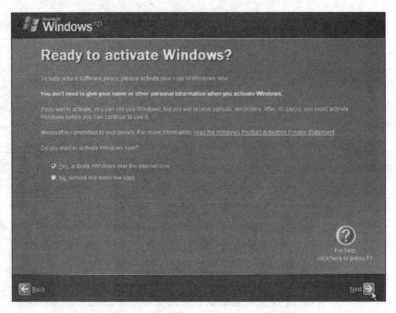

If you are already connected to the Internet, click Yes, and then click Next.

If you are not yet connected to the Internet, click No, and then click Next.

After setup is complete, the Windows XP setup program will remind you to activate and register your copy of Windows XP.

Step 18

If you have an Internet connection, click Yes, I'd Like to Register with Microsoft Now.

If you do not have an Internet connection, click No, Not at This Time.

Click Next (see Figure 5-20).

Figure 5-20   Registering Windows XP

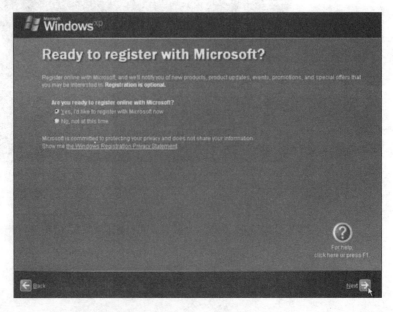

Step 19

On the Collecting Registration Information screen, fill in the fields using the information provided by your instructor and then click Next (see Figure 5-21).

Figure 5-21   Specifying the Registration Information

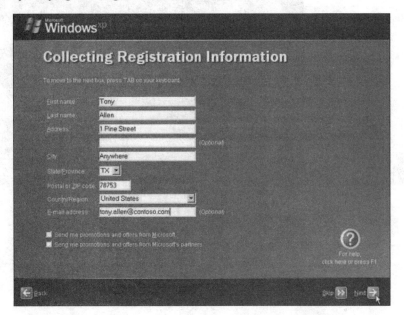

Step 20

On the Who Will Use This Computer? screen, enter the information provided by your instructor. Click Next (see Figure 5-22).

Figure 5-22   Specifying the Computer Users

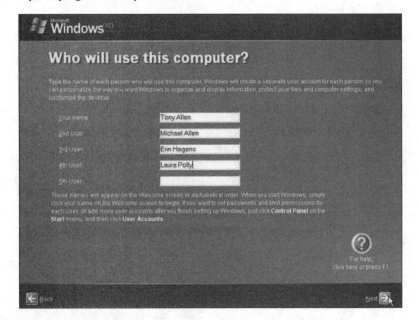

Step 21

On the Thank You screen, click Finish to complete the installation (see Figure 5-23).

Figure 5-23   Thank You Screen

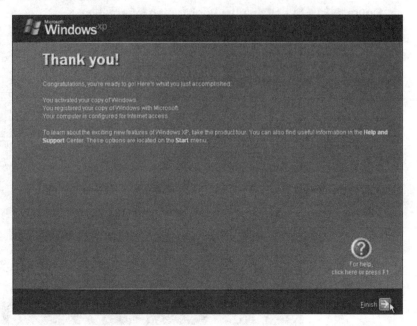

 # Lab 5.4.5: Create Accounts and Check for Updates

In this lab, you will create user accounts and configure the operating system for automatic updates after the Windows XP Professional installation process.

The recommended equipment for this lab is a computer with a new installation of Windows XP Professional.

Step 1

Boot the computer. Navigate to the Control Panel window by clicking Start, Control Panel (see Figure 5-24).

Figure 5-24   Windows XP Control Panel

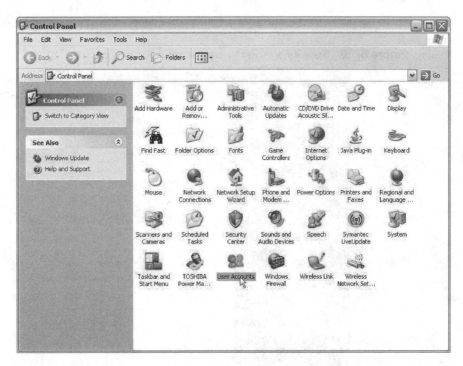

Step 2

Double-click the User Accounts icon. The User Accounts window appears (see Figure 5-25). Click Create a New Account.

Figure 5-25   Configuring Windows XP User Accounts

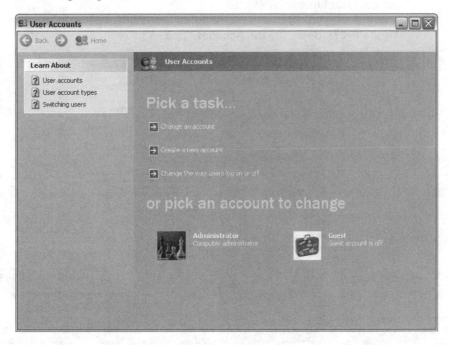

Step 3

At Name the New Account, type your name into the field and then click Next (see Figure 5-26).

Figure 5-26   Specifying the Username for a New Account

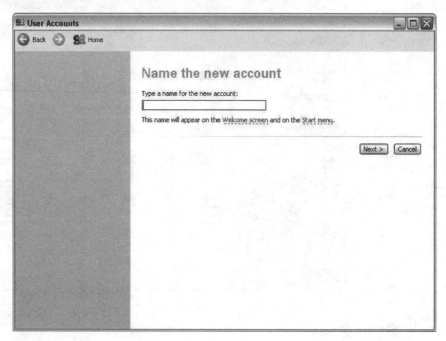

Step 4

At Pick an Account Type, leave the default setting of Computer Administrator and click Create Account (see Figure 5-27).

Figure 5-27   Selecting the Account Type

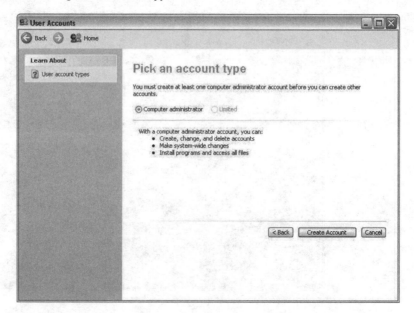

You have now finished creating a new account. Log off the computer and log back on as yourself. Leave the password field blank.

Step 5

Return to the User Accounts window of the Control Panel.

Click your account.

Click Create a Password (see Figure 5-28).

Figure 5-28   Modifying User Accounts

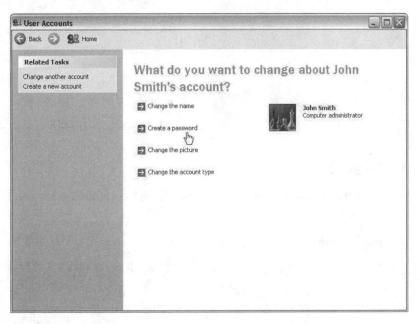

Step 6

On the Create a Password for Your Account page, type your first initial and your last name in the Type a New Password field. Example: **jsmith**

Type the same password into the Type the New Password Again to Confirm field.

Type your first initial and last name into the Type a Word or Phrase to Use as a Password Hint field.

Click Create Password (see Figure 5-29).

Figure 5-29   Changing a User Account's Password

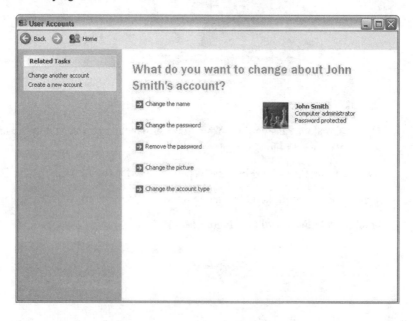

Step 7

Click the red X in the upper-right corner of the User Accounts window to close the window (see Figure 5-30).

Figure 5-30   Modifying User Accounts

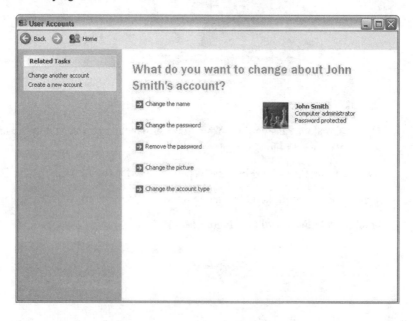

Step 8

Click Start, Control Panel (see Figure 5-31).

Double-click the Automatic Updates icon.

Figure 5-31   Windows XP Control Panel

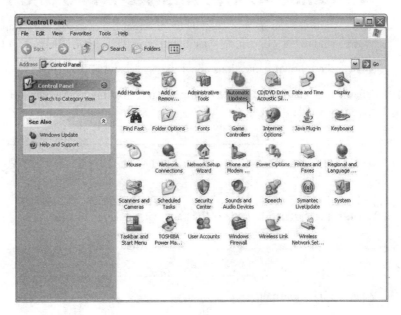

Step 9

The Automatic Updates dialog box appears.

Click the Automatic (recommended) option button.

Click OK to accept the change and close the dialog box (see Figure 5-32).

Figure 5-32   Configuring Automatic Updates

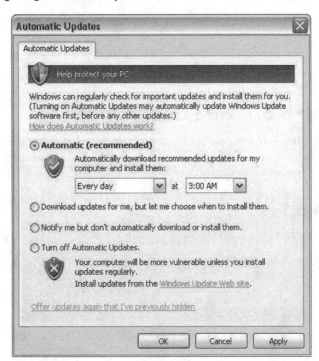

Worksheet 5.4.9: Answer NTFS and FAT32 Questions

Hard disk drives can be formatted using different file systems. NTFS and FAT32 are file systems used by the Windows XP operating system and provide different file system features.

Answer the following questions about the NTFS and FAT32 file systems:

What is the default cluster size setting when formatting a Windows NTFS partition on a hard disk drive larger than 2 GB?

_____

What is the command used to change a FAT32 partition to an NTFS partition?

_____

What is the Master File Table (MFT) and what does it contain?

_____

_____

What is NTFS journaling?

_____

_____

How does journaling help an operating system recover from system failures?

_____

_____

Why is an NTFS partition more secure than FAT32?

_____

_____

Lab 5.5.1: Run Commands

In this lab, you will open the same program by using the Windows Explorer and the run command.

The recommended equipment for this lab is a computer system running Windows XP.

Step 1

Boot the computer and log on as yourself.

Right-click the Start button, and then click Explore (see Figure 5-33).

Figure 5-33   Windows Explorer Window

Step 2

Right-click the Local Disk (C:) hard disk drive.

Click Properties, and then click the Disk Cleanup button (see Figure 5-34).

Figure 5-34   Drive Properties

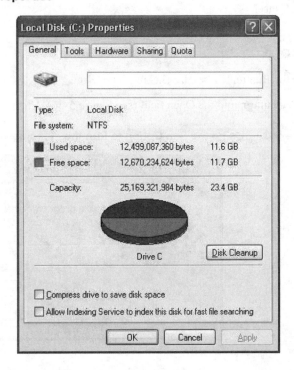

The Disk Cleanup for (C:) window appears (see Figure 5-35).

Figure 5-35   Disk Cleanup

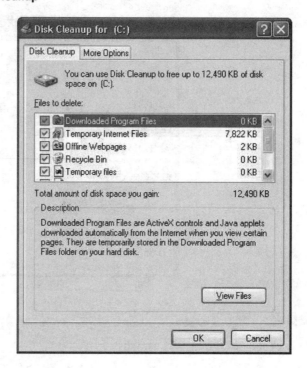

Windows calculates the amount of space used by unnecessary files.

Click Cancel.

Step 3

Open the Run dialog box by clicking Start, Run.

Type **cleanmgr** into the Open field (see Figure 5-36). Click OK.

Figure 5-36   Using the Run Option to Run the cleanmgr Command

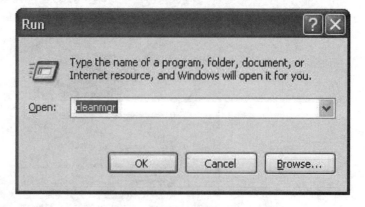

The Disk Cleanup for (C:) window opens (see Figure 5-37).

Figure 5-37   Disk Cleanup Utility

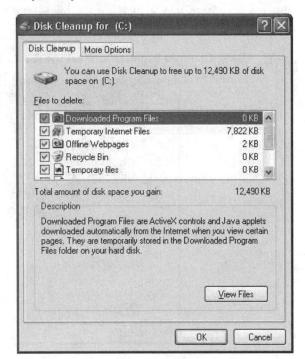

Step 4

Click the OK button.

Why should disk cleanup be performed regularly?

_____

_____

Lab 5.5.4: Install Third-Party Software

In this lab, you will install and remove a third-party software application by using the Microsoft Windows XP Professional Installation CD. The student will install the CITRIX ICA 32-bit Windows Client application.

The following is the recommended equipment for this lab:

- A computer system that is using Windows XP

- A Microsoft Windows XP installation CD

Step 1

Log on to the computer with the Administrator account.

Place the Windows XP Professional installation CD into the CD drive. Use Windows Explorer to navigate to the following folder:

D:\VALUEADD\3RDPARTY\MGMT\CITRIX

Locate the ICA32.exe application in the folder (see Figure 5-38). Click the ICA32 icon to start the installation process of the Citrix application. You might need to double-click the icon to start the installation.

Figure 5-38   Using Windows Explorer to Start the ICA32 Program

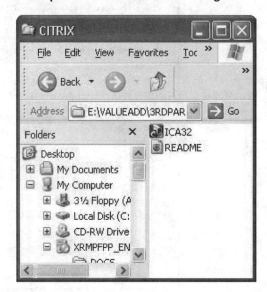

Step 2

Click Next when the InstallShield Wizard window opens (see Figure 5-39).

Figure 5-39   Welcome Screen for the Citrix ICA 32-bit Windows Client Software

A window opens displaying the file extraction progress (see Figure 5-40).

Figure 5-40   Citrix ICA 32-bit Windows Client Software Extracting Files

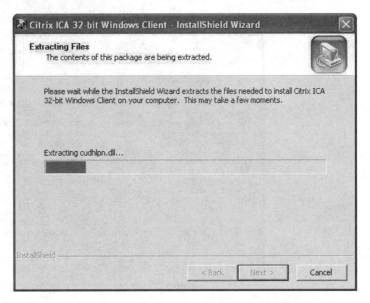

After the files have been extracted, the ICA Client Setup program begins. Click Next to begin the installation (see Figure 5-41).

Figure 5-41   Second Welcome Screen for the Citrix ICA 32-bit Windows Client Software

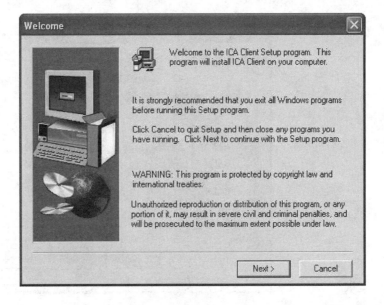

Click Yes on the License Agreement (see Figure 5-42).

Figure 5-42   Citrix License Agreement

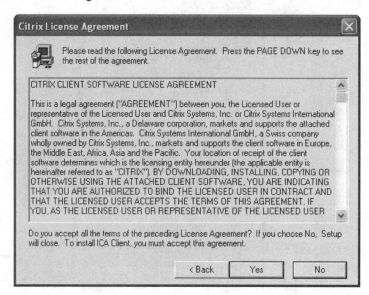

In the Choose Destination Location dialog box, use the default location, and then click Next (see Figure 5-43).

Figure 5-43   Choosing the Destination Location for the Citrix ICA 32-bit Windows Client Software

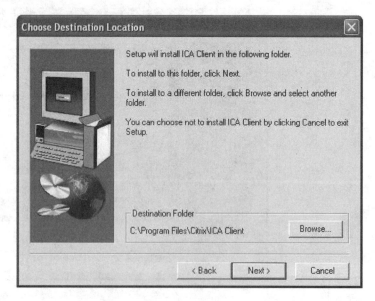

In the Select Program Folder dialog box, use the default location, and then click Next (see Figure 5-44).

Figure 5-44   Selecting the Program Folder for the Citrix ICA 32-bit Windows Client Software

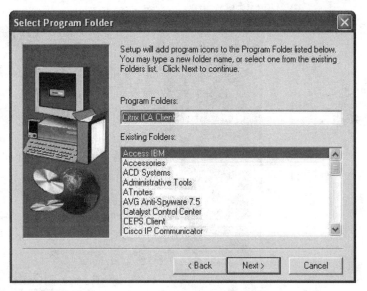

Enter student as the ClientName. Click Next (see Figure 5-45).

Figure 5-45   Specifying the ICA ClientName

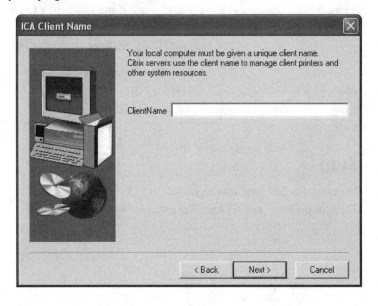

In the Select Desired Features window, leave the default choice of No. Click Next (see Figure 5-46).

Figure 5-46   Specifying the Automatic Use of Your Windows User Account for the Citrix Client Software

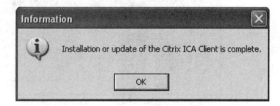

You have successfully installed the Citrix program (see Figure 5-47).

Figure 5-47   Completing the Installation of the Citrix ICA Client Software

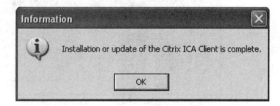

Step 3

To uninstall a program, choose Start, Control Panel, Add or Remove Programs. Click the Citrix ICA Client in the list. Click Change/Remove (see Figure 5-48).

Figure 5-48   Removing the Citrix ICA Client Software

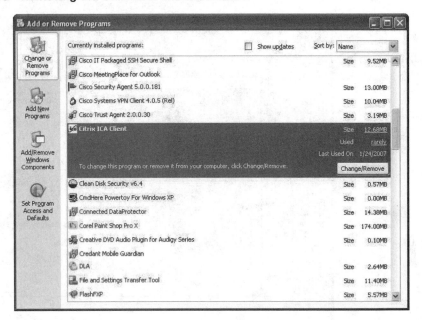

Click Yes to confirm the removal (see Figure 5-49).

Figure 5-49   Confirming the Deleting of Files

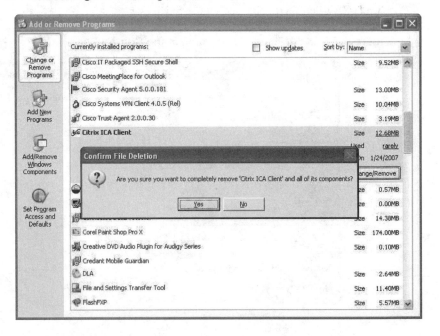

The screen in Figure 5-50 will appear, displaying the removal progress.

Figure 5-50   When the Program Is Removed, Click OK

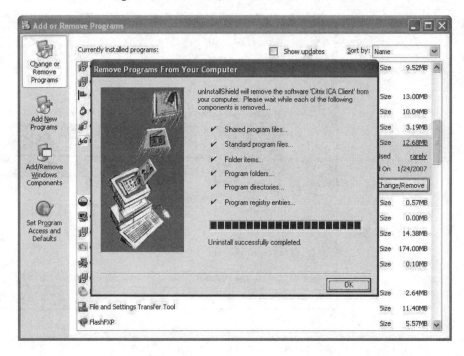

After the application removal process, the Add or Remove Programs window no longer shows the Citrix ICA Client in the list (see Figure 5-51).

Figure 5-51   Add/Remove Programs in the Control Panel

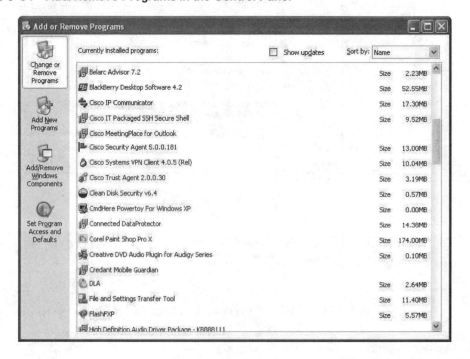

Why does Microsoft recommend using Add/Remove Programs to remove an installed application?

_____

_____

_____

Lab 5.6.2: Restore Points

In this lab, you will create a restore point and return your computer back to that point in time.

The following is the recommended equipment for this lab:

- A computer system running Windows XP
- The Windows XP installation CD

Step 1

Click Start, All Programs, Accessories, System Tools, System Restore.

Click the Create a Restore Point option button.

Click Next (see Figure 5-52).

Figure 5-52   Welcome Screen for the System Restore

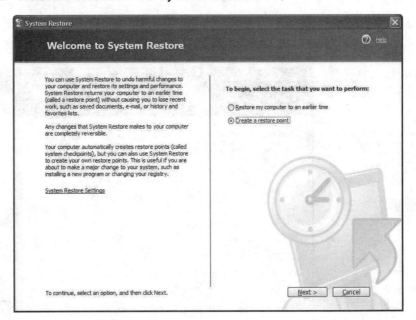

Step 2

In the Restore Point Description field, type **Application Installed**.

Click Create (see Figure 5-53).

Figure 5-53   Creating a Restore Point

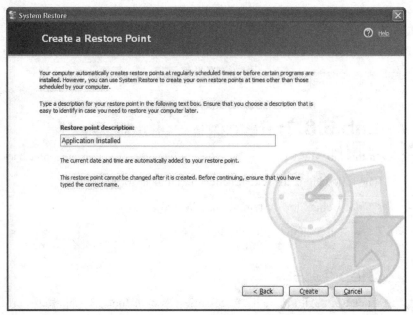

Step 3

The Restore Point Created window appears.

Click Close (see Figure 5-54).

Figure 5-54   Completing the Creation of a Restore Point

Step 4

Click Start, Control Panel, Add or Remove Programs.

Click the Add or Remove Programs icon (see Figure 5-55).

Figure 5-55   Control Panel in Category View

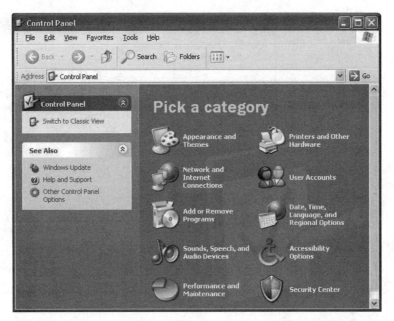

Step 5

Click Add/Remove Windows Components (see Figure 5-56).

Figure 5-56   Add or Remove Windows Components

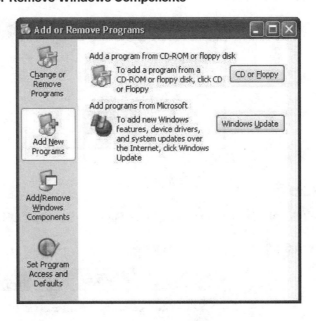

Step 6

Click the Internet Information Services (IIS) check box.

Click Next (see Figure 5-57).

Figure 5-57   Windows Components Wizard

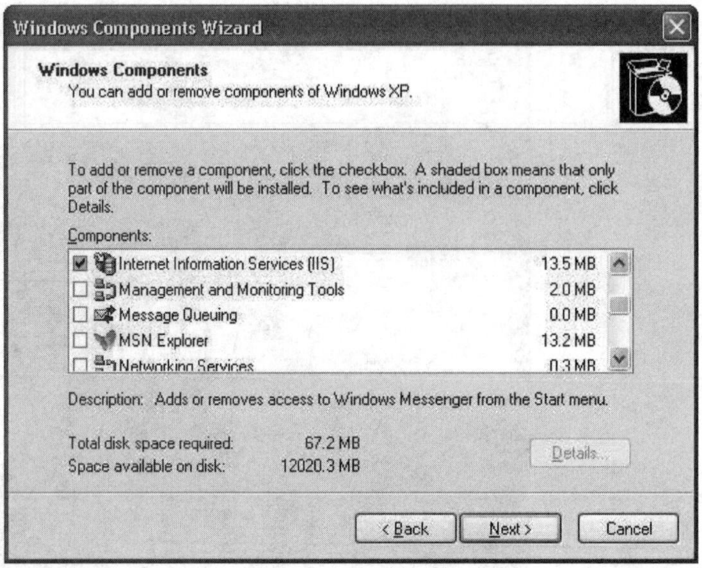

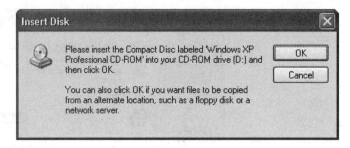

Step 7

The Insert Disk dialog box appears. Place the Windows XP installation CD into the optical drive (see Figure 5-58). Click OK.

Figure 5-58   Insert Disk Window

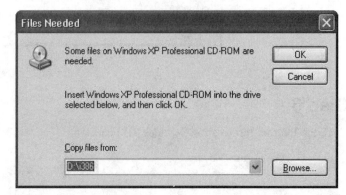

Step 8

The Files Needed window appears (see Figure 5-59). Click OK.

Figure 5-59   Files Needed Window

The Configuring Components progress window appears (see Figure 5-60).

Figure 5-60   Copying Files for the New Windows Components

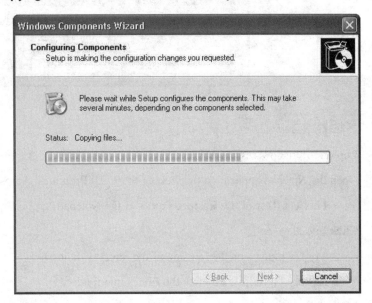

Step 9

The Completing the Windows Components Wizard window appears.

Click Finish (see Figure 5-61).

Figure 5-61   Adding Windows Components Is Finished

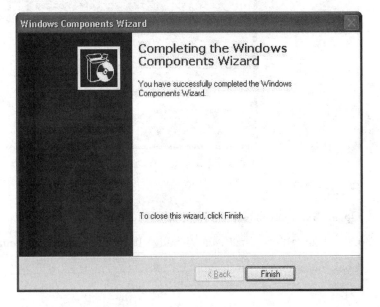

Step 10

The System Settings Change dialog box appears. Remove the Windows XP installation disk from the optical drive.

Click Yes (see Figure 5-62).

Figure 5-62   Restart Windows

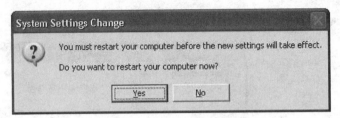

Step 11

Log on to Windows as yourself.

Open the Notepad application by clicking Start, All Programs, Accessories, Notepad.

Type **This Is a Test of the Restore Points** in the Notepad Application.

Click File, Save As.

Click My Documents on the left side of the Save As dialog box.

Type **Restore Point Test File** into the File Name field.

Click Save (see Figure 5-63).

Click File, Exit.

Figure 5-63   Using Notepad to Open a Text File

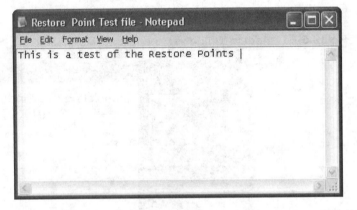

Step 12

Open IIS to confirm that you have successfully installed this service.

Click Start, All Programs, Administrative Tools, Internet Information Services (see Figure 5-64).

Click File, Exit.

Figure 5-64   Internet Information Services Management Console

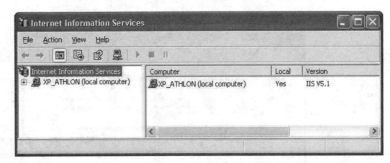

Step 13

Click Start, All Programs, Accessories, System Tools, System Restore.

Select the Restore My Computer to an Earlier Time option button.

Click Next (see Figure 5-65).

Figure 5-65   Restoring to a System Restore Point

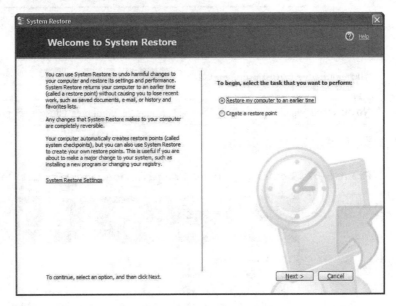

Step 14

In the Select a Restore Point window, select today's date from the calendar on the left.

Select Application Installed from the list on the right.

Click Next (see Figure 5-66).

Figure 5-66   Selecting Which Restore Point to Restore

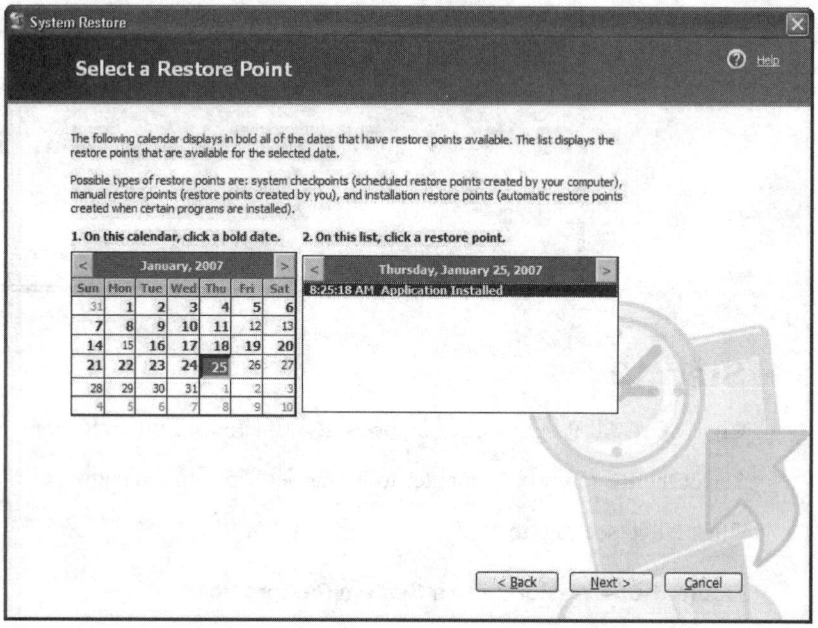

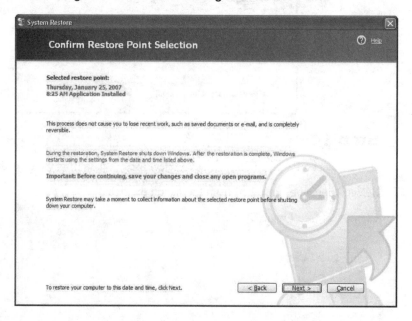

Step 15

The Confirm Restore Point Selection window appears.

Note: When you click Next, Windows will restart the computer. Close all applications before you click Next.

Click Next (see Figure 5-67).

Figure 5-67   Confirming Details Before Restoring to a Restore Point

The operating system restores to the point before the IIS application was installed.

Step 16

The Restoration Complete window appears. Click OK (see Figure 5-68).

Figure 5-68   Restore Point Has Been Restored

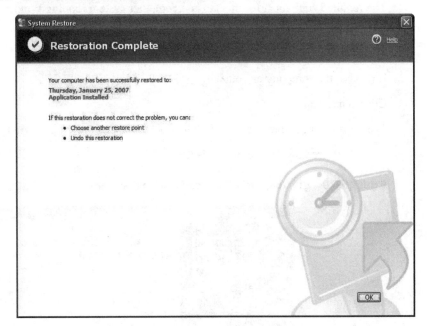

Step 17

Click Start, All Programs, Administrative Tools.

Is the Internet Information Services application listed?

Step 18

Navigate to the My Documents folder.

Open the Restore Point Test file.txt file (see Figure 5-69).

Are the contents the same?

Figure 5-69   Opening a Text File with Notepad

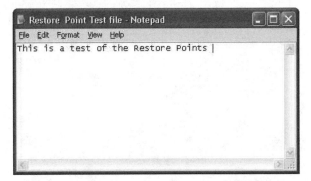

Lab 5.6.3: Windows Registry Backup and Recovery

In this lab, you will back up a computer registry. You will also perform a recovery of a computer registry. The registry is also called System State data.

The required equipment for this lab is a computer system running Windows XP.

Step 1

Log on to the computer as yourself.

Click Start, Run.

Type **ntbackup**, and then click OK. The Backup or Restore Wizard window appears.

Click Advanced Mode (see Figure 5-70).

Figure 5-70   Starting the Windows Backup Program

Step 2

The Backup Utility window appears (see Figure 5-71).

Click Backup Wizard.

Figure 5-71   Advanced Mode for the Windows Backup Program

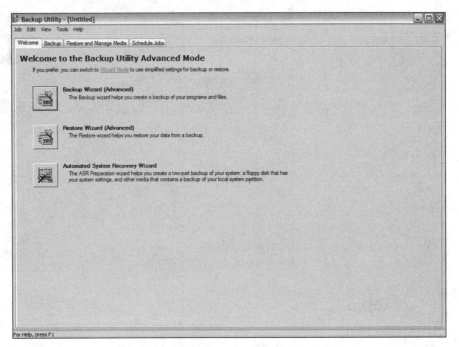

Step 3

The Welcome to the Backup Wizard window appears (see Figure 5-72).

Click Next.

Figure 5-72   Welcome Screen for the Microsoft Backup Program

Step 4

Click the Only Back Up the System State Data option button (see Figure 5-73).

Figure 5-73   Backing Up the System State Using Windows Backup Program

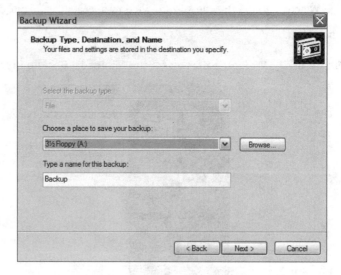

Step 5

Click Next.

The Backup Type, Destination, and Name window appears (see Figure 5-74).

Figure 5-74   Specifying the Backup Location and Name

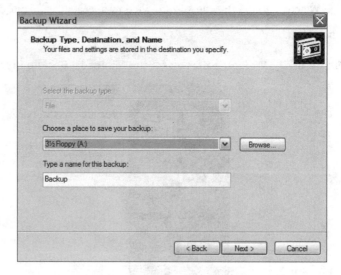

Step 6

Click Browse.

If you are asked to insert a disk into the floppy disk drive, click Cancel. The Save As dialog box appears (see Figure 5-75).

Figure 5-75   Specifying the Filename and Location of the Backup

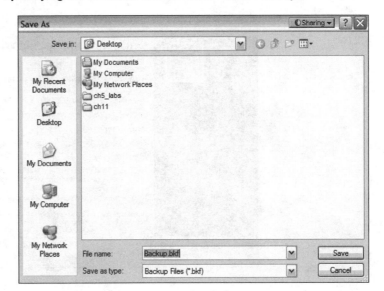

Step 7

Click the My Documents icon on the left side of the Save As dialog box.

Click Save. The Backup Type, Destination, and Name window reappears (see Figure 5-76).

Figure 5-76   Specifying the Backup Location and Name

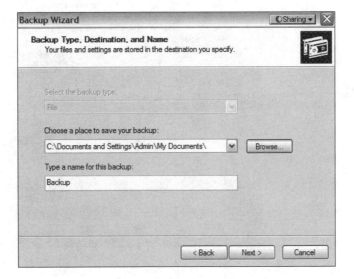

Step 8

Click Next. The Completing the Backup Wizard window appears (see Figure 5-77).

Figure 5-77   Completing the Backup Wizard

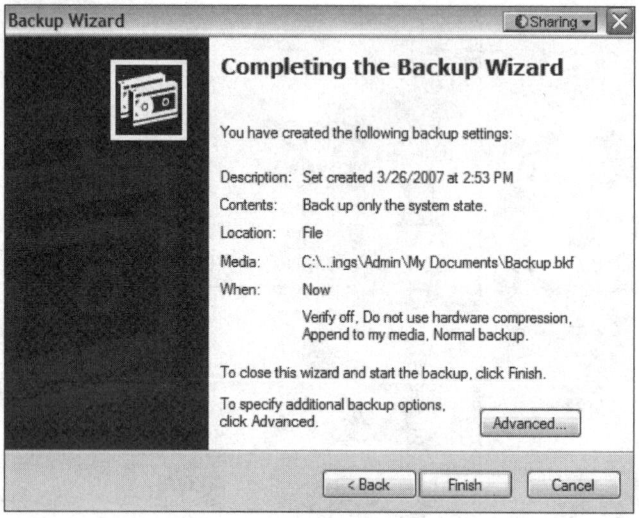

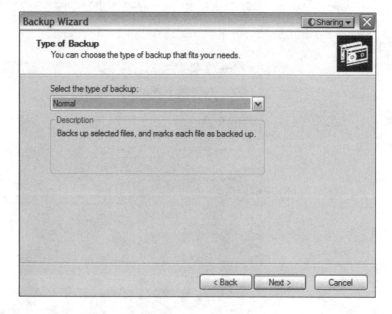

Step 9

Click Advanced. The Type of Backup window appears (see Figure 5-78).

Figure 5-78   Specifying the Type of Backup

The default backup type is Normal. If available, make sure that Backup Migrated Remote Storage Data is not checked.

Step 10

Click Next. The How To Backup window appears (see Figure 5-79).

Figure 5-79   Verification of Backup Options

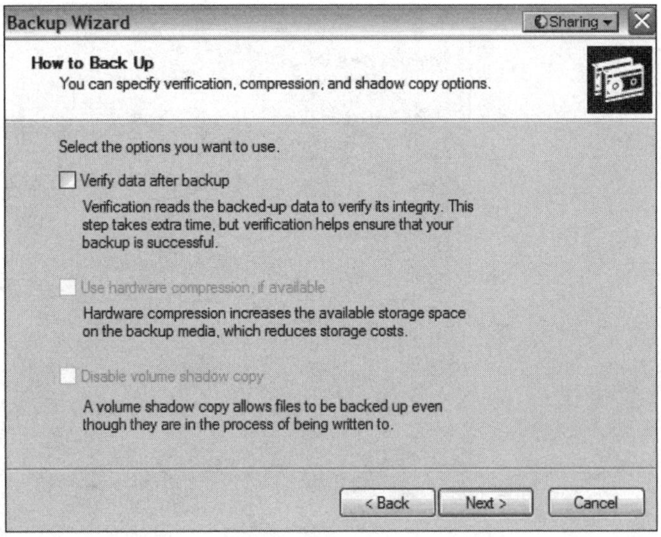

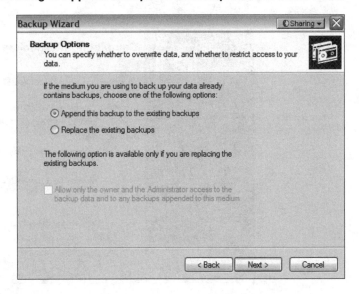

Step 11

Click the Verify Data After Backup check box, and then click Next. The Backup Options window appears (see Figure 5-80).

Figure 5-80   Choosing to Append or Replace a Backup with the Same Name

Step 12

Click Replace the Existing Backups, and then click Next. The When to Back Up window appears (see Figure 5-81).

Figure 5-81   Scheduling the Backup

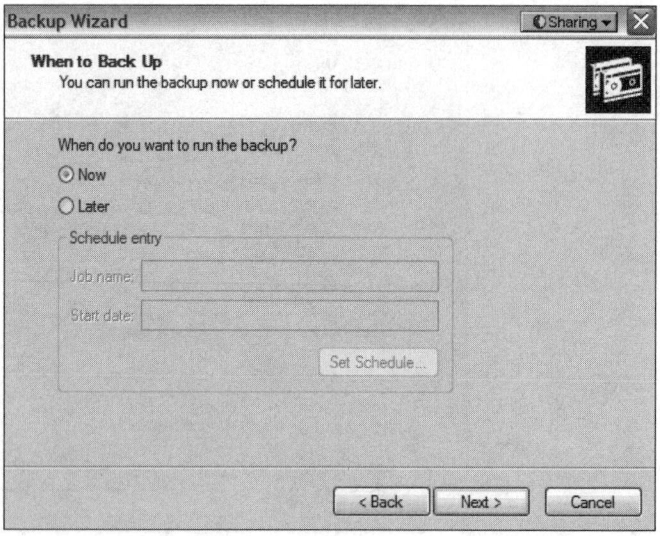

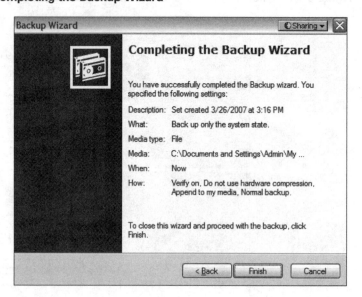

Step 13

At the When to Back Up window, click Now, and then click Next. The Completing the Backup Wizard window appears (see Figure 5-82).

Figure 5-82   Completing the Backup Wizard

Step 14

Click Finish. The Backup Progress window appears (see Figure 5-83).

Figure 5-83   Progress of the Backup

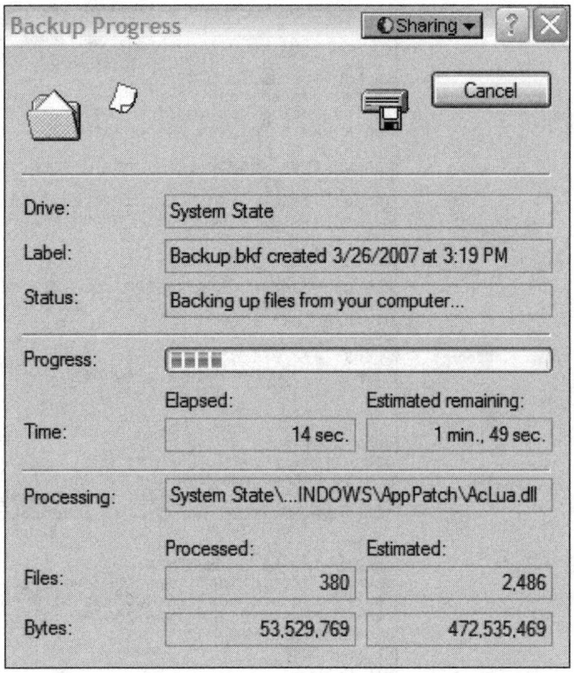

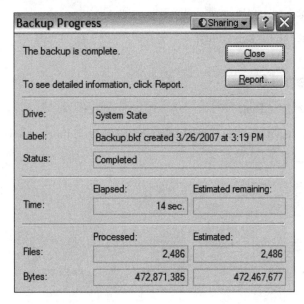

The Backup Progress window indicates that the backup is complete (see Figure 5-84).

Figure 5-84   Backup Is Complete

Step 15

Click Report. The Notepad application window appears, containing the report (see Figure 5-85).

Figure 5-85   Viewing the Backup Logs Using Notepad

Close Notepad.

In the Backup Progress dialog box, click Close.

Close the Backup Utility.

Step 16

Click Start, Run.

Type **regedit** into the Open field. The Registry Editor window appears (see Figure 5-86).

Figure 5-86   The Registry Editor

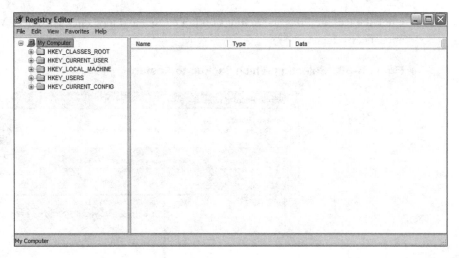

Step 17

Expand the HKEY_CURRENT_USER Registry key.

Expand the Control Panel Registry key.

Expand the PowerCfg Registry key.

Right-click the Screen Saver.Stars Registry key.

Click Delete.

Click File, Exit in the Registry Editor window.

Browse to the My Documents folder and locate the backup.bkf file.

Double-click the backup file to bring up the Backup Utility Wizard.

Click Next (see Figure 5-87).

Figure 5-87   Running the Backup/Restore Wizard

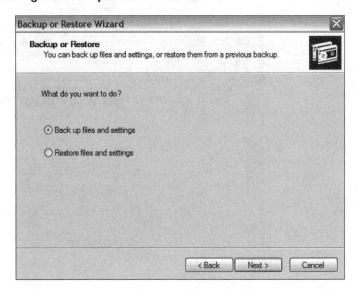

Step 18

Click the Restore Files and Settings option button, and then click Next. The What to Restore window appears (see Figure 5-88).

Figure 5-88   Selecting Which Backup to Restore

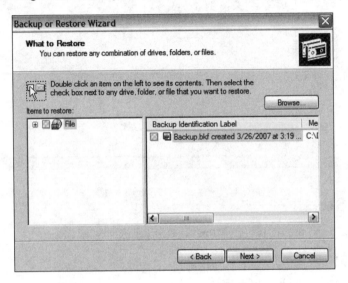

Step 19

Expand the file.

Expand the backup.bkf file.

Click the System State check box (see Figure 5-89).

Figure 5-89   Selecting the System State to Restore

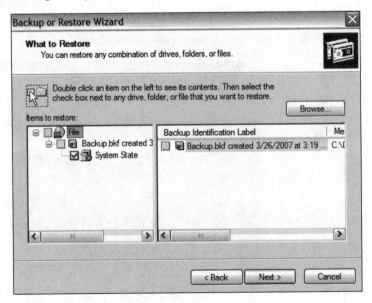

Step 20

Click Next. The Completing the Backup or Restore Wizard window appears (see Figure 5-90).

Figure 5-90   Completing the Restore Wizard

Step 21

Click Advanced. The Where to Restore window appears (see Figure 5-91).

Figure 5-91   Selecting Where to Restore To

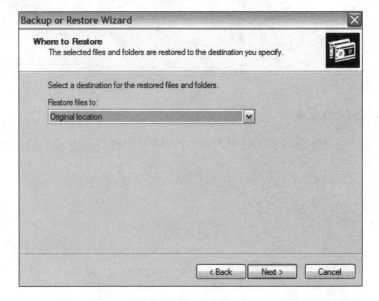

Step 22

The default restoration location is Original Location. Click Next.

The Restoring System State Will Always Overwrite Current System State Unless Restoring to an Alternate Location warning window appears (see Figure 5-92). Click OK.

Figure 5-92   Warning That the System State Can Only Be Restored to Its Original State

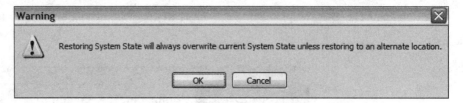

Step 23

Click the Replace Existing Files if They Are Older Than the Backup Files option button (see Figure 5-93).

Figure 5-93   Options to Replace Existing Files

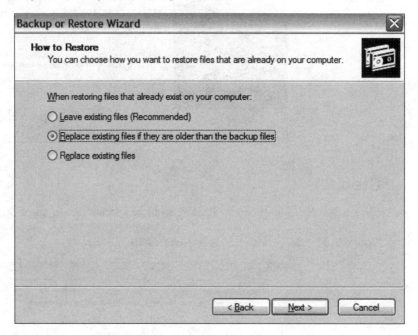

Step 24

Click Next. The Advanced Restore Options window appears (see Figure 5-94).

Figure 5-94   Advanced Restore Options

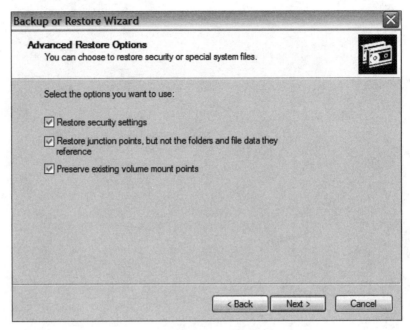

Be sure that all three check boxes are selected, and then click Next.

Click Finish. The system recovery begins by copying the files back to the computer. When prompted to restart the computer, click Yes. The computer will restart.

Step 25

Click Start, Run.

Type **regedit** into the Open field.

Click OK. You should see the Screen Saver.Stars Registry key in the Registry Editor application window.

Click File, Exit.

How does backing up the system state files save time?

_____

_____

_____

_____

CHAPTER 6

Fundamental Laptops and Portable Devices

The Study Guide portion of this chapter uses a combination of multiple-choice, matching, fill-in-the-blank, and open-ended questions to test your knowledge of laptop computers, including maintaining and troubleshooting laptop computers. This portion also includes multiple-choice study questions to help prepare you to take the A+ certification exams and to test your overall understanding of the material.

The Lab Exercises portion of this chapter includes all the online curriculum worksheets to further reinforce your mastery of the laptop and portable devices content.

Study Guide

Laptop Fundamentals

Over the past several years, laptop computers have become very popular. Although laptops are essential compact computers, configuring or troubleshooting a laptop computer brings different challenges than configuring and troubleshooting a desktop computer. Therefore, as a well-rounded technician, you need to know those differences and be prepared to work on both desktop and laptop computers.

Vocabulary Exercise: Completion

Fill in the blanks with the appropriate terms about these laptop components:

- Processors: Although desktop processors can be used in laptop computers, mobile processors make a better choice because they have less _power_ consumption and produce less _heat_. Mobile processors also have the capability to _throttle_ so that they run at lower speeds to consume less power.

- Motherboard: Laptop motherboards vary by manufacturer and are _proprietary_.

- RAM: The most common RAM that you will find in a laptop is _DDRSDRAM_. These memory chips have _172_ pins/contacts or _200_ pins/contacts and are _64_-bits wide.

- Video Card: The video card will usually be built in to the motherboard. The type of video RAM is typically _VRAM_.

- Hard Drive: Hard drives are _3½_ inches wide, and they include the _IDE_ interface or the _ATA_ interface.

- Expansion Slots: The standard expansion slots found on laptop computers are PC cards. Type I cards are used for SDRAM Flash; type II cards are used for _modem_, _NIC_, and _WIFI_; and type III cards are used for _Hard drives_. If you have two stacked card slots, it will support _2_ type II card(s) or _1_ type III card(s). Internal expansion cards include _____ cards.

- Power: Laptops run on _DC_ power or a rechargeable _Battery_. Of the types of batteries, the _Nickel Cadmium_ has the shortest battery life.

- Keyboard and Pointing Devices: The keyboard and pointing device are _integrated_ into the base of the laptop. Pointing devices found on a laptop are _Keyboard_, _Touchpad_, and _mouse_. If you want to connect a wireless mouse and keyboard to a laptop, you should use _IR Wireless_ technology.

- Monitor: The type of monitor found on laptop computers are _LCD_ monitors.

- Ports: Laptops use many of the same type of ports that a desktop computer uses. To connect a printer or an external keyboard or mouse, you can use the _USB_ port. Other common ports include serial ports, parallel ports, and VGA ports.

- External Expandability: To expand a laptop system even further, laptops can connect to a _docking station_, which will provide AC power and access to attached peripherals.

Identify the Parts of a Laptop

Fill in the blanks for the parts of a laptop pictured in the following table.

Parallel Port

USB

Graphics Port

Serial Port

CD Drawer

PCI card

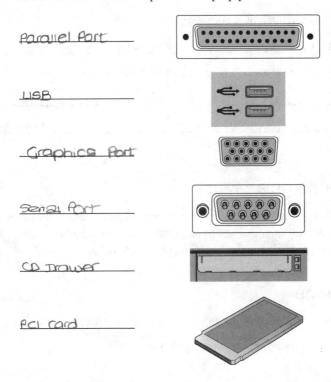

Power Management

Because mobile computers can run on battery power, users like to take advantage of the mobility this affords for as long as possible without plugging into an AC outlet or replacing batteries. Therefore, it is important that you understand the features that mobile computers offer so that you can conserve power.

Vocabulary Exercise: Matching

Match the definition on the left with a term on the right.

Definitions

a. Creates a bridge between the hardware and OS and allows technicians to create power management schemes in the operating system to get the best performance from the computer.

b. Collection of settings that manage the power usage of the computer.

c. Documents and applications are saved in RAM, allowing the computer to power on quickly.

d. Documents and applications are saved to a temporary file on the hard drive, and will take a little longer than standby to power on.

e. Allows for power management in the BIOS.

Terms

_a_ Advanced Configuration and Power Interface (ACPI)

_e_ Advanced Power Management

_d_ Hibernate

_b_ Power Schemes

_c_ Standby

Concept Questions

Answer the following power-management questions.

Describe the best method to keep the laptop computer cool.

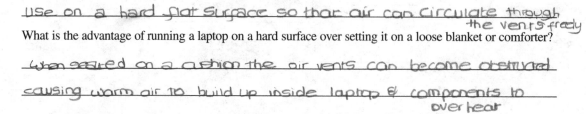

use on a hard flat surface so that air can circulate through the vents freely

What is the advantage of running a laptop on a hard surface over setting it on a loose blanket or comforter?

When seated on a cushion the air vents can become obstructed causing warm air to build up inside laptop & components to overheat

Laptop Maintenance

Similar to desktop computers, you also need to perform preventive maintenance on laptop and notebook computers. Because these devices are designed to be portable and consume less power, laptop and notebook computers require preventive maintenance that is a little different.

Concept Questions

Answer the following laptop maintenance question:

Describe the best method to clean the following components:

- Laptop keyboard:

  Either with compressed air or an anti-static vacuum.

- Ventilation:

  compressed air

- LCD:

  Damp cloth

- Touch pad:

  Damp cloth

- Floppy drive:

  Compressed air

- Optical drive:

  Commercial cleaning kit

- CD:

Moist lint-free cloth either moistened with water or

a commercial CD cleaner.

Troubleshooting Laptop Computers

Although laptop and desktop computers have different designs, troubleshooting laptop computers follows a systematic troubleshooting model similar to troubleshooting desktop computers. When troubleshooting laptop and notebook computers, you must keep in mind the features and characteristics of technology used in mobile computers compared to desktop computers.

Concept Questions

Answer the following troubleshooting laptop computers question:

In the list that follows, fill in the basic steps in troubleshooting:

Step 1.   _Gather Data from Customer_

Step 2.   _Verify the obvious issues_

Step 3.   _Try quick solutions first_

Step 4.   _Gather data from the computer_

Step 5.   _Evaluate the problem & implement the solution_

Step 6.   _Close with the customer_

Study Questions

Choose the best answer for each of the questions that follow.

1. What is the best method for connecting multiple external peripheral devices such as printer, keyboard, and mouse to a laptop computer using wireless technology?

    A. Bluetooth

    B. Microwave

    C. IrDA

    D. 802.11b

2. After you replace a touchpad, you find out that the keyboard is not functioning. What do you think the problem is?

   A. The touchpad is not seated properly.

   B. The keyboard needs to be replaced.

   C. The keyboard connector is not seated properly.

   D. The computer needs to be rebooted.

3. Where would you enable hibernation on a laptop running Windows XP?

   A. In the BIOS setup program

   B. In the power schemes

   C. In the power management applet in the Control Panel

   D. In the power hibernation applet in the Control Panel

4. A laptop has Windows XP up and running. How do you remove a PC card?

   A. Disable the device in the Device Manager.

   B. Use the Safely Remove Hardware icon to eject the device.

   C. Use the Add/Remove Hardware applet in the Control Panel.

   D. Nothing needs to be done. Just pull the PC card out.

5. What is the range of IrDA?

   A. 1 meter

   B. 3 meters

   C. 10 meters

   D. 100 feet

6. What is the best place to use the laptop?

   A. On a hard surface so that the air can flow underneath the laptop to keep it cooler

   B. 30 inches from any wall to allow good air flow

   C. In front of a fan

   D. In the carrying case

Lab Exercises

Worksheet 6.1.2: Research Laptops, Smart Phones, and PDAs

Use the Internet, a newspaper, or a local store to gather information, and then enter the specifications for a laptop, smart phone, and PDA onto this worksheet. What type of equipment do you want? What features are important to you?

For example, you may want a laptop that has an 80 GB hard drive and plays DVDs or has built-in wireless capability. You may need a smart phone with Internet access or a PDA that takes pictures.

Shop around, and in the table that follows, list the features and cost for a laptop, smart phone, and PDA. Be prepared to discuss your decisions regarding the features you select.

Equipment	Features	Cost
Laptop Computer		

continues

Equipment	Features	Cost
Smart Phone		
PDA		

Worksheet 6.2.3: Complete Docking Stations True or False Questions

Enter T for true or F for false in the space provided to correctly identify the statements that follow.

_F_ Docking stations are usually smaller than port replicators and do not have speakers or PCI slots.

_T_ The exhaust vent is an outlet through which the fan expels hot air from the interior of the docking station.

_T_ A laptop can be secured to a docking station with a key lock.

_F_ The RJ-11 modem port connects a laptop to a cabled local area network.

_F_ The Ethernet port uses an RJ-45 socket to connect a laptop to a standard telephone line.

_T_ The DVI port is a 15-pin socket that allows output to external displays and projectors.

_T_ The Line In connector is a socket used to attach an audio source.

_F_ The Eject button releases the peripherals from the docking station.

_T_ The parallel port is a socket used to connect a device such as a printer or a scanner.

Worksheet 6.3.4: Answer Laptop Expansion Questions

1. List three types of PC Cards and the thickness of each.

Type	Thickness
I	3.3mm
II	5.0mm
III	10.5mm

2. Are PC ExpressCards interchangeable with PC cards?

   No

3. What does APM use to control power management?

   Power usage operating levels

4. What does ACPI use to control power management?

   Power options

5. Can you add desktop RAM to a laptop motherboard?

   No - laptops require 'small outline' memory modules

6. Does a desktop processor use more or less power than a laptop processor of the same speed?

   More power - laptops use CPU-Throttling

7. Does a laptop processor generate more or less heat than a desktop processor?

   Less - as a result of CPU throttling & power management

Worksheet 6.4.1: Match ACPI Standards

Enter the appropriate ACPI standard (S0, S1, S2, S3, S4, S5) next to the correct power management state description:

ACPI Standard	Power Management States
S2	The CPU is off, but the RAM is refreshed to maintain the contents.
S4	The CPU and RAM are off. The contents of RAM have been saved to a temporary file on the hard disk. This state is also called Suspend to Disk. In Windows XP, this state is known as Hibernate.
S1	The CPU is not executing instructions; however, the CPU and RAM are still receiving power.
S3	The CPU is off, and the RAM is set to a slow refresh rate. This state is called Suspend to RAM. In Windows XP, this state is known as Standby.
S5	The computer is off and any content that has not been saved will be lost.
S0	The computer is on and all devices are operating at full power.

Worksheet 6.7.2: Research Laptop Problems

Laptops often use proprietary parts. To find information about the replacement parts, you may have to research the website of the laptop manufacturer.

Before you begin this activity, you need to know some information about the laptop.

Your instructor will provide you with the following information:

- Laptop manufacturer: _____
- Laptop model number: _____
- Amount of RAM: _____
- Size of the hard drive: _____

Use the Internet to locate the website for the laptop manufacturer. What is the URL for the website?

_____

Locate the service section of the website and look for links that focus on your laptop. It is common for a website to allow you to search by the model number. The list that follows shows common links that you might find:

- FAQs
- WIKIs
- Service notices
- White papers
- Blogs

List the links you found specific to the laptop and include a brief description of the information in that link.

_____

_____

_____

Briefly describe any service notices you found on the website. A service notice example is a driver update, a hardware issue, or a recall notice for a laptop component.

_____

_____

_____

Open forums may exist for your laptop. Use an Internet search engine to locate any open forums that focus on your laptop by typing in the name and model of the laptop. Briefly describe the websites (other than the manufacturer website) that you located.

_____

_____

_____

CHAPTER 7

Fundamental Printers and Scanners

The Study Guide portion of this chapter uses a combination of matching, fill-in-the-blank, and open-ended questions to test your knowledge of printers and scanners, including maintenance and troubleshooting. This portion also includes multiple-choice study questions to help prepare you to take the A+ certification exams and to test your overall understanding of the material.

The Lab Exercises portion of this chapter includes the online curriculum lab to further reinforce your mastery of the printers and scanners content.

Study Guide

Printers

A printer is a commonly used output device that prints text or pictures on paper. Today, most printers are connected through the USB or parallel ports; a few older printers are connected through the serial port. Some printers can be connected directly to the network and accessed through a network adapter. Printers can also be connected through SCSI, IEEE 1394, infrared, or wireless connections.

Vocabulary Exercise: Matching

Match the definition on the left with a term on the right.

Definitions

a. A printer that works by spraying small droplets of ionized ink onto a sheet of paper.

b. Similar to copy machines, this uses an electrophoto (EP) process to form images on paper with toner instead of ink.

c. An impact printer that prints little dots by pressing against or striking against a ribbon to form text and images.

d. A printer that prints by pressing heated pins onto a special heat-sensitive paper. These printers are often used on older fax machines.

e. Today's most common printer interface.

f. Common interface used on older printers.

g. Older interface that sent one bit at a time on cables that could be up to 50 feet long.

h. Wireless technology that offers up to 3 Mbps and range that varies from 3 to 328 feet, depending on the class of the device.

i. Wireless technology that offers 11 Mbps or 54 Mbps.

Terms

_i_   802.11

_h_   Bluetooth

_c_   Dot-matrix printer

_a_   Inkjet printer

_b_   Laser printer

_f_   Parallel port

_g_   Serial port

_d_   Thermal printer

_e_   USB port

Electrophoto (EP) Stages

Identity the six EP steps or stages to transfer the image onto a paper using a laser printer:

Step 1. _cleaning_   c

Step 2. _conditioning_   c

Step 3. _Writing_   w

Step 4. _Developing_   D

Step 5. _Transferring_   T

Step 6. _Fusing_   F

Vocabulary Exercise: Matching

Match the EP stage description on the left with a term on the right.

Descriptions

a. Laser light aimed by mirrors sweeps through the drum line by line, reducing the charge on the area of the drum where the light hits.

b. The main corona wire or primary charge roller is charged.

c. The photosensitive drum is cleaned to remove any residual toner and residual charge.

d. Toner is applied to the charged drum.

e. Toner is melted onto the paper.

f. Toner is transferred from the drum to the paper.

Terms

_c_ Cleaning

_b_ Conditioning

_a_ Developing

_e_ Fusing

_f_ Transferring

_d_ Writing

Vocabulary Exercise: Completion

Fill in the blanks with the appropriate terms about printer basics.

All printers can be divided into _monochrome_ and _Colour_ printers.

Laser scanners and toner cartridges are found on _laser printers_.

Toner, used in laser printers, is made of a fine powder of _plastic_ and _iron particles bonded_. The _iron particles_ are used to hold a charge so that the toner can be placed on the drum and eventually onto the paper. The _plastic particles_ allows the toner to flow easily while providing a sufficient melting point so that it can be fused onto the paper.

The high-voltage power supply provides the proper voltage to charge the _primary_ or _transfer corona_.

In laser printers, _turning gears_ move the paper into the proper transfer position.

The toner in laser printers is stored in the _toner cartridge_.

A _static charge eliminator_ is used to drain the charge from the paper.

Dot-Matrix printers use a printhead and ink supply to print.

Bubble jet is a Canon trade name for its _inkjet_ printers.

The printer that can be used in multipart forms is a _dot-matrix_ printer.

After physically connecting a printer to a computer, you will need to load the proper _paper_ before you can start using the printer.

The _driver_ is a software program that enables the computer and printer to communicate and to provide an interface for the user to configure the printer options.

Every printer model has a unique _language_ program.

Increasing the amount of _printer memory_ is the easiest way to improve the efficiency of a printer and allow it to handle more complex print jobs.

Print a _test page_ after installing a printer to verify that the printer is operating properly.

Most printers have a _panel_ with controls to allow you to generate test pages. This method of printing enables you to verify the printer operation separately from the network or computer.

If you get a numeric error code on the front panel of a printer, you need to consult the printer's _user manual_ to get its meaning.

Printer Troubleshooting

Identify a potential cause for each printer problem in the following table.

Problem	Cause
Printed page is blank from a laser printer.	The printer is out of toner. If the printer does have toner it could be that Transfer Corona or high-voltage power supply has failed.
Printed page is completely black on a laser printer.	Problem with laser
Recurring marks on page on a laser printer.	Dirty fusing mechanism.
Vertical black lines on page on a laser printer.	Dirty rollers
Vertical white lines on the page on a laser printer.	Blocked toner cartridge
Smudging of image or toner rubs off on a laser printer.	Paper was damp & therefore toner not fused to paper or fuser not getting hot enough.

Problem	Cause
Ghosting of image (light images of previously printed pages) on a laser printer.	The imaging drum has not fully discharged & is picking up toner from a previous image.
Unintelligible text on a laser printer.	Paper that is too rough or too smooth.
Printer not printing full color correctly on a laser or inkjet printer.	Toner running low
A horizontal line is missing in the middle of each letter on an inkjet printer.	Blocked nozzles.
Documents appear to be blurred on an inkjet printer.	Damp paper
Documents in the print queue will not print.	Problem with the print spooler

Scanners

A scanner (sometimes known as an optical scanner) is a device that can scan or digitize images on paper (much like a copy machine does) and convert them to data that the computer can use. They can then be stored in a file, displayed on the screen, added to documents, or manipulated.

Scanners are connected to the computer using a SCSI interface, parallel port, USB interface, FireWire interface, or proprietary interface. After the scanner is installed and configured, the scanner software that controls the scanner must be installed. The software allows you to choose when to scan, which areas to scan, brightness and other control settings, and saves the data into a bitmap (picture made of dots) graphic file.

A scanned page of text is treated as an image made of dots. Optical character recognition (OCR) software converts the image of the text to actual text by analyzing the shape of each character and comparing its features against a set of rules that distinguishes each character and font. Most OCR software packages will then save the text into a Word, WordPerfect, rich text format (RTF), or ASCII text file.

Vocabulary Exercise: Completion

Fill in the blanks with the appropriate terms about scanners.

The de facto standard for scanners is _flat bed scanners_.

Files with the .jpg, .bmp, and .gif filename extensions are examples of _saved image files_.

If a scanner is not responding to the scanner software, make sure it is properly _configured_ and has _power_.

Study Questions

Choose the best answer for each of the questions that follow.

1. Which of the following will you find on an impact printer?

   A. It has an ink ribbon.

   B. It has an ink cartridge.

   C. It has a printhead.

   D. It uses toner powder.

2. Which of the following will you find on an inkjet printer?

   A. It has an ink ribbon.

   B. It has an ink cartridge.

   C. It has a high voltage power supply.

   D. It uses toner powder.

3. What is used to drain the charge in the paper when printing with a laser printer?

   A. Static-charge eliminator strip or roller.

   B. The rubber cleaning blade.

   C. The laser light.

   D. None of the above.

4. Which is the fastest interface used for printers?

   A. Serial

   B. USB 1.0

   C. USB 2.0

   D. Parallel

   E. IEEE 802.11g

5. After connecting a new printer to a Windows XP Professional computer via a parallel cable, the computer will not print to the printer. What is most likely the problem?

   A. The printer is connected to the wrong port.

   B. The device drivers are not installed.

   C. The computer must be rebooted.

   D. The printer is not compatible with Windows XP.

6. Multipart forms can be printed on _____.

   A. A laser jet printer

   B. An ink jet printer

   C. A dot matrix printer

   D. Thermal printers

7. If you can print a test page from the printer itself, but cannot print from the computer, what is the first thing that the technician should check?

   A. The device drivers

   B. The cable

   C. The toner cartridge

   D. The paper tray

8. When you have ghosting (light images of previously printed pages) on the current page on your laser printer, what is most likely the problem?

   A. A bad erasure lamp or broken cleaning blade

   B. The wrong type of paper

   C. Fuser is malfunctioning

   D. Power fluctuations

9. What is usually the problem if the print on the paper from a laser printer smears when you rub it?

   A. The toner is running low.

   B. The cartridge must be changed.

   C. The printer is using the wrong type of toner.

   D. The fuser is not getting hot enough.

10. When you print with a Windows system and the print jobs and documents do not print when they are in the print queue, what do you do?

    A. Restart the print spooler.

    B. Clear the print queue.

    C. Reboot the user's computer.

    D. Reboot the printer.

11. When you try to scan a picture, the lamp does not move, yet the computer is still communicating with the scanner. What is the problem?

    A. The USB port is faulty.

    B. The USB cable needs to be replaced.

    C. The user needs another lamp.

    D. The lamp is locked in place.

Lab Exercise

Lab 7.4.2: Install All-in-One Device and Software

In this lab, you will install an all-in-one device. You will find, download, and update the driver and the software for the all-in-one device.

The recommended equipment for this lab is:

- A computer running Windows XP Professional
- An Internet connection
- An all-in-one device

Step 1

If you are installing an all-in-one device that connects to a parallel port, shut down the computer and connect the cable to the all-in-one device and computer using a parallel cable. Plug the all-in-one device power cord into an AC outlet and unlock the all-in-one device if necessary. Restart your computer.

If you are installing a USB all-in-one device, plug the all-in-one device into the computer using a USB cable. Plug the all-in-one device power cord into an AC outlet if necessary. Unlock the all-in-one device if it is locked.

Step 2

Windows detects the new hardware.

The Found New Hardware Wizard window appears.

Click the Yes, This Time Only option button, and then click Next. Figure 7-1 shows these options.

Figure 7-1   Found New Hardware Wizard

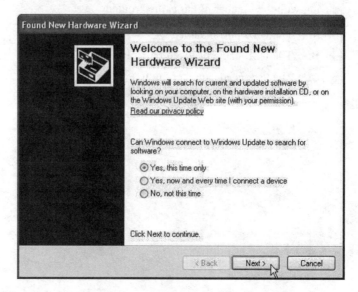

The second screen of the Found New Hardware Wizard appears as shown in Figure 7-2.

Figure 7-2   Found New Hardware Wizard Installation Options

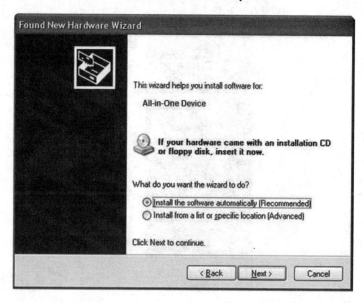

The default is Install the Software Automatically (Recommended).

Click Next.

The Please Wait While the Wizard Searches window appears as shown in Figure 7-3.

Figure 7-3   Wizard Searching Window

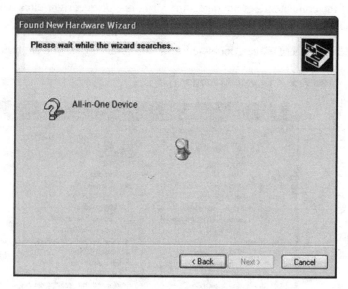

The Cannot Install This Hardware window may appear as shown in Figure 7-4.

**Figure 7-4   If the Device Driver Cannot Be Found, Cannot Install This Hardware Message
Will Appear**

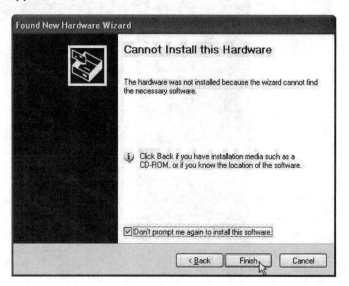

If this happens, click Finish.

If it does detect the hardware, follow the wizard to install the proper drivers.

Step 3

If the computer does not detect the all-in-one device, right-click My Computer, then choose Manage, Device Manager.

Under Other Devices, double-click the all-in-one device you are trying to install as shown in Figure 7-5.

Figure 7-5   Device Manager

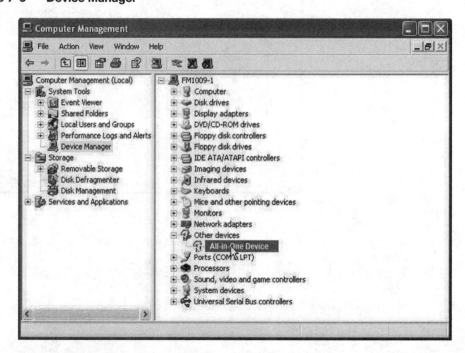

Step 4

The Properties window for the all-in-one device appears as shown in Figure 7-6.

Figure 7-6   All-in-One Device Properties Window

The Device status area shows The Drivers for This Device Are Not Installed. (Code 28).

Do not click Reinstall Driver at this time.

Click Cancel.

Step 5

Find the manufacturer and the model number of the all-in-one device.

Visit the manufacturer's website and navigate to the product downloads or support page. Download the most recent drivers and software for the model of all-in-one device that you have installed. The software and drivers must be compatible with your operating system.

Download the drivers to a temporary folder on your desktop.

Double-click the installation file that you downloaded and go through the driver installation process, as shown in Figure 7-7.

Figure 7-7   All-in-One Device Set Up

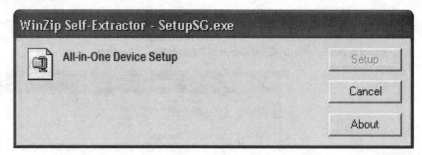

Step 6

Unplug the all-in-one device and plug it back in. Note that some parallel port devices might need a system restart to be redetected by Windows.

Because the drivers are now located on the computer, the Windows XP operating system will detect the new device every time it is reconnected.

To verify, right-click My Computer and then choose Manage, Device Manager. You should now see the all-in-one device installed under Imaging Devices on the right side of the window as shown in Figure 7-8.

Figure 7-8   Device Manager Recognizes the All-in-One Device

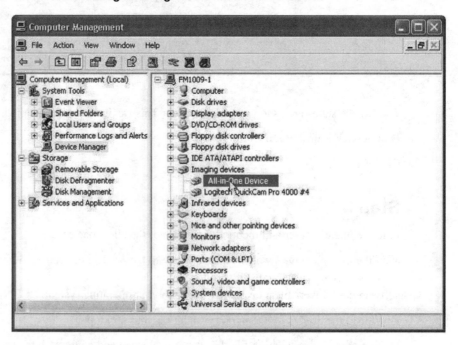

CHAPTER 8

Fundamental Networks

The Study Guide portion of this chapter uses a combination of matching, short-answer, and fill-in-the-blank questions to test your introductory knowledge of computer networks. This portion also includes multiple-choice study questions to help prepare you to take the A+ certification exams and to test your overall understanding of the material.

The Lab Exercises portion of this chapter includes all the online curriculum labs and worksheets to further reinforce your mastery of the computer network content.

Study Guide

Defining a Network

A network is two or more computers connected together to share resources. Many computers communicate with the network by a cable attached to the computer's network interface card (NIC), whereas other computers use some form of wireless technology (infrared, microwaves, or radio waves). Computers are networked according to certain protocols, such as TCP/IP, which are the rules or standards that allow computers on the network to communicate with one another. Currently, the benefits of a network include the following:

- Sharing data or access to a program loaded on the network (file sharing)
- Sharing printers (print sharing)
- Sending messages back and forth (electronic mail or e-mail)
- Sending and receiving faxes
- Accessing a modem or accessing the Internet directly
- Accessing a centralized database
- Scheduling appointments
- Providing security for the network services and resources
- Allowing for a central location of data files so that it is easier to perform a backup of essential files

Vocabulary Exercise: Matching

Match the definition on the left with a term on the right.

Definitions

a. Made up of computers within a close geographical area, such as a building or a campus, that are connected.

b. Uses long-range telecommunication links to connect networks over long distances and often consists of two or more smaller LANs.

c. A hardware address that identifies itself on the network, usually burned within or hard-coded onto a network card.

d. A networked computer where the individual users are responsible for their own resources and can decide which data and devices to share. There is no central point of control or administration in the network.

e. A model where the client requests information or services from the server. The server provides the requested information or service to the client. This model is designed for medium to large networks or networks that require enhanced security.

f. A single, one-way transmission.

g. When data flows in one direction at a time.

h. When data flows in both directions at the same time.

i. A method to transmit ordinary telephone calls over the Internet using packet-switched technology. It can also use an existing IP network to provide access to the public switched telephone network (PSTN).

Terms

_e_ client/server model

_h_ full-duplex

_g_ half-duplex

_a_ LAN

_c_ MAC address

_d_ peer-to-peer model

_f_ simplex

_b_ WAN

_i_ Voice over IP (VoIP)

Network Devices

As a computer technician, you will eventually have to connect a computer to a network. Therefore, you need to first learn the various components that make up a network and how to install and configure these components.

Vocabulary Exercise: Completion

Fill in the blanks with the appropriate terms about network devices.

A _hub_ is a traditional multiported connection point used to connect network devices via a cable segment. Different from switches, only one device can communicate through this device at a time.

A _Bridge_ is a device that connects two LANs and makes them appear as one, or that is used to connect two segments of the same LAN. Different from a gateway, it keeps traffic separated on both sides of the bridge by analyzing MAC addresses of the communicating devices to remember where each device is located. These Layer 2 devices forward or block Ethernet frames based upon destination MAC address information.

A _Switch_, also known as a switching hub, is a fast, multiported bridge that actually reads the destination MAC address of each frame and then forwards the frame to the correct port. Switches, Layer 2 devices, use _MAC Address Tables_ to determine which frames to forward within a single network.

A _router_ is a device that connects entire logical networks to each other. Routers use _MAC Addresses_ to forward packets to other networks.

A _peer to peer network_ is any hardware and software combination that connects dissimilar network environments.

Wireless Access Points provide network access to wireless devices such as laptops and PDAs.

A _Network Interface Card_, abbreviated _NIC_, is the physical interface, or connection, between the computer and the network cable. The role of this device is to prepare and send data to another computer, receive data from another computer, and control the flow of data between the computer and the cabling system.

Cable Types and Connectors

Network devices are often connected with cables. Therefore, you will need to identify the common cables used in today's networks, know their characteristics, and understand how to install them.

Vocabulary Exercise: Completion

Fill in the blanks with the appropriate terms about cable types and connectors.

Twisted Pair cabling is a type of copper cabling that is used for telephone communications and most local-area networks. A pair of wires forms a circuit that can transmit data. The pair is twisted to provide protection against _cross-talk_, which is the noise generated by adjacent pairs of wires in the cable.

Unshielded Twisted Pair is a type of twisted cable that has two or four pairs of wires. This type of cable relies solely on the cancellation effect produced by the twisted wire pairs that limits signal degradation caused by _Electromagnetic Interface_ and _Radio Frequency Interference_. It is the most commonly used cabling in _Ethernet_ networks. UTP cables have a range of _____ feet (_100_ meters).

UTP comes in several categories that are based on the number of _wires_ in the cable and the number of _twists_ per foot in those wires.

Category 3 is the wiring used for telephone connections. It has four pairs of wires and a maximum data transmission rate of up to 16 Mbps.

category 5 and *category 5e* have four pairs of wires with a maximum data transmission rate of up to 1000 Mbps. Category 5 and 5e are the most common Ethernet network cables used. Category 5e has more *twists per foot* than Category 5 wiring. These extra twists further prevent *interference* from outside sources and the other wires within the cable.

Category 6 cable often uses a plastic divider to separate the pairs of wires to prevent crosstalk interference. The pairs also have more twists than Category 5e cable.

Shielded Twisted Pair is a type of twisted-pair cable in which each pair of wires is wrapped in metallic foil to better shield the wires from noise. Four pairs of wires are then wrapped in an overall metallic braid or foil. It reduces electrical noise, or crosstalk, from within the cable. It also reduces electrical noise, EMI, and RFI from outside the cable.

Coaxial cable is a copper-cored cable surrounded by a heavy shielding. This cable used to be used to connect computers in a network but today is usually found only as part of a home broadband (such as cable TV) system.

Thick net or *10 BASE5* is a traditional Ethernet network implementation that uses coaxial cables and operates at *10* megabits per second with a maximum length of *500* meters.

Thin net or *10 BASE 2* is also a traditional Ethernet network implementation that uses coaxial cables and operates at *10* megabits per second with a maximum length of *185* meters.

RG-59 and *RG-6* coaxial cable is most commonly used for cable TV in the U.S.

A *Fibre-optic cable* is a glass or plastic conductor that transmits information using light. A fiber-optic cable is one or more optical fibers enclosed together in a sheath or jacket. Because it is made of glass, fiber-optic cable is not affected by *Electromagnetic Interface* or *radio-frequency interference*. Fiber-optic cable can reach distances of *several miles* before the signal needs to be regenerated. However, fiber-optic cabling is usually more *expensive* to use than copper cabling. The connectors are more costly and harder to assemble. And all signals have to be converted to light pulses to enter the cable and back into electrical signals when they leave it.

Multimode has a thicker core than single-mode cable and is easier to make, can use simpler light sources (LED), and works well over distances of a few kilometers or less.

Single-mode has a very thin core. It is harder to make, uses lasers as a light source, and can transmit signals dozens of kilometers with ease.

Plenum is the space above the ceiling and below the floors used to circulate air throughout the workplace. A _____ is a special cable that gives off little or no toxic fumes when burned.

A UTP cable uses *BNC* connectors.

Modems that connect to an analog phone system use *RJ-11* connectors.

The RJ-11 connector has _____ connectors, whereas the RJ-45 has _____ connectors.

A _____ uses a RG-58 coaxial cable with 50 ohm terminating resistors and a _____ uses RG-8 with 50 ohm terminating resistors. RG-6 cables use a _____ ohm terminating resistor.

A 10Base2 cable uses _____ and ___-connectors to connect computers to the network.

Two traditional fiber-optic connectors are *SC* and *ST* _____ . A new connector called the *MT-RJ* is similar to an RJ-45 connector.

Network Topologies

Network topologies give a computer technician an idea how network traffic flows over a cable system. If a device is not functioning properly or a cable is broken, understanding the topology will help you figure out where the problem is.

Vocabulary Exercise: Matching

Match the definition on the left with a term on the right.

Definitions

a. Describes the layout of the cabling and devices, as well as the paths used by data transmissions.

b. The topology that has no beginning or end, so the cable does not need to be terminated.

c. The topology that is the simplest network arrangement, in which a single cable (called a backbone, trunk, or segment) connects all the computers in series.

d. Used in bus topology to prevent signals from bouncing back when they reach the end of a backbone.

e. The most common network configuration in which all the computers in the network are connected to a central device known as a hub or switch.

f. The topology that connects all devices to each other.

Terms

_c_ bus topology

_f_ mesh topology

_a_ network topology

_b_ ring topology

_e_ star topology

_d_ terminating resistor

Networking Technology

After understanding the basics of how a network works, you are now ready to look at the various technologies and standards used in networking. By understanding these, you can make educated decisions on which technology and standards to use and how to troubleshoot them.

Concept Questions

Answer the following networking technology questions:

What IEEE standard is the Ethernet architecture?

IEEE 802.3

What access method (rules defining how a computer puts data onto the network cable and takes data from the cable) does Ethernet use?

CSMA/CD

Which access method is used in IEEE 802.11 networks?

_____

10BaseT is based on what topology?

_____ star _____

What is the maximum length of a 10BaseT cable?

_____ 100 m _____

Fast Ethernet runs at what speed?

_____ 100 Mbps _____

What type of cable does 100BaseFX use?

_____

What is the central hub used for Token Ring?

_____ multistation Access Unit _____

At what speed does FDDI run?

_____ 100 Mbps _____

What uses a special authorizing packet (token) of information to inform devices that they can transmit data?

_____ Token Ring _____

What mode do wireless devices use to connect to an access point to communicate on a wireless network?

___ Wi-fi ___

What is the maximum speed that 802.11g can run?

___ 54 Mbps ___

How fast does 802.11a run?

___ 54 Mbps ___

802.1g is backward compatible with which standard?

___ 802.11 b ___

At what radio frequency does an IEEE 802.11g wireless network operate?

___ 2.4 GHz ___

At what radio frequency does an IEEE 802.11a wireless network operate?

___ 5.0 GHz ___

What is the maximum transmission speed supported by Bluetooth?

___ 1 Mbps ___

What is the speed of a T-1 line?

___ 1.544 Mbps ___

Connecting to the Internet

The Internet is the largest network used today. Most computers that you connect to a network will most likely need to connect to the Internet. Therefore, you need to know the options that are available as well as how to install and configure these options.

Vocabulary Exercise: Matching

Match the definition on the left with a term on the right.

Definitions

a. A standard for sending voice, video, and data over digital telephone lines.

b. An ISDN connection that offers a dedicated 128 Kbps connection using two 64 Kbps B channels.

c. ISDN that offers up to 1.544 Mbps over 23 B channels in North America and Japan or 2.048 Mbps over 30 B channels in Europe and Australia.

d. An "always-on" technology that uses the existing copper telephone lines to provide high speed data communication.

e. An electronic device that transfers data between one computer and another using analog signals over a telephone line.

f. The address used on a TCP/IP network that logically identifies the computer.

g. A protocol and service that automatically hands out IP addresses to client computers.

h. The address of the nearest router or gateway so that you can communicate with other networks.

i. A set of numbers that resemble an IP address to determine which bits of an IP address make up a local host address and which bits make up the network address (subnet).

j. The protocol and service that translates from hostnames to IP addresses.

k. Technology that uses multiple signals/multiple frequencies over one cable.

Terms

_k_ broadband

____ default gateway

_d_ digital subscriber lines (DSL)

_j_ Domain Name System (DNS)

_g_ Dynamic Host Configuration Protocol (DHCP)

_h_ IP address

_a_ ISDN

_b_ ISDN Basic Rate Interface (BRI)

_c_ ISDN Primary Rate Interface (PRI)

_e_ modem

_i_ subnet mask

Network Troubleshooting Tools

When network problems occur, you have some tools available to help you troubleshoot these problems. Most of these tools are available within Windows, and you will need to know how and when to use these tools.

Concept Questions

Answer the following network troubleshooting questions:

What command can you use to see the current IP address in Windows XP?

ipconfig

What command can you use to see all IP configuration information, including DNS server information?

ipconfig /all

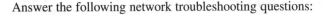

What command can you use to test connectivity with another host?

nslookup

How do you know if a cable is not connected properly or if a NIC is improperly installed or configured?

Ping 127.0.0.1 tests your NIC regardless of the actual assigned IP.

Study Questions

Choose the best answer for each of the questions that follow:

1. Which of the following IP blocks are reserved for private networks?

    A. 192.0.x.x   ?

    B. 244.0.x.x

    C. 127.0.x.x

    D. 192.168.x.x

2. Which of the following describes a transmission technology on which data can be transmitted in both directions on a signal carrier at the same time?

    A. Bidirectional

    B. Half duplex

    C. Full duplex

    D. Multidirectional

3. Which of the following is used to automate the IP configuration of network clients?

    A. DHCP

    B. WINS

    C. ARP

    D. DNS

4. Which of the following provides name resolution on the Internet, including translating from hostnames to IP addresses?

    A. DHCP

    B. DNS

    C. WINS

    D. ARP

5. Which access method is used in Ethernet?

    A. Token passing

    B. Full duplex

    C. CSMA/CA (Carrier Sense Multiple Access/Collision Avoidance)

    D. CSMA/CD (Carrier Sense Multiple Access/Collision Detection)

6. Which of the following Ethernet cable standards supports transmission speeds of more than 200 Mbps?

    A. CAT3

    B. CAT4

    C. CAT5

    D. CAT6

7. Which of the following supports the longest transmission distance?

    A. Coaxial cable

    B. UTP cable

    C. STP cable

    D. Fiber-optic cable

8. What is the minimum cable rating required for a 1000BASE-TX network?

    A. CAT3

    B. CAT5

    C. CAT5e

    D. CAT6

9. If you need to connect two computers directly to each other using FastEthernet without going through a hub or switch, what would you need?

    A. CAT3 crossover

    B. CAT5 crossover

    C. CAT3 straight

    D. CAT5 straight

10. Which media type is *not* susceptible to electromagnetic interference (EMI)?

    A. Unshielded twisted pair cable

    B. Shielded twisted pair cable

    C. Coaxial cable

    D. Fiber-optic cable

11. What is the maximum segment length of a 100BASE-TX cable?

   A. 50 meters

   B. 75 meters

   C. 100 meters

   D. 182 meters

   E. 550 meters

12. Which of the following is the connector used for 100BASE-T Ethernet cables?

   A. RJ-11

   B. RJ-45

   C. RJ-66

   D. BNC

13. How many pairs of wires are used in an RJ-45 connector?

   A. 2

   B. 3

   C. 4

   D. 5

14. Which of the following devices can be used to connect two similar network segments but keeps network traffic separate on the two segments?

   A. CSU/DSU

   B. Switch

   C. Gateway

   D. Bridge

15. At what radio frequency does an IEEE 802.11g wireless network operate?

   A. 2.4 GHz

   B. 5.0 GHz

   C. 5.4 GHz

   D. 10 GHz

16. What is the maximum transmission speed supported by IEEE 802.11g?

   A. 2 Mbps

   B. 11 Mbps

   C. 54 Mbps

   D. 248 Kbps

17. Which of the following can be used to connect a WLAN to a wired LAN?

   A. An access point

   B. A bridge

   C. A gateway

   D. A CSU/DSU

18. What can you replace a hub with that will also increase network performance?

   A. Switches

   B. Routers

   C. Bridges

   D. Gateways

19. How can you determine the connection speed and signal strength of a wireless network connection on a Windows XP computer?

   A. A wireless access point utility

   B. A wireless network adapter

   C. Wireless NIC properties

   D. Windows Device Manager

20. What command do you use to view the IP configuration of a Windows XP?

   A. ping

   B. arp -a

   C. ipconfig /all

   D. winipcfg /all

21. What command do you use to view the IP configuration of a Windows 98 computer?

   A. netstat

   B. arp /all

   C. ipconfig /all

   D. winipcfg /all

22. What command can be used to identify which computers are having an IP conflict?

   A. ping

   B. arp -a

   C. ipconfig /all

   D. winipcfg /all

23. You notice that a NIC card amber LED is continuously flashing very quickly. What is the problem?

   A. Data transmission is taking place.

   B. Transmission collisions are occurring.

   C. There is a faulty cable.

   D. The hub or switch is faulty.

24. If you can ping a website by address, but not by name, what is the problem?

   A. The web server is down.

   B. The DHCP server is down.

   C. The DNS server is down.

   D. The domain controller is down.

Lab Exercises

Worksheet 8.3.2: Identify IP Address Classes

In this worksheet, write which IP address class is appropriate in the IP Address Class column in the following table. An example has been provided for you.

IP Address	Subnet Mask	IP Address Class
10.0.0.0	255.0.0.0	A
201.18.0.0	255.255.255.0	C
99.0.0.0	255.0.0.0	A
130.130.0.0	255.255.0.0	B
80.0.0.0	255.0.0.0	A
189.12.0.0	255.255.0.0	B

Worksheet 8.9.1: Internet Search for NIC Drivers

In this worksheet, you will search the Internet for the latest NIC drivers for a network card.

Complete the following table. An example has been provided for you. Drivers are routinely updated. Manufacturers often move driver files to different areas of their websites. Version numbers change frequently. The driver in the example was found by visiting the manufacturer's (www.intel.com) website. A search for the full name of the NIC was used to find the driver download file.

NIC	URL Driver Location and Latest Version Number
Intel PRO/1000 PT Desktop Adapter	http://downloadcenter.intel.com/scripts-df-external/confirm.aspx?httpDown= http://downloadmirror.intel.com/df-support/4275/eng/PRO2KXP.exe&agr=& ProductID=2247&DwnldId=4275&strOSs=&OSFullName=&lang=eng Ver. # 12.0
3COM 905CX-TXM	
Linksys WMP54GX4	

Lab 8.9.2: Configure an Ethernet NIC to Use DHCP

In this lab, you will configure an Ethernet NIC to use DHCP to obtain an IP address.

The following is the recommended equipment for this lab:

- Linksys 300N router
- A computer running Windows XP Professional
- Ethernet patch cable

Step 1

Plug in one end of the Ethernet patch cable to Port 1 on the back of the router.

Plug in the other end of the Ethernet patch cable to the network port on the NIC in your computer.

Plug in the power cable of the router if it is not already plugged in.

Turn on your computer and log on to Windows as an administrator.

Click Start.

Right-click My Network Places, and then choose Properties. The Network Connections window appears as shown in Figure 8-1.

Figure 8-1   Network Connections Window

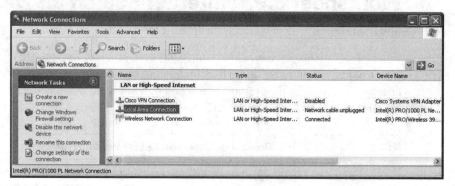

Step 2

Right-click Local Area Connection, and then choose Properties. The Local Area Connection Properties window appears as shown in Figure 8-2.

Figure 8-2   Local Area Connection Properties Window

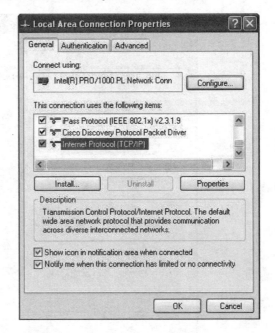

What is the name and model number of the NIC in the Connect Using field?

What are the items listed in the This Connection Uses the Following Items field?

Step 3

Choose Internet Protocol (TCP/IP).

Click Properties. The Internet Protocol (TCP/IP) Properties window appears as shown in Figure 8-3.

Figure 8-3   Internet Protocol (TCP/IP) Properties Window

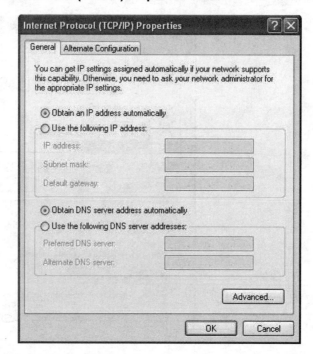

What is the IP Address, Subnet Mask, and Default Gateway listed in the fields of the Use the Following IP Address area?

_____

_____

Click the Obtain an IP Address Automatically option button.

Click OK. The Internet Protocol (TCP/IP) Properties window closes, which takes you back to the Local Area Connection Properties window.

Click OK. Restart your computer.

Step 4

Log on to Windows as an administrator.

Check the lights on the back of the NIC. These lights will blink when there is network activity.

Choose Start, Run.

Type **cmd** and click OK, as shown in Figure 8-4.

Figure 8-4   Entering cmd

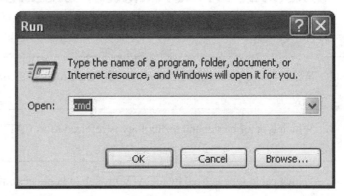

Type **ipconfig/all**, and then press the Enter key as shown in Figure 8-5.

Figure 8-5   Sample Output of the ipconfig /all Command

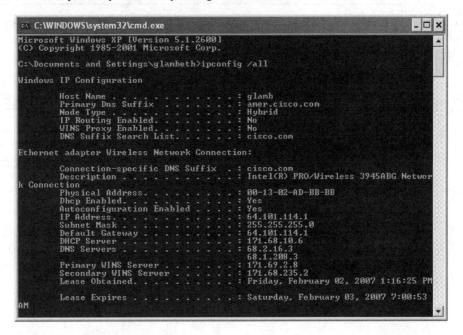

What is the IP address and subnet mask of the Ethernet Adapter Local Area Network Connection?

_____

What is the IP address of the DHCP server?

_____

On what date was the lease obtained?

_____

On what date does the lease expire?

_____

Worksheet 8.10.3: Answer Broadband Questions

1. Which types of signals are carried over a DSL cable?

   256 Kbps to 24 Mbps

2. What is the typical upload speed of a satellite broadband connection?

   56 Kbps

3. Which type of broadband technology is referred to as CATV?

4. Which cable type is used by a CATV broadband connection?

5. ISDN uses existing telephone copper wires to send and receive which types of signals?

   Digital

6. Which technology is usually an alternative when cable or DSL is not available?

   Satellite

7. What is the 16 Kbps digital line used for in an ISDN connection?

   Call setup, control & teardown

8. What is the typical download speed of a satellite broadband connection?

   500 Kbps

9. What is the maximum data rate for ISDN BRI?

   128 Kbps

10. Which device on a DSL connection requires a filter?

    Telephone - to prevent DSL signals from interfering with phone signals.

Worksheet 8.12.2: Diagnose a Network Problem

(Student Technician Sheet)

Gather data from the customer to begin the troubleshooting process. Document the customer's problem and a solution in the following work order. (See the Student Customer Sheet later in the lab for more information.)

Company Name: _Handford Insurance_

Contact: _J. Halle_

Company Address: _1672 N. 52nd Ave._

Company Phone: _555-9991_

Work Order

Generating a New Ticket

Category _Network_   Closure Code _____   Status _Open_

Type _____   Escalated _____   Pending _____

Item _Pending_   Until Date _____

Business Impacting? ☒ Yes ○ No

Summary _The customer is unable to connect to the network. Customer is not able to send or receive email._

Case ID# _____   Connection Type _____
Priority _____   Environment _____
User Platform _Windows XP_

Problem Description: _Customer cannot access network folders. Customer cannot send or receive email. Customer was able to access the network yesterday._

_____

_____

_____

_____

Problem Solution: _____

_____

_____

_____

_____

(Student Customer Sheet)

Use the contact information and problem description that follows to report the following information to a level-one technician:

Contact Information

Company Name: Handford Insurance

Contact: J. Halle

Company Address: 1672 N. 52nd Ave.

Company Phone: 555-9991

Problem Description

I am not able to connect to the network. I can log on to Windows, but I cannot get to my folders on the network. I cannot get to the Internet, either. Everything was fine yesterday because Johnny was using my computer while I was at home sick, but now it does not work. In fact, my e-mail does not work either. I tried to send e-mail, but it did not go anywhere. It just sits in my Outbox. My friend said she sent me some e-mail this morning, but I do not have it. It just is not there. What am I going to do? I have to get started on my work. My boss is going to be very upset. Can you help me get to the network? And my files? And my e-mail?

Note: After you have given the level-one tech the problem description, use the Additional Information to answer any follow-up questions the technician may ask.

Additional Information

- I am using Windows XP Pro.
- Cable connects me to the Internet.
- I am using a desktop computer.
- Everybody else in the office can access their files.
- Everybody else in the office can use e-mail.

CHAPTER 9

Fundamental Security

The Study Guide portion of this chapter uses a combination of matching, short-answer, and fill-in-the-blank questions to test your introductory knowledge of security in information technology. This portion also includes multiple-choice study questions to help prepare you to take the A+ certification exams and to test your overall understanding of the material.

The Lab Exercises portion of this chapter includes all the online worksheets and remote technician exercises to further reinforce your mastery of the fundamental security content.

Study Guide

Importance of Security

Security is a high concern and a major responsibility for network administrators. Security should also be a concern for anyone who uses a computer to connect to a network—including the Internet—or a computer that holds confidential information.

Computer security refers to the process and techniques by which digital information and related assets are protected. The goals of computer security are the following:

- Maintain integrity
- Protect confidentiality
- Assure availability

Integrity refers to the assurance that data is not altered or destroyed in an unauthorized manner. *Confidentiality* is the protection of data from unauthorized disclosure to a third party. *Availability* is defined as the continuous operation of computer systems.

A *threat* is a person, place, or thing that has the potential to access resources and cause harm. A *vulnerability* is a point where a resource is susceptible to attack. It can be thought of as a weakness. An *exploit* is a type of attack on a resource that involves a threat that takes advantage of a vulnerability in an environment. The exploitation of resources can be performed in many ways. When a threat takes advantage of a vulnerability to attack a resource, severe consequences can result.

For example, a virus is a major threat to a computer system. First, it can disrupt the operation of the computer (availability) by deleting or corrupting key files or corrupting the file system. It can also corrupt or delete data files (integrity). It can also capture information such as personal files and passwords that you type on a website (confidentiality).

Some of the tools and methods used to secure a computer are the following:

- Physical security
- Authentication
- Encryption
- Perimeter security, including firewalls and routers
- Access control, including rights and permissions

Because security is a constantly changing process and technology, to properly protect a computer you must always be on guard and adapt to the changing processes and technology. This includes adding patches to the operating system and applications, keeping the virus checker up-to-date, and being educated on the techniques and methods of possible attacks.

Vocabulary Exercise: Matching

Match the definition on the left with a term on the right.

Definitions

a. The ability to verify the identity of a user, system, or system element.

b. The process of disguising a message or data in what appears to be meaningless data to hide and protect the sensitive data from unauthorized access.

c. A system that uses two authentication methods, such as smart cards and a password.

d. The use of protocols on a public or shared network (such as the Internet) to create a secure, private network connection between a client and a server.

e. A protocol developed for transmitting private documents via the Internet/web pages; it uses a public key to encrypt data that is transferred over the connection.

f. A hardware device with software that is used to detect unauthorized activity on your network.

g. An area that is used by a company that wants to host its own Internet services without sacrificing unauthorized access to its private network.

h. A system designed to prevent unauthorized access to or from a private network.

i. A term used to describe the process of circumventing security barriers by persuading authorized users to provide passwords or other sensitive information.

j. A program designed to replicate and spread, generally without the knowledge or permission of the user.

k. Any software that covertly gathers user information through the user's Internet connection without his or her knowledge, usually for advertising purposes.

l. A combination of text used to validate the person's identity when that person logs on.

m. A seemingly useful or benign program that when activated performs malicious or illicit action, such as destroying files.

n. A type of attack on a network that is designed to make a system or network perform poorly or not at all.

o. The act of sending an e-mail to a user, falsely claiming to be an established legitimate enterprise in an attempt to scam the user into surrendering private information that will be used for identity theft.

p. A type of server that makes a single Internet connection and services request on behalf of many users to filter requests and to increase performance.

Terms

_a_   Authentication

_g_   Demilitarized zone (DMZ)

_n_   Denial of Service (DoS)

_b_   Encryption

_h_   Firewall

_f_   Intrusion Detection System (IDS)

_l_   Password

_o_   Phishing attack

_e_   Secure Sockets Layer (SSL)

_i_   Social engineering

_k_   Spyware

_m_   Trojan horse

_c_   Two-factor authentication

_d_   Virtual Private Network (VPN)

_j_   Virus

_p_   Proxy server

Concept Questions

Answer the following questions about security:

You are visiting a website to purchase several books. What do you need to use to make sure that your transactions are secure?

That the website is a 'HTTP S' - 'S' = secure

Passwords are the most common form of authentication. Can you think of any other methods for authentication?

security questions (in addition to passwords)

Biometric

What restricts traffic onto a network or onto an individual system?

Firewall

How do you combat social engineering?

Ensure users do not write down or pass on passwords

If you have a workstation at work, what should you do when you walk away from your computer?

lock your workstation. Either CTR + ALT + DEL or Windows logo + L

If you configure a VPN through a firewall, why can't the firewall inspect the traffic going through the VPN tunnel?

Wireless Security

Because wireless technology typically sends out network traffic using a broadcast wireless signal, these wireless signals can be easily captured by anyone who has a wireless card. Therefore, you have to take extra steps to make sure that your wireless network is secure by using encryption and other forms of wireless security.

Vocabulary Exercise: Completion

Fill in the blanks for the items that follow:

The _____ is a 32-character unique identifier attached to the header of packets sent over a WLAN that acts as a password when a mobile device tries to connect to an access point.

The most basic wireless encryption scheme that provides encryption over IEEE 802.11x networks is *Wired Equivalent Privacy*. To access the network, you would provide a key. If you provide the *wrong key*, you will not be able to access the network. Unfortunately, it is easy for someone with a little knowledge or experience to break the shared key because it doesn't change automatically over time. Therefore, it is recommended to use a higher form of wireless encryption.

Today, it is recommended to use *Wi-Fi Protected Access* or *Wi-Fi Protected Access 2*. To help prevent someone from hacking the key, this encryption rotates the keys and changes the way keys are derived.

_802.11_ is the wireless protocol that provides an authentication framework for wireless LANs, allowing a user to be authenticated by a central authority.

There are two ways to prevent unauthorized computers from connecting to a wireless network. One way is to configure _MAC Address Filtering_ on the wireless access point so that you can specify which computers (identified by the computer's MAC address) can connect to the wireless network. Another way is to disable the _Service Set Identifier_ so that users who want to connect to the wireless network must also know the unique identifier to connect.

Some wireless switches include an _____, which is used to prevent unauthorized wireless access to local area networks and other information assets. These systems can be used to troubleshoot security breaches and other wireless problems.

Anytime you install a new wireless switch, you should always change the default _____ and change the default _____ and _____. You should also keep the _____ updated on the system so that it has the best security available for the switch.

When implementing a wireless solution, you should perform a thorough _____ first.

Viruses

Computer viruses have been around almost as long as the modern computer has been around, and viruses are not going away anytime soon. Therefore, to protect your computer and the data that the computer is holding, you need to protect yourself against viruses.

Vocabulary Exercise: Completion

Fill in the blanks for the items that follow:

A _Virus_ is a program designed to replicate and spread, generally without the knowledge or permission of the user. Therefore, they are a huge security concern.

To help keep your system protected from viruses, you must keep your operating system _updated_, and you must use an updated _Anti-Virus software_.

A threat to computers that can cause similar problems is _Spyware_, which can monitor user activity on the Internet and transmit that information without the user's knowledge. Spyware can also generate annoying pop-ups and make your system unreliable.

Denial of Service Attacks

Denial of Service (DoS) is a form of attack that prevents users from accessing normal services, such as e-mail and web services, because the system is busy responding to an abnormally large amount of requests. Common DoS attacks work by sending enough requests for a system resource that the requested service is overloaded and ceases to operate. Simpler forms of DoS attacks include cutting a cable or shutting off the power.

Vocabulary Exercise: Matching

Match the definition on the left with a term on the right

Definitions

a. An abnormally large ping packet is sent in the hope of causing a buffer overflow that will crash the receiving computer.

b. A large quantity of bulk e-mail sent to individuals, lists, or domains, intending to prevent users from accessing e-mail.

c. Randomly opens TCP ports, tying up the network equipment or computer with a large amount of false requests, causing sessions to be denied to others.

d. Intercepts or inserts false information in traffic between two hosts.

e. Gains access to resources on devices by pretending to be a trusted computer.

f. Uses network sniffers to extract usernames and passwords to be used at a later date to gain access.

g. Changes the DNS records on a system to point to false servers where the data is recorded.

h. Another form of attack that uses many infected computers, called zombies, to launch an attack. This makes it difficult to trace the origin of the attack.

Terms

_h_ Distributed DoS (DDoS)

_g_ DNS poisoning

_b_ E-mail bomb

_d_ Man-in-the-middle

_a_ Ping of death

_f_ Replay

_e_ Spoofing

_c_ SYN flood

Study Questions

Choose the best answer for each of the questions that follow:

1. You have multiple users who work for your company that need to connect to your network servers when they are on the road. What would you suggest as a solution?

    A. Configure a company server to accept incoming VPN connections from authorized remote users.

    B. Configure an ISDN line to your network servers.

    C. Configure a web server to use SSL.

    D. Install digital certificates on the servers and the workstations.

2. What should you do if you want to prevent unauthorized computers from connecting to your wireless network?

   A. Install an IDS on your wireless network.

   B. Configure MAC address filtering on the wireless access point.

   C. Enable SSID broadcast.

   D. Use WEP encryption.

3. What is the most basic encryption used in today's wireless network?

   A. WEP

   B. VPN

   C. WPA2

   D. SSL

4. If you specify the wrong WEP key, what would happen?

   A. Data that you see on the screen would be garbled.

   B. You would not be able to access the wireless network.

   C. You would attach to the next available wireless network.

   D. You could only send data but not receive data.

5. You have a laptop that you use while you are on the road. Which of the following would be the best to protect your system while you are on the road?

   A. Use HTTPS on your laptop.

   B. Use digital certificates on your laptop.

   C. Use WEP.

   D. Use a personal firewall.

6. What is a recommended method of wireless encryption?

   A. WPA

   B. WEP

   C. PAP

   D. SSL

7. You are monitoring a server and you find several incidents of unauthorized access to certain key data files. What should you do?

   A. Reboot the server.

   B. Shut down the server.

   C. Report the incident as a security violation by following company procedures or policies.

   D. Change the administrator password.

8. While you are at the front desk, you notice that the security guard had let an unidentified person into the server room, which is protected by a locked door and code. The unidentified person said he was sent by the president of the company, but was not. What type of attack would this be?

    A. A man-in-the-middle attack

    B. IP spoofing

    C. Halloween attack

    D. Social engineering

9. What do you do if an SSL certificate is no longer valid in Internet Explorer and you need to access a website that uses SSL?

    A. Create a new SSL certificate.

    B. Clear the SSL cache.

    C. Allow SSL with revoked or expired certificates.

    D. Delete temporary Internet files.

10. If you are configuring two-factor authentication to be implemented when users are accessing your corporate network, what else can they use besides passwords?

    A. Smart cards

    B. DNA scan

    C. IP address

    D. Username

Lab Exercises

Worksheet 9.1.0: Security Attacks

In this activity, you will use the Internet, a newspaper, or magazines to gather information to help you become familiar with computer crime and security attacks in your area. Be prepared to discuss your research with the class.

1. Briefly describe one article dealing with computer crime or a security attack.

_____

_____

2. Based on your research, could this incident have been prevented? List the precautions that might have prevented this attack.

_____

_____

Worksheet 9.2.1: Third-Party Antivirus Software

In this activity, you will use the Internet, a newspaper, or a local store to gather information about third-party antivirus software.

1. Using the Internet, a newspaper, or a local store, research two antivirus software applications. Based on your research, complete the following table:

Company/Software Name Website URL	Software Features Subscription Length (Month/Year/Lifetime) Cost

2. Which antivirus software would you purchase? List reasons for your selection.

_____

_____

Worksheet 9.4.2: Operating System Updates

In this activity, you will use the Internet to research operating system updates. Be prepared to discuss your research with the class.

1. Which operating system (OS) is installed on your computer?

_____

2. List the configuration options available for updating the OS.

_____

_____

_____

_____

_____

3. Which configuration option would you use to update the OS? List the reason for choosing a particular option.

_____

_____

4. If the instructor gives you permission, begin the update process for the OS. List all security updates available.

_____

Remote Technician 9.5.2: Gather Information from the Customer

(Student Technician Sheet)

Gather data from the customer to begin the troubleshooting process. (See the Student Customer Sheet later in the lab for customer information.) Document the customer's problem in the following work order.

Company Name: _____

Contact: _____

Company Address: _____

Company Phone: _____

Work Order

Generating a New Ticket

Category _____   Closure Code _____   Status _____

Type _____   Escalated _____   Pending _____

Item _____   Pending Until Date _____

Business Impacting?   ○ Yes   ○ No

Summary _____

_____

Case ID# _____   Connection Type _____

Priority _____   Environment _____

User Platform _____

Problem Description: _____

_____

_____

_____

_____

Problem Solution: _____

_____

_____

_____

_____

(Student Customer Sheet)

Use the contact information and problem description here to report the following information to a level-one technician:

Contact Information

Company Name: Organization of Associated Chartered Federations, Inc.

Contact: Henry Jones

Company Address: 123 E. Main Street

Company Phone: 480-555-1234

Category: Security

Problem Description

I am not able to log in. I was able to log in yesterday and all days previously. I tried to log in with a different computer but was unsuccessful there also. I received an e-mail last week about changing my password, but I have not changed my password yet.

Note: After you have given the level-one tech the problem description, use the Computer Configuration to answer any follow-up questions the technician may ask.

Computer Configuration

Windows XP Pro

I do not know when it was last updated.

There is some kind of antivirus program that used to run when I started the computer, but I haven't seen it recently.

CHAPTER 10

Communication Skills

The Study Guide portion of this chapter uses short-answer questions to test your knowledge of communication skills. This portion also includes multiple-choice study questions to help prepare you to take the A+ certification exams and to test your overall understanding of the material.

The Lab Exercise portion of this chapter includes the online curriculum worksheets and class discussions to further reinforce your mastery of communication skills.

Study Guide

Dealing with the Customer

When repairing computers, you may be repairing the computer for someone who works within the same company as you or for a customer who contacted you. One of the main responsibilities is to satisfy the customer or client. Your job or business depends on the customer, so you must be skilled at dealing with people.

You will find a range of computer users and customers. Some of these people will be very knowledgeable about computers, and other people can barely turn them on. Some people will be easy to work with, and others will be more difficult. Although you can show some people how to use the computer properly, you will find it is sometimes harder to fix people's attitudes than it is to fix a hardware or software problem.

When dealing with customers, you should follow certain guidelines:

- Always be courteous. Try to smile and say positive things to the customer whenever you can.

- Focus on the customer and don't get distracted.

- Be concerned with the customer's need.

- Don't belittle a customer, a customer's knowledge, or a customer's choice of hardware or software.

- Don't complain to the customer and don't make excuses.

- Stay calm. Don't get angry.

- If you give a customer a component that appears to be defective or faulty, offer an immediate replacement.

- Be professional. Dress appropriately for the environment. Don't take over a person's workspace without asking.

- Follow proper personal hygiene.

- Be dependable and follow up on the service. If you will miss an appointment or will be late, call the customer to let him or her know.

- Allow the customer to complain.

- Allow the customer to explain the problem, and listen carefully.

- Don't do anything until you have interviewed the user.

- Always ask permission first.

- Keep things neat, tidy, and out of the client's way.

- Explain how to prevent future problems without condescension and disrespect.

- Try not to use industry jargon or acronyms when explaining the problem and solution to the customer.

- If a customer is unhappy with you, your company, or a product, an apology can go a long way. If it is not your fault, you can still apologize for the situation. In addition, find out how you can make things better.

Concept Questions

Answer the following questions about dealing with a customer:

When you are communicating with a customer, what kind of statements should you use?

clear without jargon

As mentioned before, you should allow the customer to explain the problem while you listen carefully. Why is this important?

So that you can try & evaluate what may have caused the problem.

If you are totally clear on the problem or situation, you should always do what first?

Repeat the problem back to the customer.

When you get a call from the customer, you should always remain in control of the call. What else should you do?

Ask relevant questions to try & understand problem.

When you are listening for meaning to what a customer is saying, you are checking with the customer to see that you correctly heard and understood the statement. What is this known as?

Active listening

Study Questions

Choose the best answer for each of the questions that follow:

1. A customer calls and complains that the computer you just repaired is still not working properly. What should you do?

    A. Apologize and explain that is a different problem than the one you repaired.

    B. Explain that the customer did something wrong.

    C. Refer the customer to another repair facility.

    D. Offer to replace any new components you installed or reservice the computer.

2. What is the last thing you should do to complete a service call?

    A. Hand the customer the bill.

    B. Thank the customer for his or her business.

    C. Explain why the repair took so long.

    D. Tell the customer how he or she could have repaired the problem.

3. A customer complains because she has been on hold for a long time and has been transferred several times. What should you do?

    A. Apologize for the inconvenience and offer to help her now.

    B. Give her your home phone number or cellular phone number.

    C. Tell her the best time to call back.

    D. Explain how busy you are.

4. Which of the following techniques are *not* recommended when explaining the problem? (Choose two.)

    A. Use pictures, graphs, and charts.

    B. Use analogies and examples.

    C. Use industry jargon and acronyms.

    D. Give information explaining every detail.

5. You are troubleshooting a computer that will not boot. Unfortunately, you determined that you will need to reinstall the operating system. What should you tell the customer?

    A. You will need to rebuild the system from scratch.

    B. You need to reinstall the operating system and data loss may occur.

    C. You will need to format the hard drive and reinstall all software.

    D. You will need to upgrade the operating system.

6. You have been asked by your customer to install an application that the customer does not have a license for. What should you do?

    A. Notify law enforcement.

    B. Notify the customer that he or she will need to install the software.

    C. Do not install the software. Notify the customer of the legal ramifications if the application is installed.

    D. Take the initiative by ordering a software license for the customer.

Lab Exercise

Worksheet 10.1.0: Technician Resources

In this worksheet, you will use the Internet to find online resources for a specific computer component. Search online for resources that can help you troubleshoot the component. In the following table list at least one website for each of the following types of resources: online FAQs, online manuals, online troubleshooting site, blogs, and online help sites. Give a brief description of the content on the site. Be prepared to discuss the usefulness of the resources you found.

Component to research:

_____

_____

Type of resources	Website address
FAQ	
Manual	
Online troubleshooting site	
Blog	
Online help site	

Class Discussion 10.2.2: Controlling the Call

In this activity, discuss positive ways to tell customers negative things. There are four scenarios.

1. Demonstrate a positive way to tell a customer that you cannot fix the component and that the customer will have to purchase a new component. The customer's name is Fred. You have been helping him conduct a variety of tests on his computer. After attempting several solutions, it has become apparent that his hard drive is beyond repair.

- _____

- _____

- _____

- _____

- _____
  _____

- _____
  _____

- _____

2. Demonstrate a positive way to tell a customer that you cannot fix a computer component because it falls outside the scope of that customer's SLA with your company. The customer's name is Barney.

- _____

- _____

- _____
  _____

- _____

3. Demonstrate how you would put a customer on hold. You have forgotten one of the steps for setting up a user account for Windows XP and need to ask a fellow worker the instructions for that step. The customer's name is Wilma.

- _____

- _____

- _____

- _____

- _____
  _____

4. Demonstrate how you would transfer a customer to another technician. You have not learned how to configure the security feature on the wireless router used by the customer (Betty) and need to transfer the call to a knowledgeable technician.

- _____

- _____

- _____

- _____

- _____
  _____

- _____

Class Discussion 10.2.3: Identifying Difficult Customer Types

In this activity, identify difficult customer types.

Try to choose only one customer type for each scenario:

- Rude Customer

- Very Knowledgeable Customer

- Inexperienced Customer

- Angry Customer

- Talkative Customer

Scenario 1: The customer asks you to repeat the last three steps you just gave. When you do, the customer says that you did not say the same thing and asks if you know how to fix the problem. The customer then goes into an explanation of what he thinks you should know and asks if you have ever done this before.

Scenario 2: When you ask the customer to explain the problem, the customer starts by telling you how the computer is acting up and that it happened after their grandson was over for a visit last weekend. The customer explains that their grandson is taking computer courses and knows a lot about computers. The customer asks what computer courses you have taken and from where. When asked a close-ended question, the customer gives a quick yes and goes on to explain how wet and cold the weather is where he or she lives.

Scenario 3: The customer tells you how frustrated he is about the Internet not working. When the customer is asked if the computer is on, he replies with "Nothing shows when I click on the little picture on the TV." The technician restates the question, "Is the computer plugged in to the wall?" The customer's reply is "Not all of the cables. There are too many for me to know where they all go." The customer then informs you that a friend set everything up.

Scenario 4: The customer tells you how frustrated he is about the new color printer not working. He explains that he was told that he only needed to plug in two different cords and that everything would work. You ask the customer to check some obvious issues with the printer. He responds by asking how long this will take and tells you that the only reason he bought the printer was because he was told it was the easiest printer on the market to install.

Scenario 5: When the customer is asked to explain the problem, the customer goes into great technical detail about how the new external hard drive is not showing up in the Device Manager. You ask him to click Start, My Computer to see if it is showing up there. Instead of doing as you ask, the customer provides details of all the different settings and configurations and updates he has tried.

Class Discussion 10.3.0: Customer Privacy

In this activity, discuss the importance of respecting customer privacy.

1. You are working on a customer's computer, and you need to log off as the administrator and log on as the customer. You have not talked with the customer about her own access to the computer. You see a note with the customer's access information. Do you log on as the customer to test the system and log off? Why or why not?

_____

_____

_____

2. You are out on an office call. When you leave the customer's office, which is in an open public area, you leave your briefcase behind. It contains work order forms from all the customers you serviced that day. When you contact the office where you left the briefcase, you are told that no one has seen it. What should you do to protect your customers, and why?

_____

_____

_____

3. A new customer calls you with concerns about privacy regarding using a computer and the Internet. List several security concerns you should discuss.

_____

_____

CHAPTER 11

Advanced Personal Computers

The Study Guide portion of this chapter uses a combination of fill-in-the-blank and open-ended questions to test your advanced knowledge of personal computers. This portion also includes multiple-choice study questions to help prepare you to take the A+ certification exams and to test your overall understanding of the material.

The Lab Exercises portion of this chapter includes all the online curriculum hands-on labs, worksheets, and remote technician exercises to further reinforce your mastery of the personal computers content.

Study Guide

Motherboards

In previous chapters, you have learned about the basics of a motherboard. In this chapter, we take a closer look at the motherboard, including configuring the BIOS and looking at the function of the chipset.

Concept Questions

Answer the following questions about motherboards:

What is the function of the BIOS?

when the computer is booted the Basic Input Output System performs a check of all the internal components. This check is called a Power On Self Test.

If a hardware problem is found during bootup, how does the system notify you of the problem?

A beep code alerts the technician that there is a problem.

I have a system that has AMI BIOS. What do three beeps and eight beeps mean during bootup?

- Three beeps: *memory failure*
- Eight beeps: *Video memory failure*

Describe what the North Bridge component holds:

The primary chip in a chipset that controls the processor, memory & video buses

Describe what the South Bridge component holds:

A second chip that typically incorporates the PCI, IDE/SATA & USB buses

If you want to change the boot sequence so that every time your system boots, it tries to boot from the CD drive, what do you need to do?

Set boot sequence in BIOS to boot to CD

RAM

In previous chapters, you looked at the different technology and packages for RAM and how to install RAM. In this chapter, you need to understand how the motherboard affects and limits the RAM.

Concept Questions

Answer the following questions about RAM:

When installing RAM, how do you know how much more the system will accommodate?

Although Windows XP will accommodate up to 4GB of RAM you have to check what is compatible with the Motherboard

What would happen if the RAM is not physically installed correctly?

Can cause serious damage to Motherboard if incorrectly aligned & shorts the main system bus.

Cooling the System

Heat is an enemy of any computer system. Therefore, you need to make sure that the computer and its components stay cool enough to operate properly. This includes looking at the fan that comes with the case, additional fans, and the processor thermal solution.

Concept Questions

Answer the following questions about cooling the system:

What is the primary component within a PC that keeps it cool?

case Fan

Newer motherboards and cases have been redesigned to keep the PC cooler. How do these designs accomplish this?

Because the processor is one of the hottest running components within the PC, what is used to keep the processor cool besides the power supply?

Heat Sink Fan

To provide a good thermal connectivity between the processor and cooling devices, you must apply what?

Thermal compound

What would happen if the processor overheats?

Power Supply

By now, you understand that the power supply supplies electricity to the computer. Of course, if you use your computer in various countries, you may need to know how the electricity varies. You also need to understand that your system often has to deal with power fluctuations. Therefore, you need to know the problems that these power fluctuations can cause and how to combat these problems.

Concept Questions

Answer the following power supply questions:

What is the primary function of the PC power supply?

To provide the necessary electrical power to make the PC operate.

What voltage does the power supply use when in the United States, and what voltage does the power supply use when it is in Europe?

Between 110 and 120 volts in America

Between 220 and 240 volts in Europe.

If the power supply voltage is configured incorrectly, what would happen?

In America it would cause very little damage running the PC at half the power it was expecting - it probably wouldn't boot up. In Europe running the PC at 115V could irreparably damage the power supply.

Four types of devices can protect a PC against power fluctuations. Describe each one that is listed:

- Surge Protector: *Helps protect against damage from surges and spikes. It diverts extra electrical voltage on the line to the ground.*

- Line Conditioner: _____

- Standby Power Supply (SPS): *Helps protect against potential electrical power problems by providing a back up batter to supply power when the incoming voltage drops below the normal level*

- Uninterruptible Power Supply (UPS): *Helps protect against potential electrical problems by supplying electrical power to a PC or device. The battery is constantly recharging while the PC is connected to the power source.*

Hard Drive

The hard drive holds most of the data that people work with and often contains the user's programs. Therefore, it is important that you know how to install and configure hard drives.

Concept Questions

Answer the following hard drive questions:

When connecting a parallel IDE drive to a cable, how is it determined which drive is the master drive and which drive is the slave drive?

The jumper settings on the device will determine whether the device is the slave or master. The position on the cable can also determine this - the master drive will be positioned at the end of the cable & the slave in the middle.

What is the difference between two different parallel IDE cables that each have 40-pin connectors, but one cable has 40 conductors and the other has 80 conductors?

Both cables have 40 pins on the connectors but the one with 80 conductors include another 40 wires to act as grounds to improve the cable's ability to handle high-speed signals.

How many IDE drives can you connect on a parallel IDE cable?

2 drives.

When you configure SCSI drives, what unique settings must each drive have?

Each drive must have a SCSI ID.

When you connect SCSI drives on a SCSI cable, explain how termination is used.

SCSI chains use termination to prevent the signal reflecting back up the wire, creating an echo. Most devices on a PC have termination built in. With SCSI chains you must only terminate the ends of the chain. The devices not on the end of the cable must not be terminated.

If you are using wide SCSI, how many devices can you connect to a SCSI cable or chain?

Up to 15.

How many pins does a narrow SCSI cable have, and how many pins does a wide SCSI cable have?

Narrow SCSI has 50 or 68 pins

Wide SCSI has 68 or 80 pins.

What SCSI IDE number is normally assigned to the CD-ROM drive?

What must you do to make sure that hard drives operate properly?

Redundant Array of Inexpensive Disks (RAID)

To help with data protection, there is redundant array of inexpensive disks (RAID)—two or more drives used in combination to create a fault-tolerance system to protect against physical hard drive failure and to increase the hard drive performance. A RAID configuration can be accomplished with either hardware or software and is usually used in network servers. Note that RAID does not replace a good backup, because it does not protect against data corruption or viruses.

Concept Questions

Answer the following questions about RAID:

Fill in the following table:

Common Raid Level	Common Name	Minimum Number of Disks	Description
0	Striping	2	Fastest form of RAID that spreads the data among multiple disks.
1	Disk mirroring/ disk duplexing	2	Duplicates data between two drives. If one drive fails, you keep on working.
5	Striping with parity	3	Uses striping that spreads the data among multiple disks but also includes byte error correction so that if one drive fails, the system can still function and the data can be rebuilt on the replaced drive.

What happens if one of the drives fails in a RAID 0 configuration?

All data is lost

Video Systems

The last major component of a computer is the video system, which consists of the video card (which is sometimes built in to the motherboard) and the monitor. Because the monitor is the primary output device, it is often the most visible part of the computer. You need to know how to install, configure, and troubleshoot video systems.

Concept Questions

Answer the following questions about video systems:

If you turn on your computer and nothing shows up on the monitor, what do you check first?

Check that the power is on.

Magnetic fields, such as those generated by speakers, may distort the images and cause discoloration on isolated areas on a CRT monitor screen. What can you do to restore the image and remove the discoloration?

Degauss the monitor - usually a button can be pushed to do this.

What would happen if the video card that you are using in a computer system has faulty memory?

Bizarre screen outputs followed shortly by a screen lockup.

Performance Bottlenecks

Besides looking at each component that makes up the PC, you sometimes have to look at all the components working together to determine the power of the PC and to determine a system bottleneck.

Concept Questions

Answer the following questions about performance bottlenecks:

What are the four general components or subsystems that can have performance bottlenecks within a PC?

? *Hard Disk Drive*

? *Graphics Card*

? *RAM*

? *Printer*

If your hard drive was running fine but has gotten slower over several months, what should you try first to make the hard drive fast again?

Defragment the drive.

For some games, your video system must perform well enough to enjoy the full effects of the game. If your video game appears choppy, what can you do to increase video performance?

Upgrade the Graphics Card.

Study Questions

Choose the best answer for each of the questions that follow:

1. Which of the following has the fastest throughput?

   A. Floppy drive
   B. RAM
   C. An IDE hard disk drive
   D. A SCSI hard disk drive

2. Which of the following are fault tolerant?

   A. RAID 0
   B. RAID 1
   C. RAID 5
   D. RAID 1 and 5

3. How do you determine which drive is the master drive in a parallel IDE system?

    A. The device that was installed first

    B. A twist in the cable

    C. The jumper settings

    D. The newer drive

4. If a system has a dual controller for parallel IDE drives, how many drives can it support?

    A. 1

    B. 2

    C. 4

    D. 6

5. Which of the following components on the motherboard usually house the IDE connectors?

    A. RTC

    B. ROM BIOS

    C. North Bridge

    D. South Bridge

6. What is the minimum number of hard drives required for RAID level 0?

    A. 1

    B. 2

    C. 3

    D. 4

7. Which RAID provides disk mirroring?

    A. RAID 0

    B. RAID 1

    C. RAID 2

    D. RAID 5

8. Which of the following is the SCSI ID number generally recommended for the CD-ROM?

    A. ID 0

    B. ID 1

    C. ID 2

    D. ID 3

    E. ID 7

9. What is the maximum data transfer rate that USB 2.0 offers?

    A. 11 Mbps

    B. 128 Mbps

    C. 100 Mbps

    D. 480 Mbps

10. If you have a large drive consisting of 275 GB of data, what should you use to back it up regularly?

    A. CD-RW

    B. Dual-layer DVD-R

    C. An external hard drive

    D. A digital linear tape (DLT)

11. When installing an IDE CD-ROM on a computer that already has a single IDE hard drive configured as the master drive on the primary controller, what would you configure the CD-ROM drive for?

    A. Master on the primary IDE controller

    B. Master on the secondary IDE controller

    C. Slave on the primary IDE controller

    D. Slave on the secondary IDE controller

12. The maximum number of IDE devices that can be installed in an ATX computer is _____.

    A. 1

    B. 2

    C. 3

    D. 4

13. Your system has become sluggish after you've owned it for nine months. What is the first thing you should do to improve performance?

    A. Add more RAM.

    B. Upgrade the CPU.

    C. Add a larger hard drive.

    D. Defragment the hard drive.

14. You are installing four SCSI drives on a computer. When troubleshooting hard drive problems, what should you check?

    A. All hard drives must be terminated, and the SCSI IDs must be numbered consecutively starting with 0 (0, 1, 2 and 3).

    B. You must terminate all drives, and all drives must have the same ID as the controller card.

    C. You must terminate the two ends of the SCSI chain, and each drive must have a unique ID.

    D. You must terminate the host adapter and make sure it has a unique ID.

15. After upgrading the processor, your system shuts down automatically after 10–15 minutes of use. Why is this happening?

    A. The processor has been overclocked to the point where it runs faster than what it was designed for.

    B. The processor is overheating.

    C. The processor is not using the correct voltage.

    D. The pin on the processor is bent and not seated properly.

16. A user reports that nothing shows up on the monitor. When you look at the system, you notice that there are lights on the computer. What should you check first?

   A. Make sure the voltage is set correctly on the power supply.

   B. Make sure the monitor is turned on.

   C. Make sure that the video cable is connected to the computer and monitor.

   D. Make sure that the power cable is connected to the computer.

17. What kind of device protects your computer from sudden spikes in power?

   A. Power conditioner

   B. Generator

   C. Surge protector

   D. Resistor pack

18. What kind of device protects your computer from brownouts?

   A. Line conditioner

   B. Surge protector

   C. Resistor pack

   D. Standby power supply

19. When you need to degauss a CRT monitor because the two corners are discolored because of some speakers you had near your monitor, what should you do?

   A. Run the degauss utility in Windows.

   B. Temporarily move the speakers to the front of the monitor so that it can realign itself.

   C. Turn the monitor off for a minimum of one hour.

   D. Use the controls on the monitor and run the degauss routine.

20. You live in the United States and you accepted a six-month contract in France. What should you do to prevent damage to your computer?

   A. Purchase the correct power adapter for France.

   B. Change the voltage selector on the power supply to 220 voltage.

   C. Use a surge protector while overseas.

   D. Use a line conditioner.

Lab Exercises

Worksheet 11.1.0: Job Opportunities

In this activity, you will use the Internet, magazines, or a local newspaper to gather information for jobs in the computer service and repair field. Try to find jobs that require the same types of courses that you are presently taking. Be prepared to discuss your research in class.

Research three computer-related jobs. For each job, write the company name and the job title in the column on the left. Write the job details that are most important to you, as well as the job qualifications in the column on the right. An example has been provided for you.

Company Name and Job Title	Details and Qualifications
Gentronics Flexible Solutions/ Field Service Representative	Company offers continuing education. Work with hardware and software. Work directly with customers. Local travel.
	A+ certification preferred.
	Installation or repair experience of computer hardware and software not required.
	Requires a valid driver license.
	Reliable personal transportation.
	Mileage reimbursement.
	Ability to lift and carry up to 50 lbs.
	Installation of NIC cards.
	Experience with POS equipment (preferred).

Which of the jobs that you found in your research would you like to have? Explain why you are interested in this job. An example has been provided for you.

_____

_____

_____

_____

Gentronics Flexible Solutions Field Service Representative—I am not able to travel far away from my family and this job allows me to travel locally. Also, this job offers educational opportunities so that I can advance further in the IT field.

Worksheet 11.3.7: Research Computer Components

In this activity, you will use the Internet, a newspaper, or a local store to gather information about the components you will need to upgrade your customer's computer. Be prepared to discuss your selections.

Your customer already owns the case described in the following table. You will not need to research a new case.

Brand and Model Number	Features	Cost
Cooler Master CAC-T05-UW	ATX Mid Tower	
	ATX, Micro ATX compatible form factor	
	5X External 5.25" drive bays	
	1X External 3.5" drive bay	
	4X Internal 5.25" drive bays	
	7 expansion slots	
	USB, FireWire, audio front ports	

Research a power supply that is compatible with the components that your customer owns. The new component must have improved performance or additional capabilities. Enter the specifications in the following table:

Brand and Model Number	Features	Cost
Antec SP-450	450 Watt	$60.99
	Dual +12V rails	
	> 70% Efficiency	
	ATX12V form factor	

Research a motherboard that is compatible with the components that your customer owns. The new component must have improved performance or additional capabilities. Enter the specifications in the following table:

Brand and Model Number	Features	Cost
GIGABYTE GA-965P-DS3	LGA 775	
	DDR2 800	
	PCI Express x16	
	SATA 3.0 Gbps interface	
	1.8 V-2.4 V RAM voltage	
	1066/800/533 MHz Front Side Bus	
	Four Memory Slots	
	Dual Channel Memory Supported	
	1XATA100 connector	
	RAID 0/1	
	4X USB 2.0	
	ATX Form Factor	

Research a CPU that is compatible with the components that your customer owns. The new component must have improved performance or additional capabilities. Enter the specifications in the following table:

Brand and Model Number	Features	Cost
Intel Core 2 Duo E6300 BX80557E6300	LGA 775	$183.00
	1.86 GHz Operating Frequency	
	1066 MHz Front Side Bus	
	2M shared L2 Cache	
	64 bit supported	
	Conroe Core	

Research a heat sink/fan assembly that is compatible with the components that your customer owns. The new component must have improved performance or additional capabilities. Enter the specifications in the following table:

Brand and Model Number	Features	Cost
Intel	LGA 775	
Stock heat sink/fan80 mm fan	2 pin power	
	Under recommended socket weight	
	Included with CPU	

Research RAM that is compatible with the components that your customer owns. The new component must have improved performance or additional capabilities. Enter the specifications in the following table:

Brand and Model Number	Features	Cost
Patriot	240-Pin DDR2 SDRAM	$194.99
PDC22G6400LLK	DDR2 800 (PC2 6400)	
	Cas Latency 4	
	Timing 4-4-4-12	
	Voltage 2.2 V	

Research a hard disk drive that is compatible with the components that your customer owns. The new component must have improved performance or additional capabilities. Enter the specifications in the following table:

Brand and Model Number	Features	Cost
Western Digital	40 GB	$37.99
WD400BB	7200 RPM	
	2 MB Cache	

Research a video adapter card that is compatible with the components that your customer owns. The new component must have improved performance or additional capabilities. Enter the specifications in the following table:

Brand and Model Number	Features	Cost
XFX PVT71PUDD3	PCI Express X16 600 MHz Core clock 256 MB GDDR3 1600 MHz memory clock 256-bit memory interface	$189.99

List three components that must have the same or compatible form factor:

List three components that must conform to the same socket type:

List two components that must utilize the same front side bus speed:

List three considerations when you choose memory:

What component must be compatible with every other component of the computer?

What determines compatibility between a motherboard and a video card?

Lab 11.4.1: Install a NIC

In this lab, you will install a NIC, verify NIC operation, and manually configure an IP address.

The following is the recommended equipment for this lab:

- Computer running Windows XP Professional
- PCI NIC

- Driver files for PCI NIC on CD or floppy disk
- Antistatic wrist strap
- Tool kit

Step 1

Log on to the computer as an administrator.

Click the Start button. Right-click My Computer, and then choose Properties (see Figure 11-1).

Figure 11-1   Opening the Computer Properties

The System Properties window appears (see Figure 11-2).

Figure 11-2   System Properties

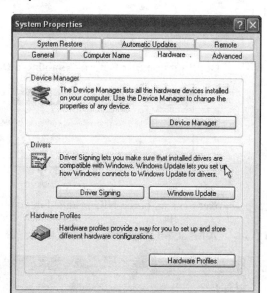

Choose the Hardware tab, and then click the Device Manager button. The Device Manager window appears.

Step 2

Expand Network Adapters.

Right-click the NIC installed in your computer, and then choose Disable (see Figure 11-3).

Figure 11-3   Disabling a Device in Device Manager

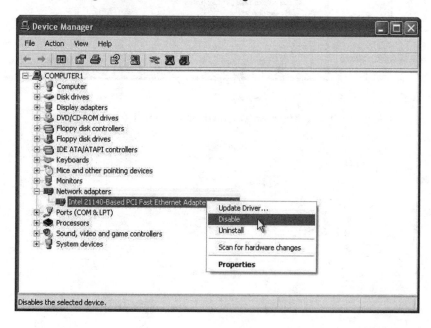

The Disabling This Device Will Cause It to Stop Functioning confirmation window appears (see Figure 11-4).

Click Yes.

Figure 11-4   Confirmation Box Before Disabling a Device

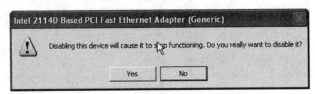

A red X appears over the icon of the NIC installed in your computer (see Figure 11-5).

Figure 11-5   A Disabled Device in Device Manager

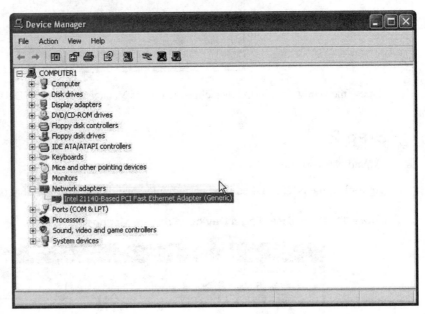

Close the Device Manager window (see Figure 11-6).

Figure 11-6   System Properties

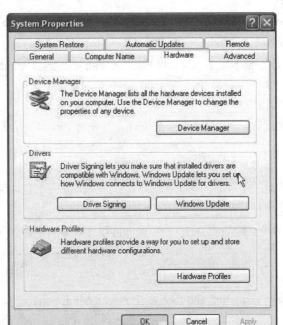

Close the System Properties window, and turn off your computer.

Step 3

Who is the manufacturer of the new NIC?

_____

What is the model number of the new NIC?

_____

What slot type is used to connect the new NIC to the motherboard?

_____

Step 4

If a switch is present on the power supply, set the switch to 0 or Off.

Unplug the computer from the AC outlet.

Unplug the network cable from the computer.

Remove the side panels from the case.

Step 5

Choose an appropriate slot on the motherboard to install the new NIC. You might need to remove the metal cover near the slot on the back of the case.

Make sure the NIC is properly lined up with the slot. Push down gently on the NIC. Secure the NIC mounting bracket to the case with a screw.

Step 6

Replace the case panels.

Plug in the network cable to the new NIC.

Plug in the power cable to an AC outlet.

If a switch is present on the power supply, set the switch to 1 or On.

Step 7

Boot your computer, and then log on as an administrator.

Choose Start. Right-click My Computer, and then choose Properties.

The System Properties window appears. Choose the Hardware tab, and then click the Device Manager button.

Step 8

The Device Manager window appears. Expand Network Adapters (see Figure 11-7).

Figure 11-7   Network Devices Within the Device Manager

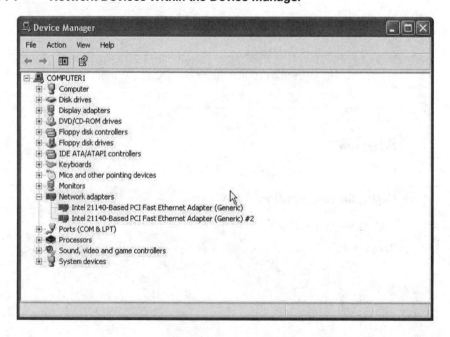

How many Network adapters are present (enabled and disabled) in the list?

If the new card icon has a red X over it, right-click that icon and then click Enable (see Figure 11-8).

Figure 11-8   Second NIC Enabled

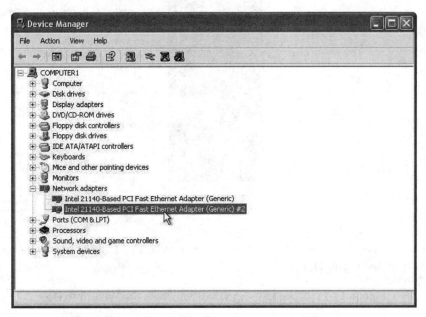

Right-click the new NIC icon, and then choose Properties.

Choose the Driver tab. Click the Update Driver button (see Figure 11-9).

Figure 11-9   Driver Properties of a Device

The Hardware Update Wizard appears. If you are prompted to connect to Windows Update, click the No, Not This Time option button, and then click Next (see Figure 11-10).

Figure 11-10   Starting the Hardware Update Wizard

Choose the Install from a List or Specific Location (Advanced) option button, and then click Next (see Figure 11-11).

Figure 11-11   Specifying What You Want the Wizard to Do

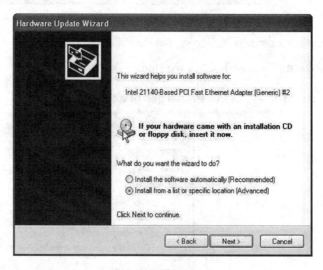

Insert the CD or floppy disk with the new NIC drivers, and then click Next (see Figure 11-12).

Figure 11-12   Specifying Where to Load the Drivers From

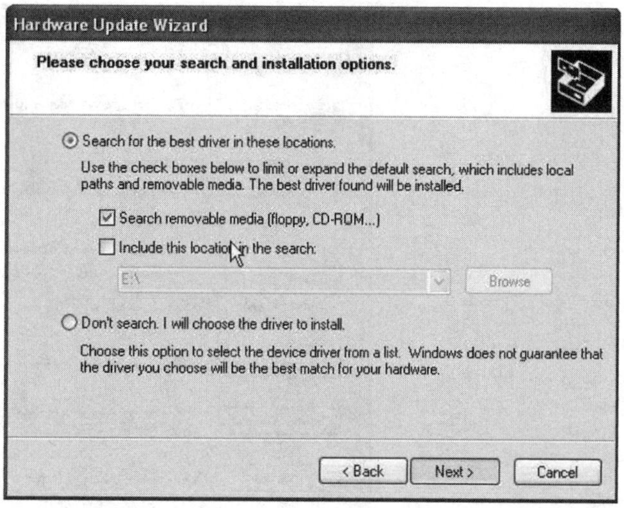

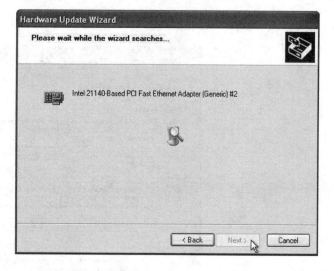

The Please Wait While the Wizard Searches window appears (see Figure 11-13).

Figure 11-13   Wizard Searching for the Appropriate Driver

Click Finish after Windows installs the new driver. The Hardware Update Wizard window closes. Click Close (see Figure 11-14).

Figure 11-14   Driver Properties

The NIC Properties window closes. Close the Device Manager (see Figure 11-15).

Figure 11-15   System Properties

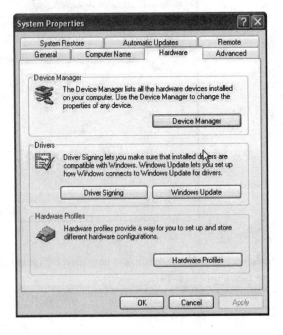

Step 9

Choose Start, Run (see Figure 11-16).

Figure 11-16   Selecting the Run Option to Run a Command or Program

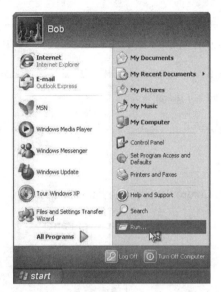

Type **cmd** into the Open field, and then click OK (see Figure 11-17).

Figure 11-17   Typing cmd to Open a DOS Window

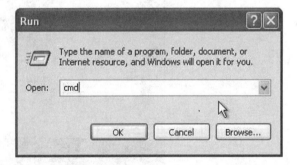

The C:\WINDOWS\System32\cmd.exe window appears. Type **ipconfig** and press Enter. The settings of the new NIC are displayed (see Figure 11-18).

Figure 11-18   Executing the ipconfig Command at a Command Window

What is the IP address?

_____

What is the subnet mask?

_____

What is the default gateway?

_____

Step 10

Choose Start, Control Panel (see Figure 11-19).

Figure 11-19   Opening the Control Panel

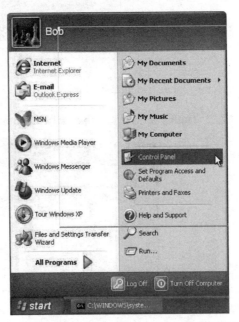

Click Network and Internet Connections (see Figure 11-20).

Figure 11-20   Control Panel

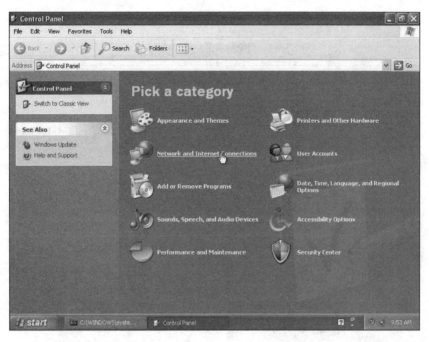

The Network and Internet Connections window appears. Click Network Connections (see Figure 11-21).

Figure 11-21   Control Panel Network and Internet Connections

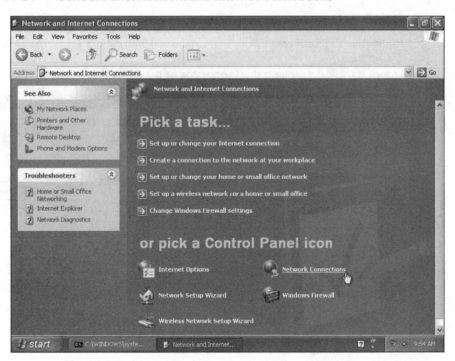

The Network Connections window appears (see Figure 11-22).

Figure 11-22   Network Connections

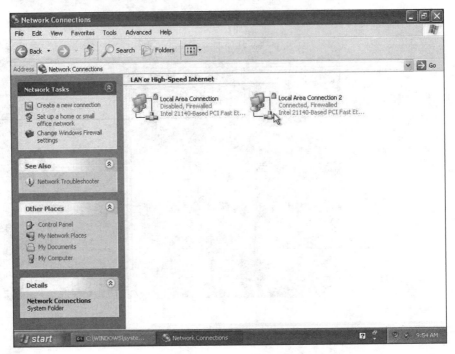

Step 11

Right-click the connected Local Area Connection and choose Properties (see Figure 11-23).

Figure 11-23   Opening the Properties of the Local Area Connection

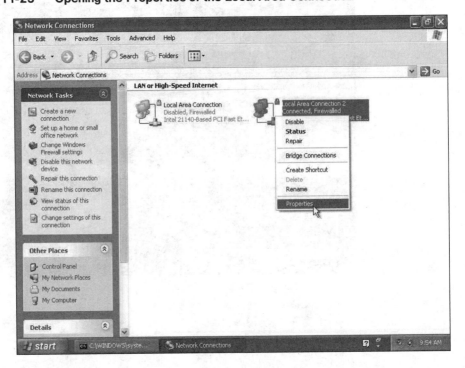

The Local Area Connection Properties window appears. Choose Internet Protocol (TCP/IP) and click Properties (see Figure 11-24).

Figure 11-24   Local Area Connection Properties

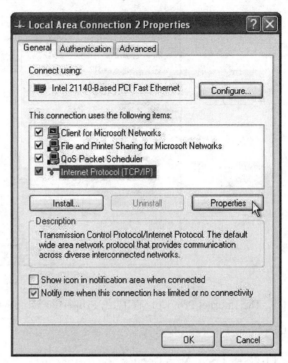

Click the Use the Following IP address option button.

Note: Use the IP address, subnet mask, and default gateway you wrote down earlier in the lab to fill in the following three fields:

Type the IP address assigned to your computer into the IP Address field.

Type the subnet mask assigned to your network into the Subnet Mask field.

Type the default gateway assigned to your network into the Default Gateway field (see Figure 11-25).

Figure 11-25   Internet TCP/IP Properties

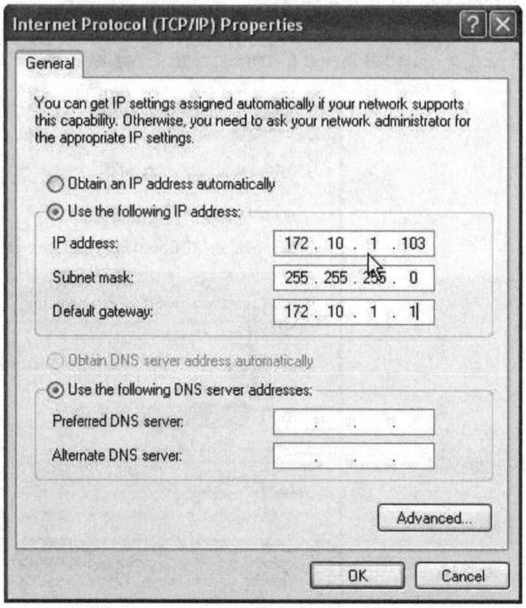

Click OK. The Internet Protocol (TCP/IP) Properties window closes.

Click Close (see Figure 11-26).

Figure 11-26   Local Area Connection Properties

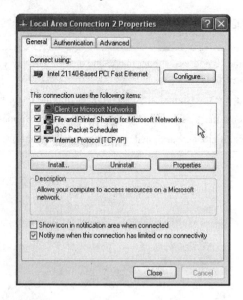

The Local Area Connection Properties window closes.

Step 12

The C:\WINDOWS\System32\cmd.exe window is revealed.

Type **ipconfig /all**, and then press Enter (see Figure 11-27).

Figure 11-27   ipconfig /all Command

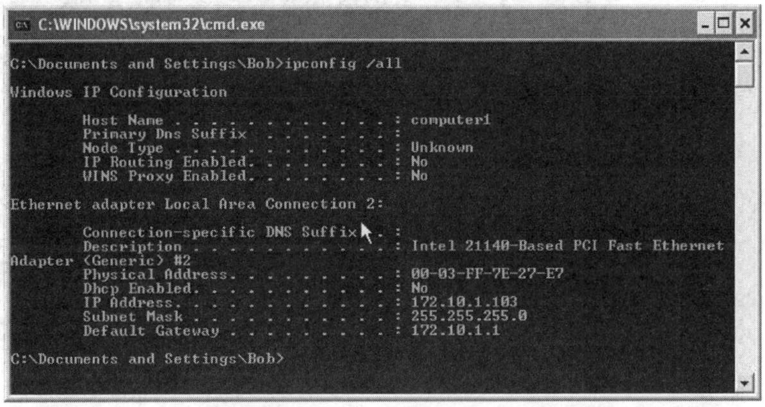

Does the NIC have DHCP enabled?

Type **ping** and your IP address. For example, **ping 172.10.1.103** (see Figure 11-28).

Figure 11-28   Using the ping Command to Test Network Connectivity

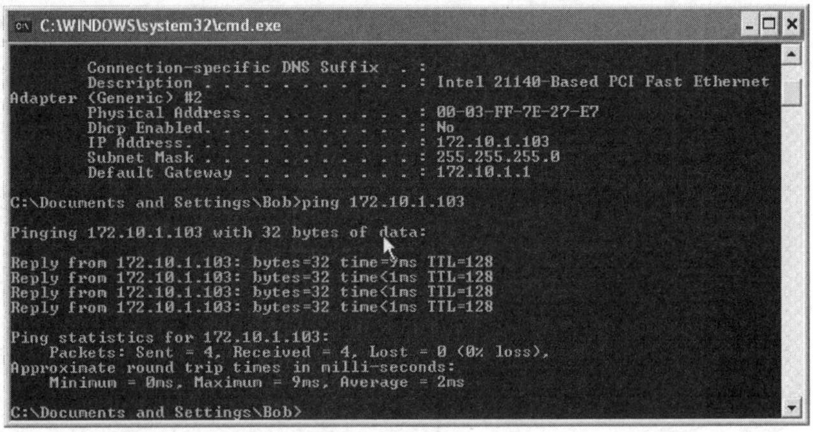

Write one of the replies of your **ping** command.

Type **exit,** and then press Enter (see Figure 11-29).

Figure 11-29 Using the exit Command to Close the Command Window

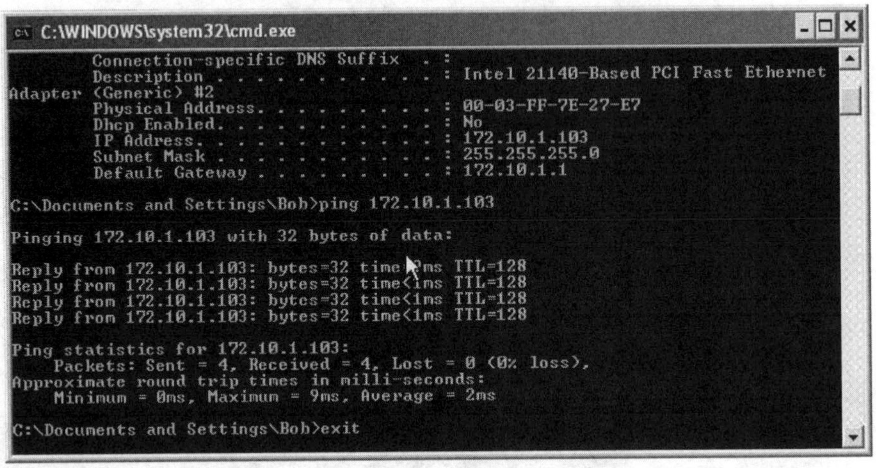

C:\WINDOWS\system32\cmd.exe
Connection-specific DNS Suffix . :
Description . . . . : Intel 21140-Based PCI Fast Ethernet
Adapter (Generic) #2
Physical Address. . . . . : 00-03-FF-7E-27-E7
Dhcp Enabled. . . . . : No
IP Address. . . . . : 172.10.1.103
Subnet Mask . . . . : 255.255.255.0
Default Gateway . . . . : 172.10.1.1
C:\Documents and Settings\Bob>ping 172.10.1.103
Pinging 172.10.1.103 with 32 bytes of data:
Reply from 172.10.1.103: bytes=32 time=9ms TTL=128
Reply from 172.10.1.103: bytes=32 time<1ms TTL=128
Reply from 172.10.1.103: bytes=32 time<1ms TTL=128
Reply from 172.10.1.103: bytes=32 time<1ms TTL=128
Ping statistics for 172.10.1.103:
Packets: Sent = 4, Received = 4, Lost = 0 (0% loss),
Approximate round trip times in milli-seconds:
Minimum = 0ms, Maximum = 9ms, Average = 2ms
C:\Documents and Settings\Bob>exit

Step 13

Choose Start, Control Panel (see Figure 11-30).

Figure 11-30 Opening the Control Panel

Bob
Internet
Internet Explorer
E-mail
Outlook Express
MSN
Windows Media Player
Windows Messenger
Windows Update
Tour Windows XP
Files and Settings Transfer Wizard
All Programs
My Documents
My Recent Documents
My Pictures
My Music
My Computer
Control Panel
Set Program Access and Defaults
Printers and Faxes
Help and Support
Search
Run...
Log Off
Turn Off Computer
start
C:\WINDOWS\syste...

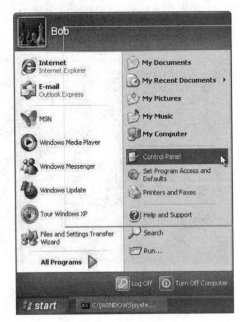

Click Network and Internet Connections (see Figure 11-31).

Figure 11-31   Control Panel

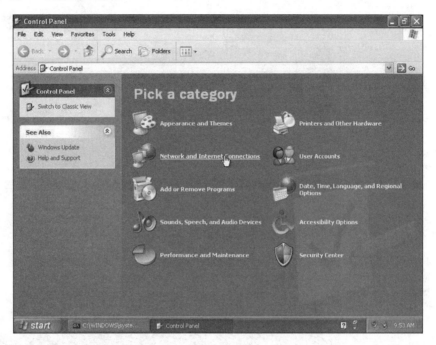

The Network and Internet Connections window appears. Click Network Connections (see Figure 11-32).

Figure 11-32   Control Panel Network and Internet Connections

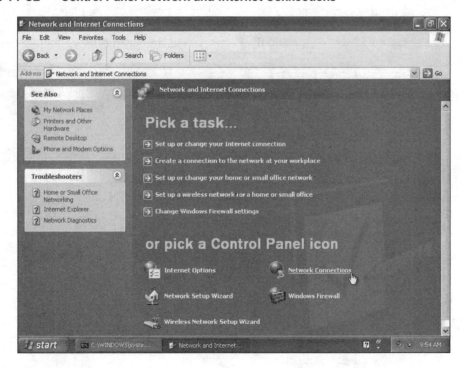

The Network Connections window appears (see Figure 11-33).

Figure 11-33   Network Connections

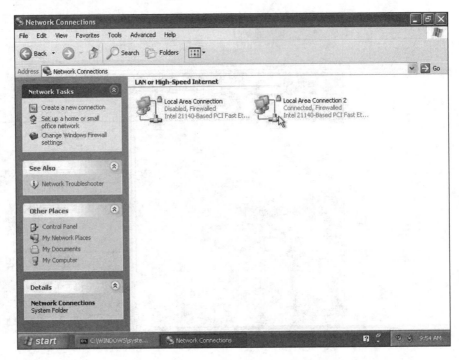

Step 14

Right-click the connected Local Area Connection and choose Properties (see Figure 11-34).

Figure 11-34   Opening the Properties of the Local Area Connection

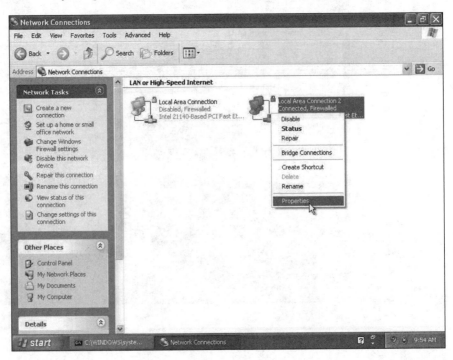

The Local Area Connection Properties window appears.

Choose Internet Protocol (TCP/IP) and click Properties (see Figure 11-35).

Figure 11-35   Local Area Connection Properties with the Client for Microsoft Networks Highlighted

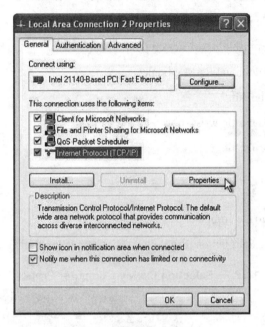

Click the Obtain an IP Address Automatically option button.

Click OK. The Internet Protocol (TCP/IP) Properties window closes.

Click Close (see Figure 11-36).

Figure 11-36   Local Area Connection Properties with the Internet Protocol (TCP/IP) Highlighted

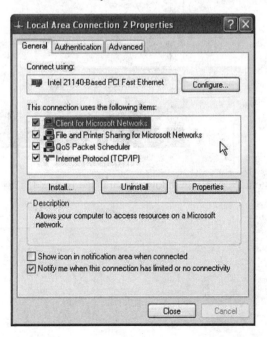

The Local Area Connection Properties window closes.

Lab 11.4.3: Install Additional RAM

In this lab, you will install additional RAM.

The following is the recommended equipment for this lab:

- Computer running Windows XP Professional
- Available RAM slot on motherboard
- Additional RAM module(s)
- Tool kit
- Antistatic wrist strap
- Antistatic mat

Step 1

Log on to the computer as an administrator.

Click the Start button. Right-click My Computer and then choose Properties (see Figure 11-37).

Figure 11-37   Selecting the My Computer Properties

The System Properties window appears (see Figure 11-38).

Figure 11-38   System Properties

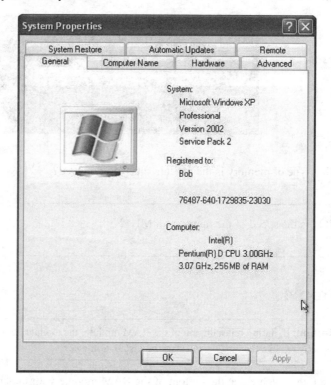

How much RAM is installed in your computer?

Close the System Properties window.

Step 2

Shut down your computer.

If a switch is present on the power supply, set the switch to 0 or Off.

Unplug the computer from the AC outlet, and remove the side panels from the case.

Put on the antistatic wrist strap, and then clip it to the case.

Step 3

Press down on the retainer tabs at each end of a slot. The memory module will be lifted out of the memory slot. Remove the memory module (see Figure 11-39).

Figure 11-39   RAM DIMM Slots

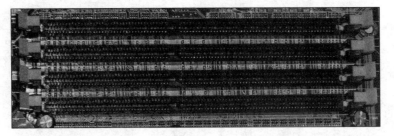

What type of memory is the module that you removed?

_____

What is the speed of the memory in MHz?

_____

Step 4

Caution: If, during reinstallation of the RAM module, the module does not fit correctly or does not install easily, carefully remove the module and start the installation again.

Align the notch(es) at the bottom of the RAM module with the key(s) in the RAM slot. Place the RAM module in the slot, and then push down firmly on the RAM module until the module is fully seated in the slot and the retainer tabs hold the module in place.

Press each retainer tab in toward the memory module to make sure that the RAM is held in place by the retainer tabs.

Install the RAM modules provided by your instructor.

Step 5

Remove the antistatic wrist strap from the case and from your wrist, and then replace the case panels.

Plug the power cable into an AC outlet.

If a switch is present on the power supply, set the switch to 1 or On.

Boot your computer (see Figure 11-40), and then log on as an administrator.

Figure 11-40   The POST Showing the Amount of RAM a System Has

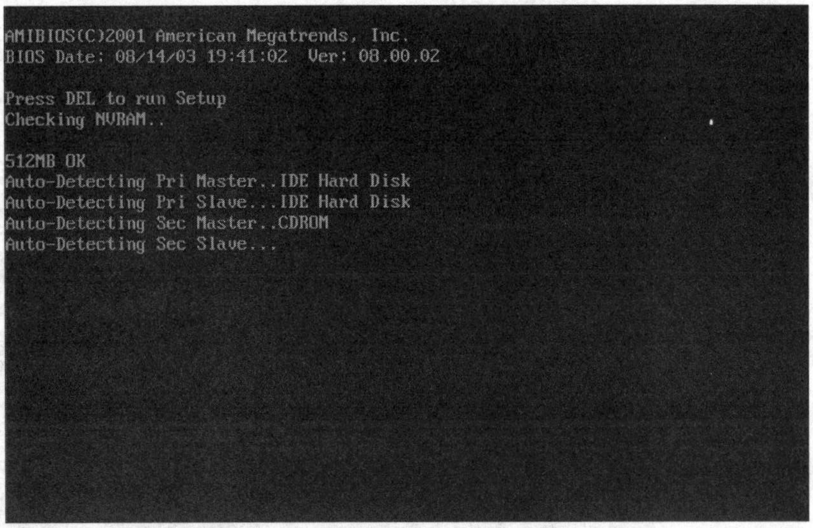

```
AMIBIOS(C)2001 American Megatrends, Inc.
BIOS Date: 08/14/03 19:41:02  Ver: 08.00.02

Press DEL to run Setup
Checking NVRAM..

512MB OK
Auto-Detecting Pri Master..IDE Hard Disk
Auto-Detecting Pri Slave...IDE Hard Disk
Auto-Detecting Sec Master..CDROM
Auto-Detecting Sec Slave...
```

Open the System Properties window.

How much RAM is installed in your computer?

Lab 11.4.4: BIOS File Search

In this lab, you will identify the current BIOS version and then search for BIOS update files.

The following is the recommended equipment for this lab:

- Computer running Windows XP Professional
- Internet access

Step 1

Boot your computer.

During POST, BIOS information is displayed onscreen for a short period of time (see Figure 11-41).

Figure 11-41   POST Showing the Amount of RAM and the Number of IDE Drives and Optical Drives

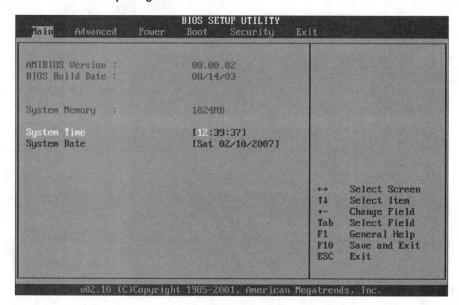

```
AMIBIOS(C)2001 American Megatrends, Inc.
BIOS Date: 08/14/03 19:41:02  Ver: 08.00.02

Press DEL to run Setup
Checking NVRAM..

1024MB OK
Auto-Detecting Pri Master..IDE Hard Disk
Auto-Detecting Pri Slave...Not Detected
Auto-Detecting Sec Master..CDROM
Auto-Detecting Sec Slave...Not Detected
```

Do not log on to Windows.

What key or combination of keys is used to run Setup on your computer?

Restart your computer and enter Setup.

Step 2

The BIOS Setup Utility screen appears (see Figure 11-42).

Figure 11-42   BIOS Setup Program

```
                    BIOS SETUP UTILITY
   Main    Advanced    Power    Boot    Security    Exit

   AMIBIOS Version :          08.00.02
   BIOS Build Date :          08/14/03


   System Memory    :         1024MB

   System Time                [12:39:37]
   System Date                [Sat 02/10/2007]




                                              ↔    Select Screen
                                              ↑↓   Select Item
                                              ←-   Change Field
                                              Tab  Select Field
                                              F1   General Help
                                              F10  Save and Exit
                                              ESC  Exit

        v02.10 (C)Copyright 1985-2001, American Megatrends, Inc.
```

Who is the manufacturer of the BIOS?

_____

Which BIOS version is installed in your computer?

_____

_____

_____

Caution: Do not update your BIOS.

_____

What is the current BIOS version available for the motherboard?

_____

What features, if any, have been added to the new BIOS version?

_____

What changes, if any, have been made to the new BIOS version to fix problems?

_____

What are the instructions to update the new BIOS version?

_____

_____

_____

Lab 11.4.5: Install, Configure, and Partition a Second Hard Drive

In this lab, you will change the boot order, install a second hard drive, create partitions, and map drive letters to partitions.

The following is the recommended equipment for this lab:

- Computer running Windows XP Professional
- Unpartitioned IDE hard disk drive
- IDE cable with a free connection
- Antistatic wrist strap
- Tool kit

Step 1

Boot your computer, and then enter the BIOS setup (see Figure 11-43).

Figure 11-43   BIOS Setup Program

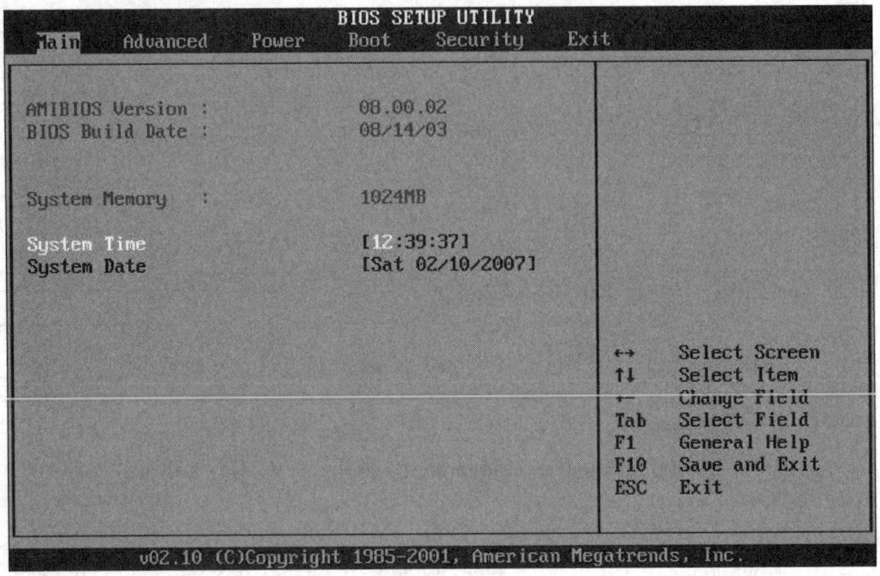

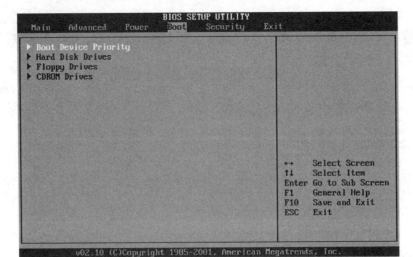

Use the left-arrow and right-arrow keys to move between tabs in the BIOS. Use the up-arrow and down-arrow keys to move between items in each tab.

Navigate the BIOS setup program screens to the boot order configuration settings screen (see Figure 11-44).

Figure 11-44   Boot Menu Within the BIOS Setup Program

Select the Boot Device Priority. The Boot Device Priority may also be called the Boot Options or the Boot Order.

Press the Enter key (see Figure 11-45).

Figure 11-45   Boot Device Priority Screen

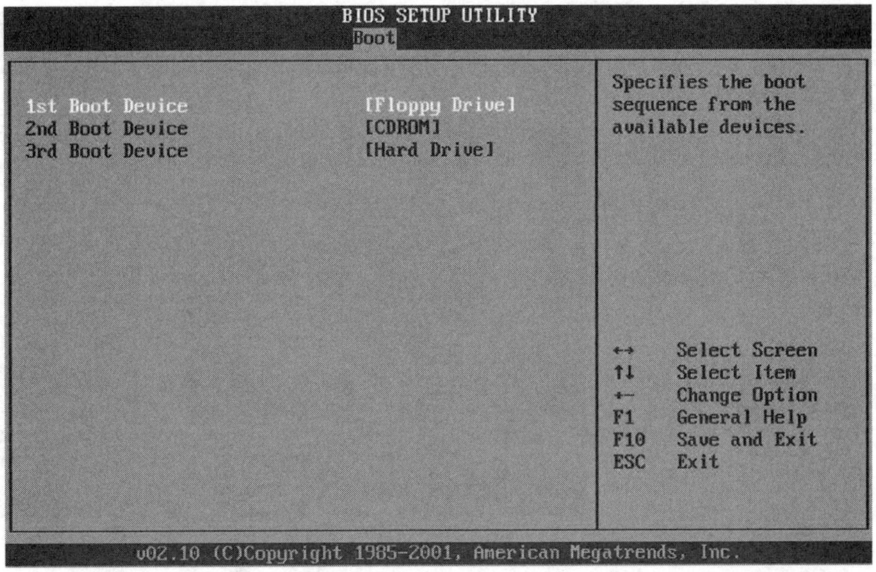

Change the order of the boot devices to the following:

1. CD-ROM

2. Hard Drive

3. Floppy Drive

4. Any other boot option available

On which screen was the boot device order found?

_____

Save the changes to the BIOS and exit the BIOS utility by pressing the F10 key.

Step 2

Confirm the change to the BIOS settings if you are prompted. The computer will restart.

Do not log on to Windows.

Shut down your computer.

If a switch is present on the power supply, set the switch to 0 or Off.

Unplug the computer from the AC outlet.

Remove the side panels from the case.

Put on the antistatic wrist strap, and then clip it to the case.

Step 3

Many hard drives will have the jumper settings indicated in a diagram on the drive. Follow the diagram to determine where the jumper will be installed (see Figure 11-46).

Figure 11-46   Jumper Settings for a Hard Drive

Move the Master/Slave jumper on the installed hard disk drive to the Master position if it is in any other position.

Move the Master/Slave jumper on the second hard disk drive to the Slave position if it is in any other position.

Insert the second hard disk drive into the computer and attach it with the proper screws.

Plug the middle connector of the IDE cable into the second hard disk drive.

Plug a four-pin Molex power connector into the second hard disk drive.

Check the jumper settings and cable connections on both hard disk drives to make sure the settings are correct and the cables are secured.

Remove the antistatic wrist strap from the case and from your wrist, and then replace the case panels.

Plug the power cable into an AC outlet.

If a switch is present on the power supply, set the switch to 1 or On.

Boot your computer.

Step 4

The new hard disk drive will be detected by the computer during the POST routine (see Figure 11-47).

Figure 11-47 POST Screen

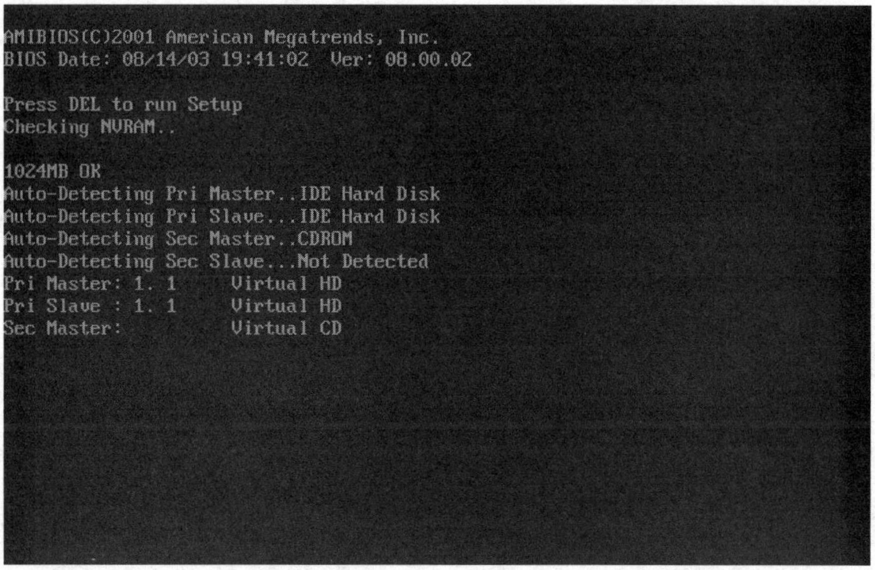

AMIBIOS(C)2001 American Megatrends, Inc.
BIOS Date: 08/14/03 19:41:02 Ver: 08.00.02
Press DEL to run Setup
Checking NVRAM..
1024MB OK
Auto-Detecting Pri Master..IDE Hard Disk
Auto-Detecting Pri Slave...IDE Hard Disk
Auto-Detecting Sec Master..CDROM
Auto-Detecting Sec Slave...Not Detected
Pri Master: 1. 1 Virtual HD
Pri Slave : 1. 1 Virtual HD
Sec Master: Virtual CD

If you are prompted to accept changes to the computer, Press the F1 key.

Log on to Windows as an administrator.

Step 5

Click the Start button, and then right-click My Computer**.**

Choose Manage. The Computer Management window appears.

Click Disk Management (see Figure 11-48).

Figure 11-48 Selecting Disk Management in the Computer Management Console

Computer Management
File Action View Window Help
Computer Management (Local)
System Tools
Event Viewer
Shared Folders
Local Users and Groups
Performance Logs and Alerts
Device Manager
Storage
Removable Storage
Disk Defragmenter
Disk Management
Services and Applications
Connecting to Logical Disk Manager service...

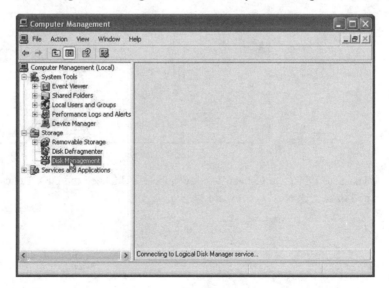

The Initialize and Convert Disk Wizard window appears. Click Next (see Figure 11-49).

Figure 11-49   Starting the Initialize and Convert Disk Wizard

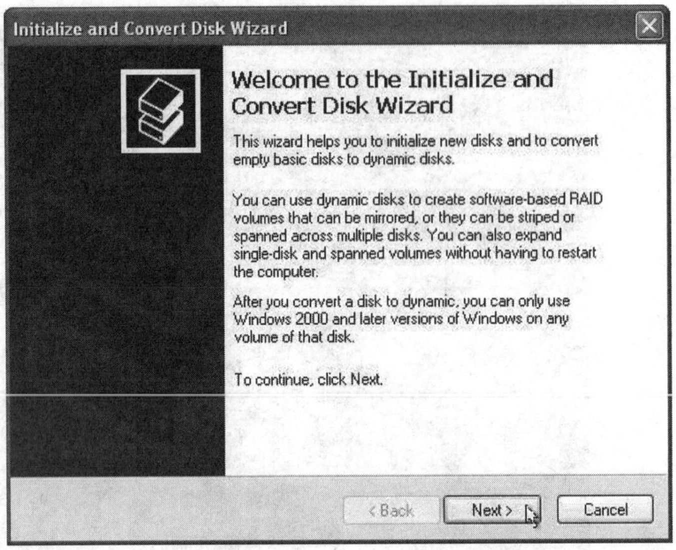

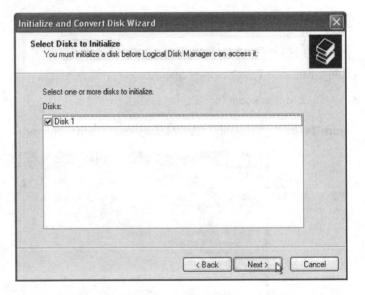

The Select Disks to Initialize window appears. Check the Disk 1 check box, and then click Next (see Figure 11-50).

Figure 11-50   Initializing a Disk

The Select Disks to Convert window appears. Uncheck the Disk 1 check box if it is already checked, and then click Next (see Figure 11-51).

Figure 11-51   Deselecting a Disk to Be Converted to a Dynamic Disk

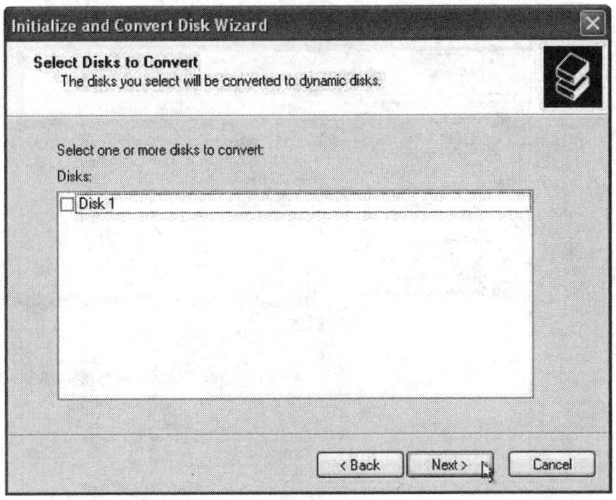

The Completing the Initialize and Convert Disk Wizard window appears.

Verify that you will Initialize: Disk 1 and Convert: None, and then click Finish (see Figure 11-52).

Figure 11-52   Completing the Initialize and Convert Disk Wizard

Step 6

The Disk Management area of Computer Management appears (see Figure 11-53).

Figure 11-53   Disk Management Console

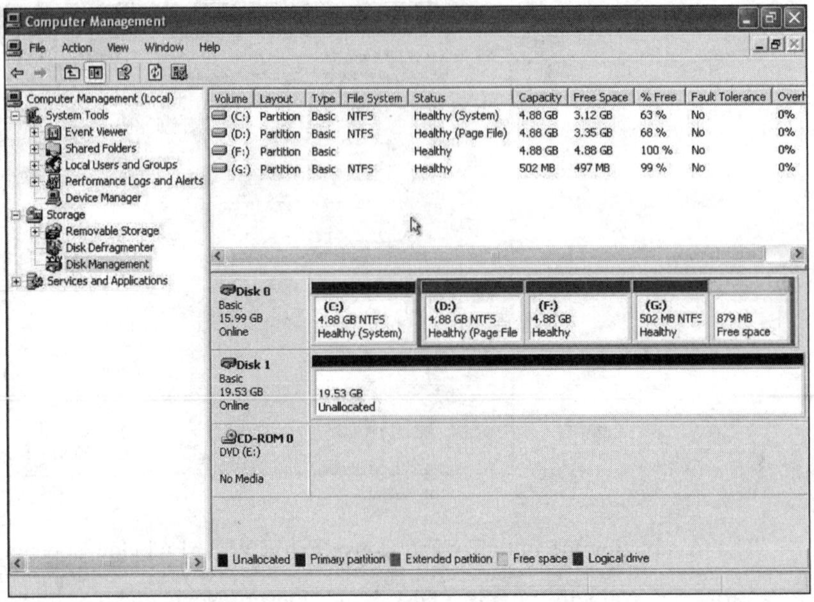

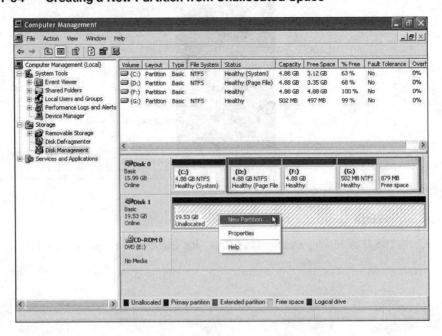

Note: If the hard disk drive is shown as offline or missing, the hard disk drive may be corrupted.

Right-click the Unallocated space of Disk 1 and choose New Partition (see Figure 11-54).

Figure 11-54   Creating a New Partition from Unallocated Space

The New Partition Wizard window appears (see Figure 11-55). Click Next.

Figure 11-55   Starting the New Partition Wizard

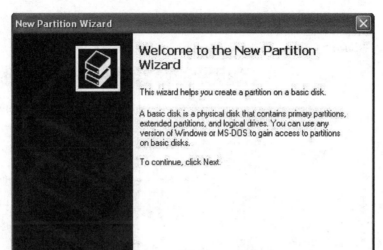

The Specify Partition Size window appears.

Type **5000** into the Partition Size in MB field, and then click Next (see Figure 11-56).

Figure 11-56   Specifying the Size of the Partition

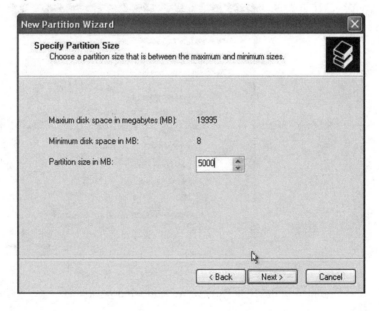

The Assign Drive Letter or Path window appears.

Click the Assign the Following Drive Letter option button.

Choose M from the Assign the Following Drive Letter drop-down box, and click Next (see Figure 11-57).

Figure 11-57   Assigning the Driver Letter for a New Partition

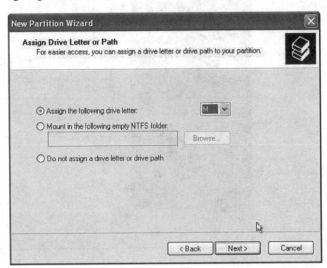

The Format Partition window appears (see Figure 11-58). Click Next.

Figure 11-58   Options to Format a Partition

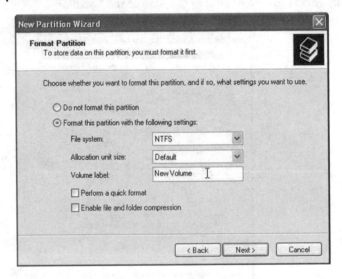

The Completing the New Partition Wizard window appears.

Verify that the settings you have chosen match the settings shown in the Completing the New Partition Wizard window, and then click Finish (see Figure 11-59).

Figure 11-59   Completing the New Partition Wizard

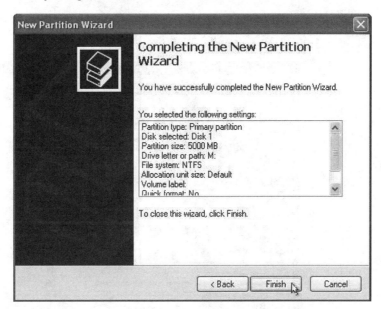

Windows formats the new partition and the status of the Volume changes to Healthy (see Figure 11-60).

Figure 11-60   Computer Management Console

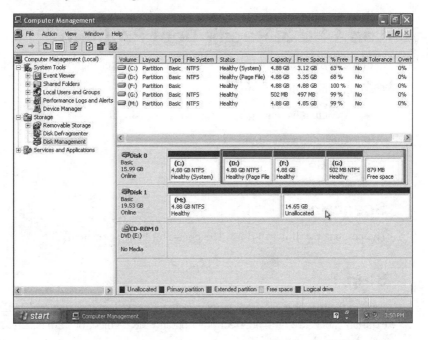

Step 7

Create a second partition in the unallocated space of Disk 1 with the drive label N:.

Step 8

Choose Start, My Computer.

The Hard Disk Drives section of My Computer now shows the two new volumes, M: and N: (see Figure 11-61).

Figure 11-61   My Computer Window

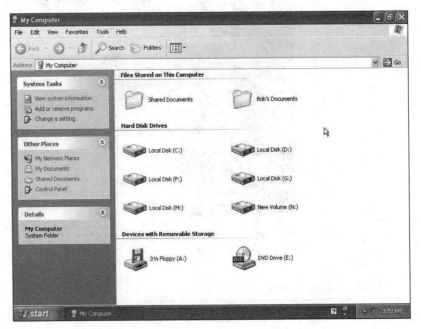

Lab 11.6.3: Repair Boot Problem

In this lab, you will troubleshoot and repair a computer that does not boot.

The following is the recommended equipment for this lab:

- A computer running Windows XP Professional
- Antistatic wrist strap
- Tool kit

Scenario

The computer will not start up. The computer beeps constantly.

Step 1

Unplug the power cable from the computer. Check the other external cables. Make sure all other external cables are in the correct position and the connections are secure. Make sure any power switches are set to Off or 0.

Step 2

Open the case and check all internal data and power cable connections. Check the adapter cards and RAM modules to make sure they are seated completely.

Step 3

Remove your antistatic wrist strap. If there is a power switch on the power supply, turn it to On or 1. Turn on the computer.

What steps did you perform to fix the computer?

Remote Technician 11.6.3: Repair Boot Problem

(Student Technician Sheet)

In this lab, you will gather data from the customer, and then instruct the customer on how to fix a computer that does not boot. Document the customer's problem in the following work order:

Company Name: _JH Travel, Inc._

Contact: _Dan Handy_

Company Address: _204 N. Main Street_

Company Phone: _1-866-555-0998_

Work Order

Generating a New Ticket

Category _Hardware_   Closure Code _____   Status _Open_____

Type _____   Escalated _Yes_____   Pending _____

Item _____   Pending Until Date _____

Business Impacting? ☒ Yes ○ No

Summary _The computer will not start up. The computer beeps constantly._
_____

Case ID# _____   Connection Type _____

Priority _2_____   Environment _____

User Platform _Windows XP Pro_____

Problem Description: _Computer will not boot. Customer does not know the manufacturer of the_
BIOS. Cannot identify error from beep sequence. Customer did not hear any strange sounds
from the computer. Customer does not smell smoke or burning electronics.
_____
_____

Problem Solution: _____
_____
_____
_____
_____

(Student Customer Sheet)

Use the contact information and problem description to report the following information to a level-two technician:

Contact Information

Company Name: JH Travel, Inc.

Contact: Dan Handy

Company Address: 204 N. Main Street

Company Phone: 1-866-555-0998

Problem Description

Okay, so I work with cars all the time and I know how they work, but I do not know how my computer works. This morning was pretty slow because I guess more and more people are using those Internet travel sites. So, after my morning coffee, I decided to figure out what makes my computer work. I opened up the case and just started looking at the different things inside. When I put everything back together, everything seemed to fit and I didn't see any leftover parts. Now it does not work at all. It beeps at me all the time.

Note: After you have given the level-two tech the problem description, use the Additional Information to answer any follow up questions the technician may ask.

Additional Information

Windows XP Pro.

Computer has no new hardware.

Computer has not been moved recently.

Except for the beeping, I did not hear any other strange sounds from the computer.

I do not smell any electronics burning or smoke.

Computer looks the same as it did yesterday.

CHAPTER 12

Advanced Operating Systems

The Study Guide portion of this chapter uses open-ended questions to test your knowledge of operating systems. This portion also includes multiple-choice study questions to help prepare you to take the A+ certification exams and to test your overall understanding of the material.

The Lab Exercises portion of this chapter includes all the online curriculum hands-on labs and remote technician exercises to further reinforce your mastery of the operating systems content.

Study Guide

Using the Command Prompt

Although DOS has been a dead operating system for many years, executing DOS commands at the command prompt/DOS window still comes in handy. Therefore, you should know the various DOS commands and how to use them.

Concept Questions

Answer the following questions about commands.

Identify what the following commands do:

- CLS: _Clear the screen_
- DIR: _Display the contents of a directory (folder)_
- CD: _Change the directory (folder)_
- MD: _Make a new directory_
- RD: _Remove a directory_
- DEL: _Delete one or more files in current directory_
- COPY: _copies files to a new location_
- XCOPY: _copies directories & all subdirectories to a new location_
- DISKCOPY: _Copy disk_
- DISKCOMP: _compare disk ?_
- FORMAT: _Make ready to receive data_

- REN: _Rename ? a file_
- ATTRIB: _Change file attributes_

For most commands, how can you display what options it has available to it?

If you are in Windows XP, what are the two ways you can open a command prompt window?

Run > Start > cmd

If you want to edit a text file, what programs can you use at the command prompt, and what program can you use in the Windows GUI interface?

What command would you use at the command prompt to format the D: drive?

_____

What command would you use at the command prompt to copy the report.doc file from its current folder to the D drive?

_____

Installing Windows 2000 and Windows XP

As a computer technician, you will need to know how to install Windows, particularly Windows XP. Therefore, you need to be familiar with the keys to press to get special options and basic steps in installation. When the installation is finished, you then need to complete postinstallation tasks.

Concept Questions

Answer the following questions about installing Windows.

What is the executable command that you would use to perform a clean installation of Windows XP?

_____Format NTFS_____

What is the executable command that you would use to upgrade Windows 2000 to Windows XP?

_____D:\i386\winnt32_____

What key do you press to specify a SCSI or RAID controller driver during installation of Windows 2000 or Windows XP?

_____

If you create a disk image of a Windows XP box and you want to copy the disk image to another computer, you must run a utility so that the computer has a unique computer name and other identifiers on the network. What is this utility?

_____Sysprep_____

What do you use the Windows update website for?

To download security packs & updates onto computer to enable OS to be
more efficient & secure.

In Windows XP, how do you install the new Windows firewall and Windows Security Center?

_____

How do you configure Windows XP to automatically download and install updates?

Access Automatic Updates screen from Control Panel the click on
Automatic (recommended)

Windows Folder Structure

When troubleshooting many Windows problems and when trying to recover data files, you need to understand the Windows folder structure. By knowing the folder structure, you will be able to locate start-up files, programs that automatically start during boot, program files, and user data and configuration programs.

Concept Questions

Answer the following questions about the Windows folder structure.

What is the default folder that holds the Windows files for Windows 95, Windows 98, Windows Millennium, and Windows XP?

Windows folder on C: drive

What is the default folder that holds the Windows files for Windows 2000?

If you have a user with a login name of Pat on Windows XP, where would you find the folder on the C: drive for the user's desktop?

Within my documents

If you have a user with a login name of Pat on Windows XP, where would you find the folder on the C: drive for the user's My Documents?

Within My Computer

In Windows XP, where do the majority of your program files reside?

Program Files within My Computer

What would you do if you want a program to automatically start up every time you turn on your computer and a user logs on?

Msconfig allows you to set programs that will run at start up

To access Msconfig, choose Start > Run, type MsConfig & press ENTER.

You are logged in to a computer as Pat. When you install a program and the program needs to create temporary files that are needed for an installation, where are the temporary installation files stored? In addition, how does Windows know how to store the files in this folder?

Control Panel and Administrative Tools

As you work with Windows, you will need to be able to configure the different parts of Windows. In this section, you will look at the most common tools that allow you to configure Windows.

Concept Questions

Answer the following questions about the Control Panel and administrative tools.

What is the main system configuration utility used in Windows?

msconfig

What utility would you use to verify that the proper device driver is loaded?

Device Manager

If you want to change the resolution that your video system is using, what applet would you use in the Control Panel?

Display settings Applet

If you want to install Internet Information Server (IIS) in Windows XP, what applet would you use?

What does a yellow exclamation point in Device Manager indicate?

There is a problem with the hardware

What does a red X in Device Manager mean?

The hardware is disabled

Which applet do you use in the Control Panel to roll back a driver in Windows XP?

Add Hardware

What is the paging file in Windows 2000 or Windows XP or the swap file used in Windows 95, Windows 98, and Windows Millennium?

Virtual Memory

What is the name of the paging file in Windows 2000?

What the name of the paging file in Windows 98?

How do you manage or configure the virtual memory in Windows XP?

Start > Control Panel > Performance & maintenance > System > Advanced > Performance > Setting > Advanced

What administrative tool do you use to view your system and application logs and manage your disks?

Disk Management   Start   right-click My Computer Manage > Disk Management

If you wanted to stop the server service, what program would you use?

Services   start right click 'my computer' select Manage Click plus sign next to services and Applications

The Registry is a central database Windows uses to hold most of the configuration of Windows and its applications. What utilities would you use to make changes in the Registry?

Regedit

Fonts

American Standard Code for Information Interchange (ASCII), generally pronounced, "ASK-ee," is a character encoding based on the English alphabet and is used to represent text in computers, communications equipment, and other devices that work with text. The original ASCSII standard defined codes for 128 characters; 95 are printable characters (including uppercase and lowercase characters, digits, and punctuation characters) and 33 nonprinting characters, used as control characters that affect how text is processed. Text files consist of ASCII characters.

Extended ASCII extends the 128-character set to 256 characters that include the original seven-bit ASCII characters, characters to accommodate some European languages, and special characters to be used in line drawing. An Extended ASCII character takes up one byte (eight bits) of data.

Today, Windows uses Unicode for its text. Unicode employs a 16-bit coding scheme that allows for 65,536 distinct characters. Unicode supports all modern languages and includes representations for punctuation marks, mathematical symbols, and dingbats/wingdings (special characters or symbols). Because they establishe a unique code for each character in each script, Windows NT-based operating systems can ensure that the character translation from one language to another is accurate.

Concept Questions

Answer the following questions about fonts.

How would you add a font to your computer?

_____

What utility can you use to view your fonts and the Unicode characters?

Character Map

Disk Management

Because every computer has one or more hard drives, you will need to learn how to manage those disks, including how to create, delete, and format partitions. One of the primary tools is the Disk Management Console, which can be found as part of the Computer Management Console.

Concept Questions

Answer the following questions about disk management.

List the advantages of using NTFS over FAT32:

(1) Security - NTFS views individual files & folders as objects & provides security for those objects through a feature called Access control List (ACL)

(2) NTFS enables you to compress individual files & folders to save space on HDD

(3) NTFS enables encryption of files using its Encrypting File System (EFS)

(4) NTFS supports Disk Quotas enabling Administrators to set limits on drive space usage for users

(5) NTFS enables you to adjust the cluster sizes

(6) NTFS utilises an enhanced file allocation table called the Master File Table (MFT)

What is the maximum size of a FAT32 volume that Windows XP supports?

2 TB or 2048 GB

If you need to convert the FAT32 volume (Drive D:) to an NTFS volume, what command do you need to execute?

convert d:/fs : NTFS

Windows Boot Options

One of the troubleshooting tools that you have in Windows is the advanced boot menu, which allows you to select different modes with certain features enabled or disabled. Therefore, you need to know how to access the advanced boot options and which mode to select.

Concept Questions

Answer the following questions about Windows boot options.

When you have multiple versions of Windows 2000 and XP on a computer, what file holds the configuration information that displays the boot menu so that you can choose which operating system to load during startup?

boot.ini

During boot, what key do you press to access the Advanced Boot options?

If you want to start the computer with only basic drivers and files needed including loading VGA driers and with no network components, what mode would you start?

Safe Mode

If you have a faulty video driver or you loaded the incorrect video driver, what mode can you use so that you fix this problem?

Enable VGA Mode

If you load a driver or load a program and now your computer does not boot properly, what mode can you load?

Recovery Console

Troubleshooting Tools

Besides the advanced boot options, you also have other troubleshooting tools available in Windows, including the Signature Verification tool, the System Configuration utility, System File Checker, Windows Registry Checker and various disk tools. You also need to know how to run the backup utility so that you can back up and restore files.

An NTFS partition keeps a backup copy of the most critical parts of the MFT in the middle of the disk, reducing the chance that a serious drive error can wipe out both the MFT & NFT copy

Concept Questions

Answer the following questions about troubleshooting.

Microsoft recommends using only signed drivers because poorly written drivers can cause a wide range of problems. What tool can you use to verify that all drivers are digitally signed?

select "Block- Never install unsigned driver software" in Driver signing Options

What tool can you use to view all programs and services that start during boot and that allows you to stop any program and service from starting during boot?

msconfig

What utility scans and verifies the versions of all protected system files after you restart your computer?

System File Checker

If your computer doesn't boot at all for Windows 2000 or Windows XP, even in safe mode, the best thing is to use the Recovery Console. The Recovery Console provides a command-line interface that will let you repair system problems using a limited set of command-line commands, including enabling or disabling services, repairing a corrupted master boot record, or reading and writing data on a local drive. There are two ways to start the Recovery Console. What are they?

from Windows Installation CD-Rom

What command do you use in the Recovery Console that can repair or replace a partition boot sector on the system partition?

fixboot

What command do you use in the Recovery Console that will fix the master boot record (MBR)?

fixmbr

What tool can you use in Windows 98 that will scan the system Registry for invalid entries and other problems?

REGCLEAN

What can you use to recover from a system crash (in Windows 98 and Windows XP) that will restore key files and the Registry for problems where safe mode and last known configuration mode does not work?

- Windows 98: _____
- Windows XP: *system Restore*

If your system crashes and you cannot figure out the problem, you can send a physical memory dump to Microsoft or another software company. Where do you configure the type of dump that is saved when a system crash occurs?

_____

You are ready to install a new application. However, when you load it, Windows XP experiences several problems. Therefore, you would like to roll it back to the same configuration before you installed the application. What should you do?

Press F8 & go to Last Know Good Configuration

What tool should you use to protect your e-mails and data documents?

Anti-Virus software / Windows Firewall

You discover that your C drive is filling up. What tool can you use to free some disk space?

Disk Cleanup

What tool in Windows 98 do you use to check for disk errors?

What tool in Windows XP do you use to check for disk errors?

chkdsk

What parameter do you need to add to chkdsk to actually fix the errors that it finds?

"Scan for and attempt recovery of bad sectors"

Describe the Nonsystem Disk or Disk Error and list some of the methods to fix it.

If the CD-Rom is set as the bootable drive then an error message like this may occur. The settings within BIOS need to be changed so that the operating system is set to boot from the hard disk drive.

What are some of the causes of the No Operating System Found error message?

That there are missing files or files that the computer is unable to find. The problem can be rectified by using a start up disk to attempt a repair.
In XP use the recovery console on the XP CD-ROM.

Study Questions

Choose the best answer for each of the questions that follow:

1. When using characters in Windows, what code does Windows use?

    A. ASCII
    B. UNICODE ✓
    C. IDBC
    D. Morse

2. What command do you use to clear the screen at the command prompt?

    A. ECHO OFF
    B. CLS ✓
    C. REM
    D. CD

3. What command would you use from the command prompt on a Windows XP computer to defragment your D drive?

    A.   SCANDISK D:

    B.   DEFRAG D: ✓

    C.   DF D:

    D.   FRAG D: /U

4. Which utility in Windows would you use to select and copy characters from any installed font?

    A.   System utility

    B.   Font utility

    C.   Font Map

    D.   Character Map ✓

5. What command do you use to convert the D: drive from a FAT partition to a NTFS partition without losing data?

    A.   format d: /fs:ntfs

    B.   convert d:

    C.   convert d: /fs:ntfs ✓

    D.   upgrade d:

6. When installing Windows XP, which key do you press to load SCSI or RAID drivers that are not included with the Windows XP installation CD?

    A.   F4

    B.   F6

    C.   F8

    D.   F10

7. Which of the following does the NTFS *not* support or is not an advantage of NTFS?

    A.   Recovers from some disk-related errors automatically ✓

    B.   Security using directory and file permissions

    C.   Utilizes disk space more efficiently than FAT and FAT32

    D.   Security using encryption

    E.   Support of quotas to specify the amount of disk space a user can use

8. Which of the following can you use to find and fix disk errors on a Windows 98 machine?

    A.   Defrag

    B.   Scandisk ✓

    C.   Fdisk

    D.   Convert

9. Which of the following files is used for virtual memory in a Windows XP machine?

    A.   PAGEFILE.SYS

    B.   WIN386.SWP

    C.   NTLDR

    D.   BOOT.SYS

10. In Windows XP, where do you configure the virtual memory settings?

   A. Open the Control Panel, double-click the System applet, and select the Advanced tab.

   B. Open the Control Panel, double-click the System applet, and click the Device Manager button.

   C. Open the Control Panel, double-click the System applet, and select the Performance tab. ✓

   D. Open the Control Panel and double-click the Paging applet.

11. What utility can you use to troubleshoot startup problems by allowing you to disable startup programs and services?

   A. Msconfig.exe ✓

   B. Regedit.exe

   C. Device Manager

   D. Add/Remove Programs

12. When using the Recovery Console in Windows XP, which command is used to fix the Windows volume boot sector?

   A. Fixmbr

   B. Footfix

   C. Diskpart

   D. Fixboot

13. What feature is installed with Service Pack 2 on Windows XP that would prevent a program from communicating over the network?

   A. An improved firewall

   B. An antivirus program

   C. User Account Control

   D. Enhanced NTFS permissions

14. How do you back up the Registry in Windows? (Choose all that apply.)

   A. Windows Registry Checker

   B. System Restore

   C. System File Checker

   D. Microsoft Backup utility

15. You are ready to make some system changes to a Windows XP computer. You want to create a restore point so that if there is a problem, you can go back to the restore option before the changes. What do you need to do?

   A. Run the Microsoft backup program.

   B. Run the System Restore application. ✓

   C. Run the Registry Checker and specify the backup option.

   D. Run the Last Known-Good Configuration option.

16. Why is it important to keep Windows updated using the Windows update website or automatic updates?

   A. To keep your system secure and to install critical updates ✓

   B. To keep your system fast

   C. To keep your system optimized for the newest games

   D. To keep your system from overheating

Lab Exercises

Lab 12.2.2: Advanced Installation of Windows XP

In this lab, you will install a Windows XP Professional operating system by using an answer file for automation. You will customize partition settings and create an administrative user and limited users.

The following is the recommended equipment for this lab:

- A computer with a new installation of Windows XP Professional

- Windows XP Professional installation CD

- A blank, formatted floppy disk

Step 1

Log on to the computer.

Insert the Windows XP Professional CD into the CD-ROM drive.

Click Perform Additional Tasks (see Figure 12-1).

Figure 12-1   Welcome to Windows XP Screen

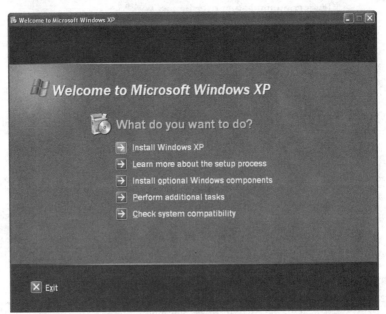

Step 2

Click Browse This CD (see Figure 12-2).

Figure 12-2   Options Available When You Click Perform Additional Tasks

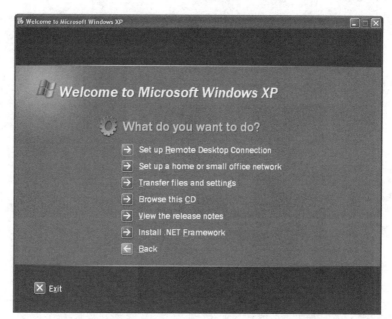

Double-click the Support folder.

Double-click the Tools folder.

Double-click Deploy.CAB.

Highlight all the files by clicking Edit, Select All.

Right-click setupmgr.exe, and then click Extract.

Click Make New Folder to create a folder on the C: drive.

Name the folder Deploy.

Click Extract to extract the files from the CD to C:\Deploy.

Browse to C:\Deploy (see Figure 12-3).

Figure 12-3   Deploy Folder

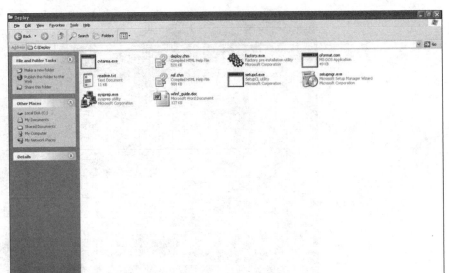

Step 3

Double-click setupmgr.exe.

Step 4

The Setup Manager window appears (see Figure 12-4).

Figure 12-4   Welcome to Setup Manager Wizard

Click Next.

The Create New button should be checked by default. Click Next (see Figure 12-5).

Figure 12-5   Creating a New Answer File

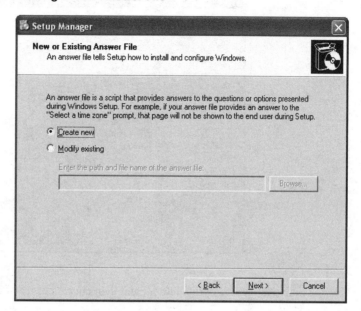

Click the Unattended Setup option button (see Figure 12-6).

Figure 12-6   Selecting the Type of Setup

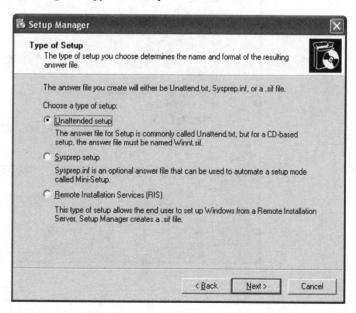

Note that a CD-based answer file name must be Winnt.sif.

Click the Windows XP Professional option button, and then click Next (see Figure 12-7).

Figure 12-7   Specifying Which Version of Windows the Answer File Is Made For

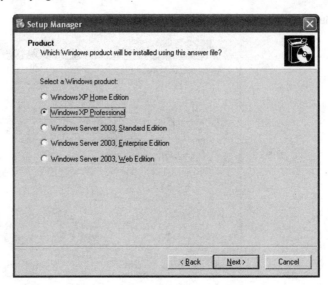

Click the Fully Automated option button, and then click Next (see Figure 12-8).

Figure 12-8   Selecting the Amount of User Interaction

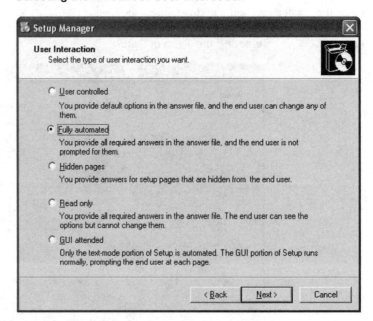

Click the Set Up from a CD option button, and then click Next (see Figure 12-9).

Figure 12-9   Specify Where the Distribution Share Is Located

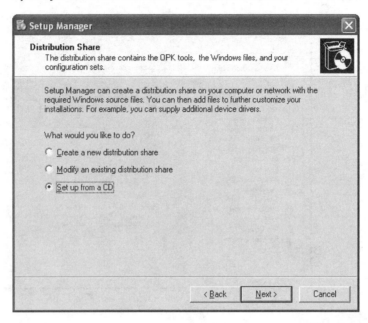

Click the I Accept the Terms of the License Agreement check box, and then click Next (see Figure 12-10).

Figure 12-10   License Agreement

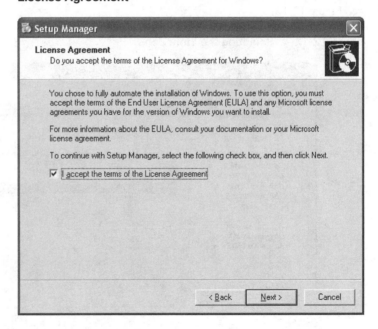

Click Name and Organization in the list on the left.

Type the name and the organization name provided by your instructor (see Figure 12-11).

Figure 12-11   Specifying the Name and Organization for the Windows Installation

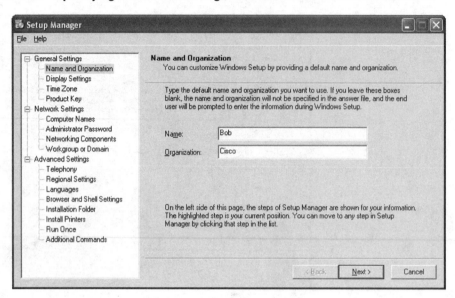

Click Next.

Click Time Zone in the list on the left.

Click the time zone for your location from the Time Zone drop-down box, and then click Next (see Figure 12-12).

Figure 12-12   Selecting the Time Zone

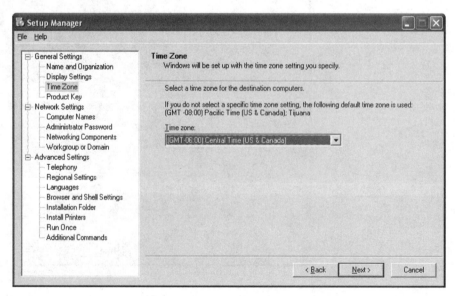

Highlight Product Key in the list on the left.

Type the Windows XP Professional product key supplied by your instructor in the Product Key fields (see Figure 12-13).

Click Next.

Figure 12-13   Specifying the Product Key

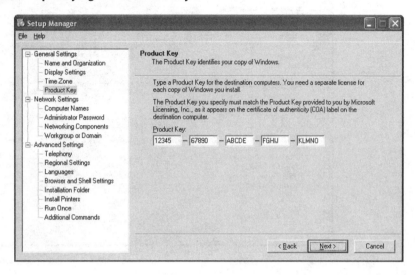

Click Computer Names in the list on the left.

Type the computer name provided by your instructor in the Computer Name field, and then click Add.

The computer name will then display in the Computers to Be Installed field. Click Next (see Figure 12-14).

Figure 12-14   Specifying Computer Names

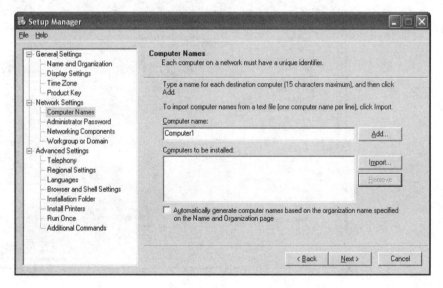

Click Administrator Password in the list on the left.

Type the first initial of your first name and your complete last name into the Password and Confirm Password fields (for example, jsmith).

Click Next (see Figure 12-15).

Figure 12-15   Specifying the Administrator Password

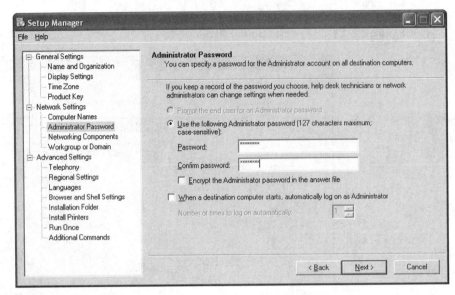

Click Workgroup or Domain in the list on the left.

Click the Workgroup option button.

Type the Workgroup name LabGroup1 into the Workgroup field, and then click Next (see Figure 12-16).

Figure 12-16   Specifying the Name of the Workgroup

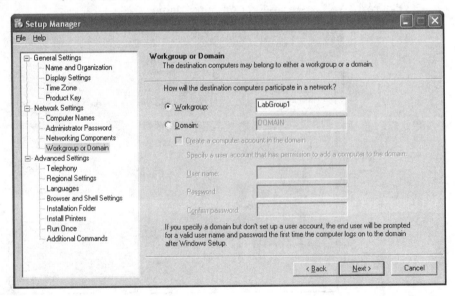

Click Additional Commands in the list on the left, and then click Finish (see Figure 12-17).

Figure 12-17   Specify Additional Commands During the Setup Manager

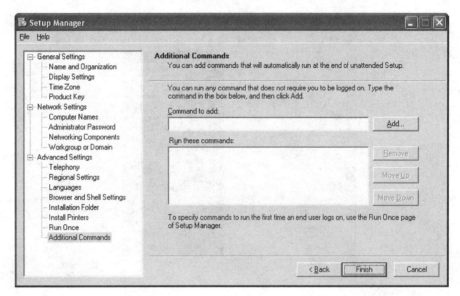

Type **C:\Deploy\unattend.txt** into the Path and Filename field if it is not already displayed (see Figure 12-18).

Click OK.

Figure 12-18   Specifying the Location of the Answer File

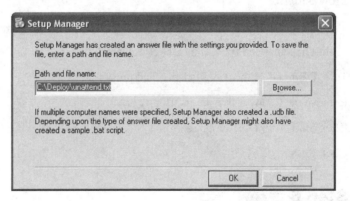

Click File, Exit (see Figure 12-19).

Figure 12-19   Completing Setup Manager

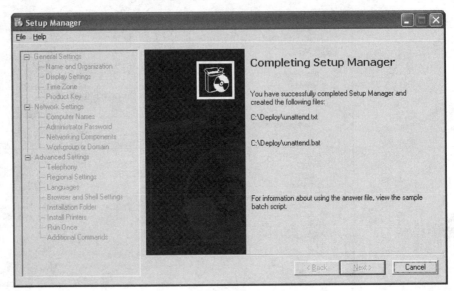

Step 5

Browse to C:\Deploy.

Right-click unattend.txt, and then click Copy.

Browse to A:\.

Click File, Paste.

Right-click unattend.txt, and then click Rename.

Type **Winnt.sif** as the new filename, and press Enter.

Remove the floppy disk from the floppy drive.

Click Start, Turn Off Computer.

Click Restart.

Step 6

When the Press Any Key to Boot from CD message appears, press any key on the keyboard. Insert the floppy disk. The system will inspect the hardware configuration (see Figure 12-20).

Figure 12-20   Inspecting Your Computer for Installation

The Windows XP Setup screen appears while the program loads the necessary files (see Figure 12-21).

Figure 12-21   The Beginning of Windows Installation

Step 7

The Welcome to Setup screen appears. Press Enter (see Figure 12-22).

Figure 12-22   Windows XP Installation Welcome Screen

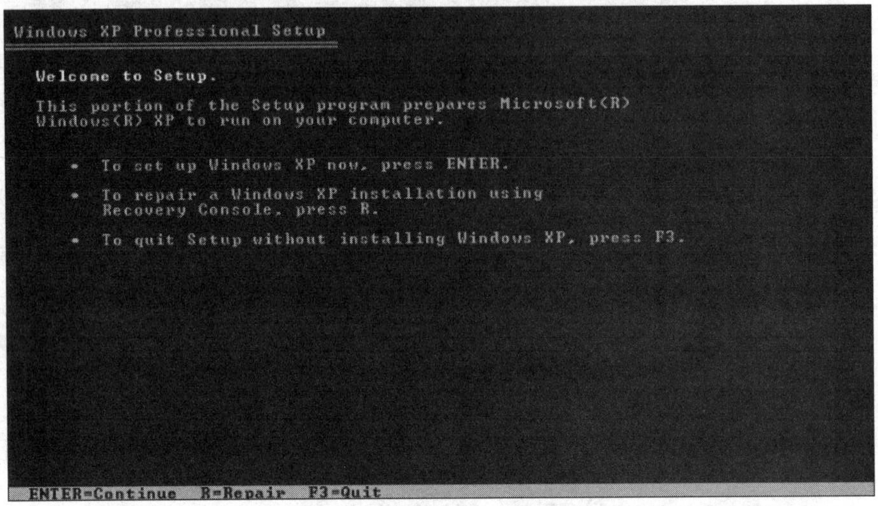

The Windows XP Licensing Agreement screen appears. Press F8 (see Figure 12-23).

Figure 12-23   Windows XP License Screen

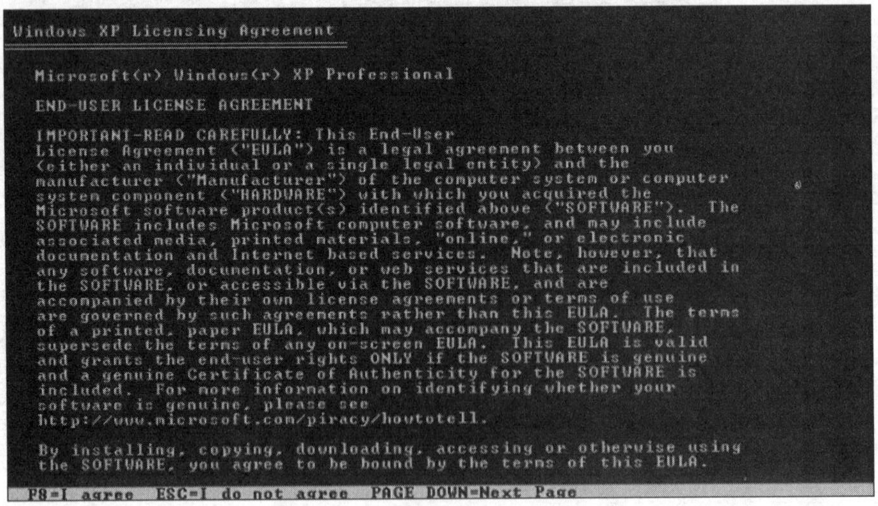

Windows XP Professional Setup will search to determine whether another operating system already exists on the hard drive (see Figure 12-24).

Figure 12-24 Searching for Previous Versions of Windows

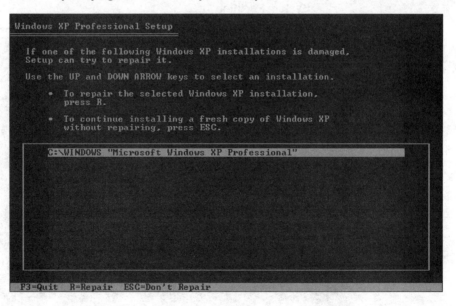

Press Esc (see Figure 12-25).

Figure 12-25 Specifying Whether to Repair or Replace a Previous Version of Windows

Press the D key (see Figure 12-26).

Figure 12-26   Deleting a Previous Partition

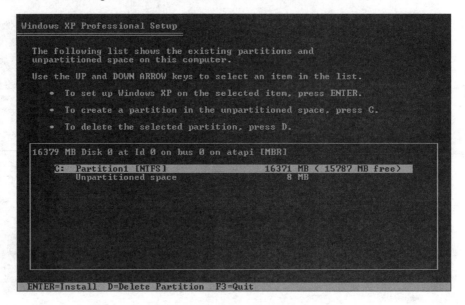

Press Enter (see Figure 12-27).

Figure 12-27   Warning Screen Specifying That If You Press the D Key, It Will Delete a System Partition

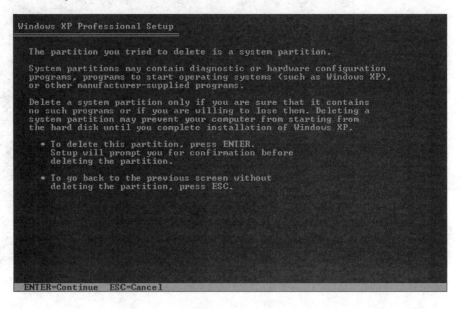

Press the L key (see Figure 12-28).

Figure 12-28   Screen to Delete a Partition

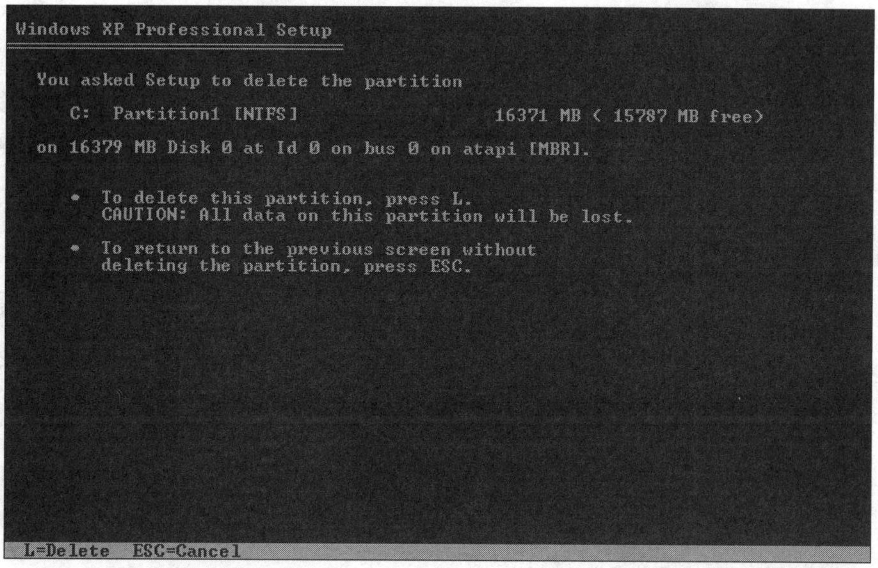

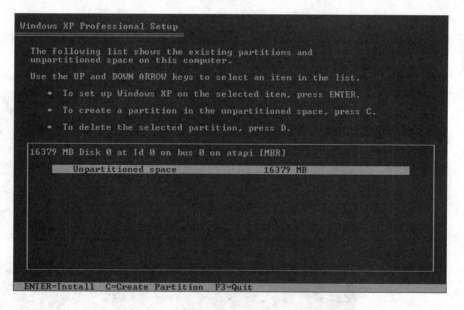

Press the C key (see Figure 12-29).

Figure 12-29   Screen to Create a New Partition

Type **5000** into the Create Partition of Size (in MB) field.

Press the Enter key (see Figure 12-30).

Figure 12-30   Specifying the Size of the New Partition

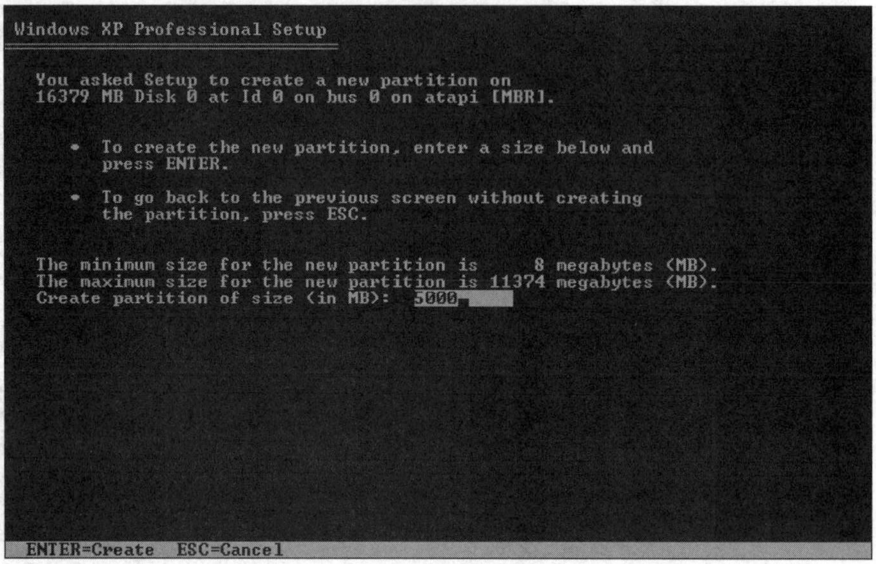

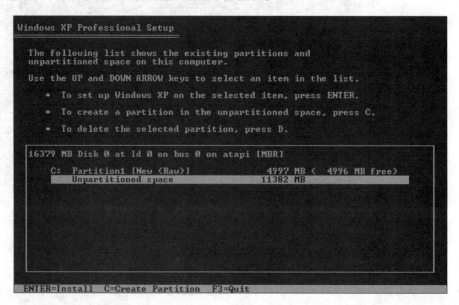

Press the down-arrow key to select Unpartitioned Space.

Press the C key (see Figure 12-31).

Create another partition of 5000 MB.

Repeat this process one more time. You will have three partitions of 5000 MB each.

Figure 12-31   Screen to Create Additional Partitions

Select C: Partition1 and press the Enter key (see Figure 12-32).

Figure 12-32   Specifying Which Partition to Install Windows Into

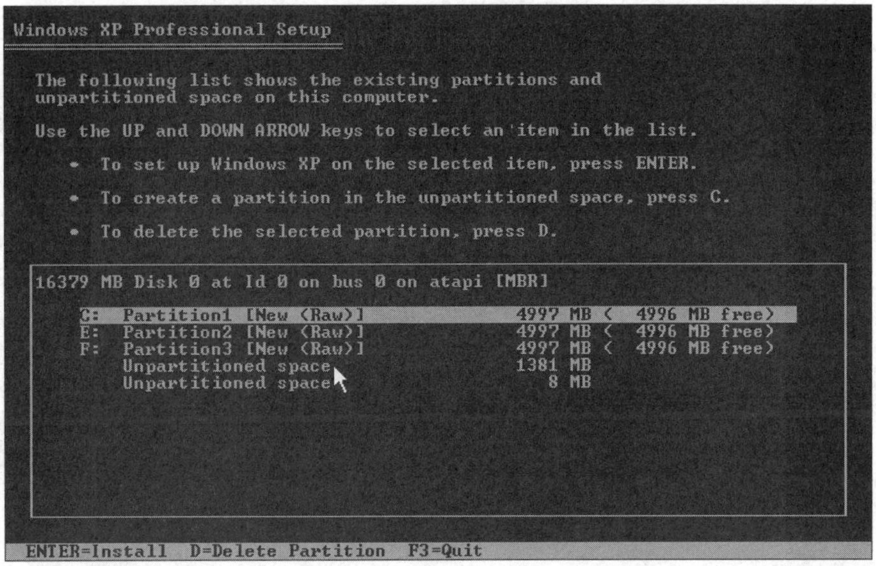

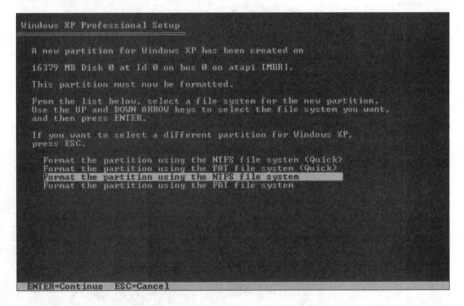

Select Format the Partition Using the NTFS File System (see Figure 12-33).

Figure 12-33   Selecting to Format the New Partition

Do not select Format the Partition Using the NTFS File System <Quick>.

Press the Enter key.

The Please Wait While Setup Formats the Partition screen appears (see Figure 12-34).

Figure 12-34   Formatting the New Partition

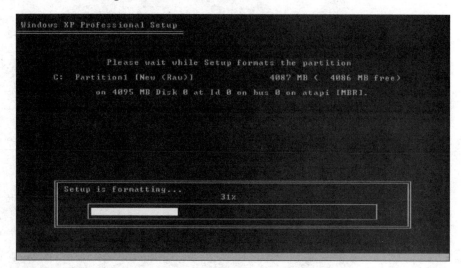

The system will restart automatically.

After the system restarts, the message Press Any Key to Boot from CD appears. Do not press any keys.

The installation should continue without prompting you for any settings.

The system will restart automatically.

After the system restarts, the message Press Any Key to Boot from CD appears. Do not press any keys.

Step 8

The Welcome to Microsoft Windows screen appears (see Figure 12-35).

Figure 12-35   Welcome to Microsoft Windows Screen

Click Next.

Click the Help Protect My PC by Turning On Automatic Updates Now option button (see Figure 12-36).

Figure 12-36   Help Protect Your System By Turning on Automatic Updates

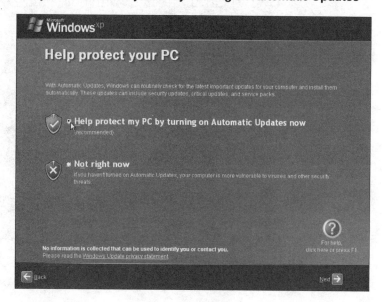

Click Next.

Click the Yes, This Computer Will Connect Through the Local Area Network or Home Network option button (see Figure 12-37).

Figure 12-37   Specifying How Your Computer Will Connect to the Internet

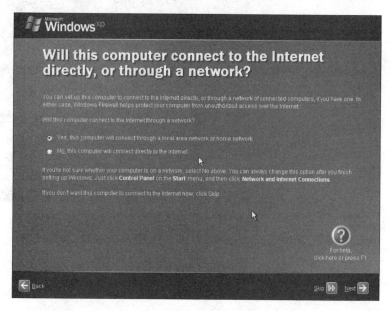

Click Next.

Click the No, Not at This Time option button, and then click Next (see Figure 12-38).

Figure 12-38   Registering Windows with Microsoft

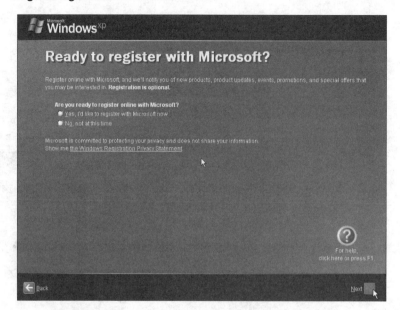

Type the name provided by your instructor into the Your Name field (see Figure 12-39).

Figure 12-39   Specifying Which Users Will Use the Windows XP Computer

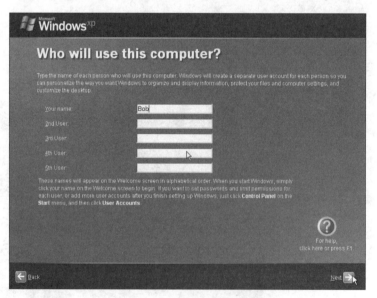

Click Next. The Thank you screen appears (see Figure 12-40).

Figure 12-40   Installation Is Complete

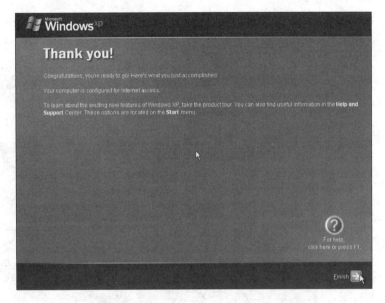

Click Finish.

Step 9

The Windows XP Professional desktop appears. Click Start, Control Panel (see Figure 12-41).

Figure 12-41   Opening the Control Panel from the Start Button

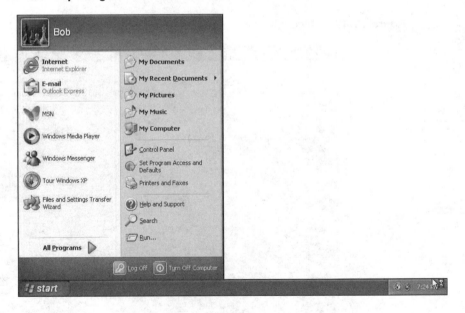

Step 10

Click User Accounts (see Figure 12-42).

Figure 12-42   Control Panel

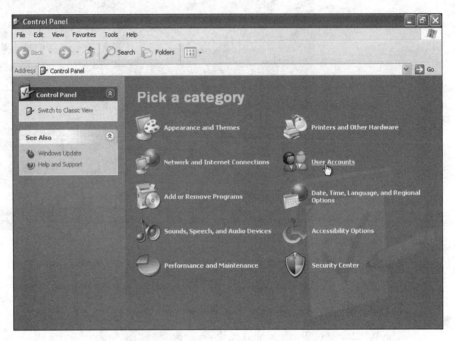

Click Create a New Account from the Pick a Task list (see Figure 12-43).

Figure 12-43   Managing User Accounts

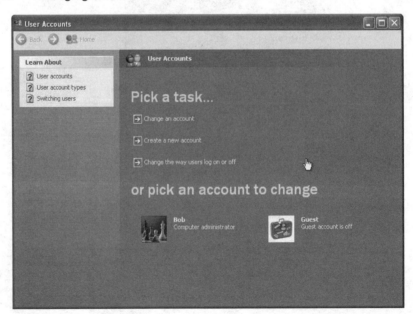

Type the name provided by your instructor into the Type a Name for the New Account field (see Figure 12-44).

Figure 12-44   Specifying the Name of the New Account

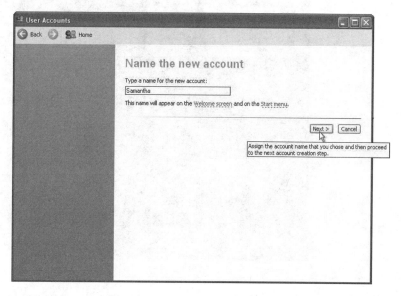

Click Next.

Click the Limited option button (see Figure 12-45).

Figure 12-45   Specifying the Type of Account

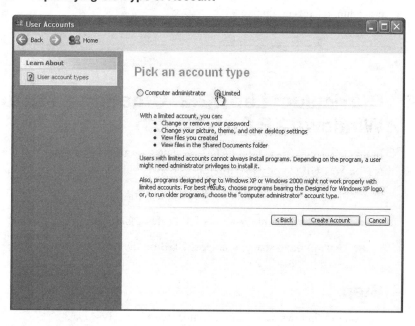

Click Create Account. The User Accounts window appears (see Figure 12-46).

Figure 12-46   Managing User Accounts Within the Control Panel

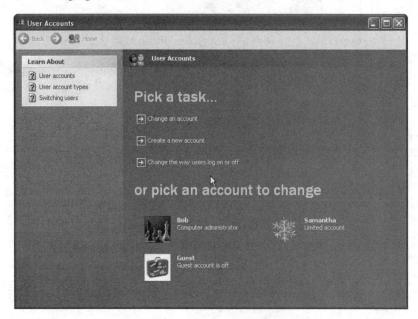

Create a second limited user. Your instructor will provide the name of the user.

What was the name of the file used to automate the installation located on the floppy disk?

_____

How do you think automating the installation will help the IT Department if they have to repeat the procedure on 100 computers?

_____

Curriculum Lab 12.2: Creating a Partition in Windows XP Pro (12.2.3)

In this lab, you will create a FAT32 formatted partition on a disk. You will convert the partition to NTFS. You will identify the differences between the FAT32 format and the NTFS format.

The following is the recommended equipment for this lab:

- Computer running Windows XP Professional
- Unpartitioned space of at least 1 GB on the hard disk drive

Step 1

Log on to Windows as an administrator (see Figure 12-47).

Figure 12-47   Windows XP Login Screen

Step 2

Click Start.

Right-click My Computer, and then click Manage (see Figure 12-48).

Figure 12-48   Opening Computer Management By Selecting the Manage Option

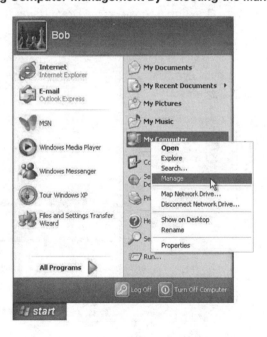

Step 3

The Computer Management window appears (see Figure 12-49).

Figure 12-49   Computer Management Console

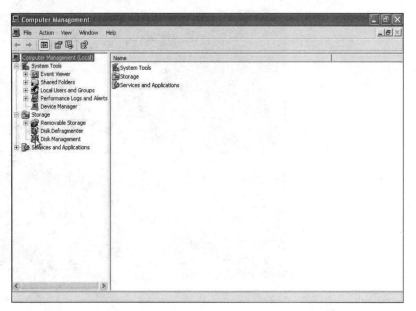

Click Disk Management on the left side of the screen.

Right-click the green-outlined block of Free Space.

Click New Logical Drive (see Figure 12-50).

Figure 12-50   Creating a New Logical Drive Using the Disk Management Console

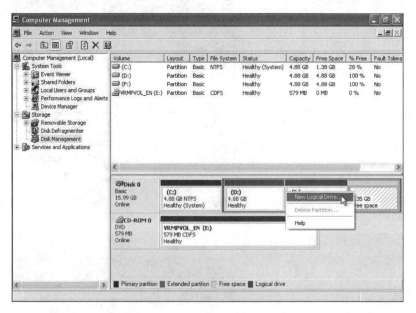

Step 4

The New Partition Wizard window appears (see Figure 12-51). Click Next.

Figure 12-51   Starting the New Partition Wizard

Click the Logical Drive option button, and then click Next (see Figure 12-52).

Figure 12-52   Selecting the Type of Partition

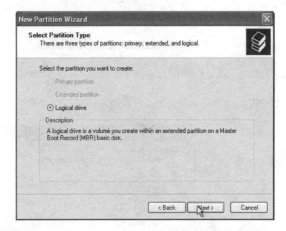

Type **500** into the Partition Size in MB field (see Figure 12-53).

Figure 12-53   Specifying the Size of the New Partition

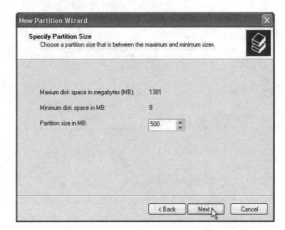

Click the Assign the Following Drive Letter option button.

Select G from the drop-down menu (see Figure 12-54).

Figure 12-54   Specifying the Drive Letter

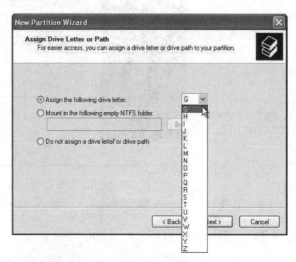

Click Next.

Click the Format This Partition with the Following Settings option button (see Figure 12-55).

Figure 12-55   Formatting the Partition

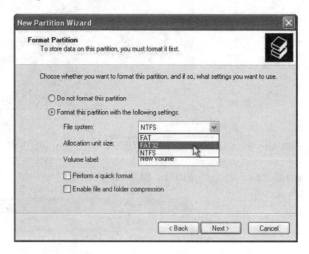

Click Next.

Click Finish (see Figure 12-56).

Figure 12-56   Completing the New Partition Wizard

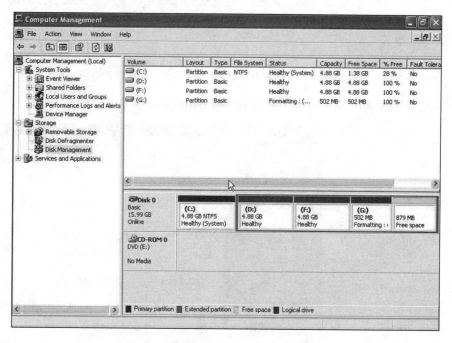

Step 5

The Computer Management window reappears while the new volume is formatted (see Figure 12-57).

Figure 12-57   New Partition Is Formatting

The Computer Management window shows the new Healthy volume (see Figure 12-58).

Figure 12-58   The Disk Management Console Showing the Status of Each Partition

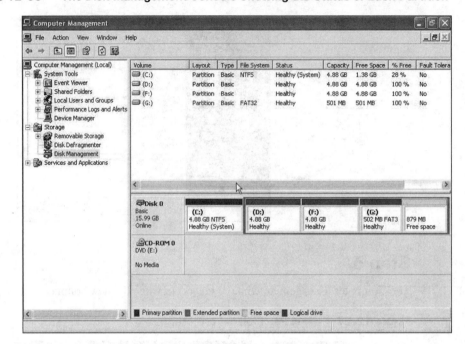

Step 6

Open My Computer. Click the Local Disk (G:) drive (see Figure 12-59).

Figure 12-59   My Computer Showing the New Drive

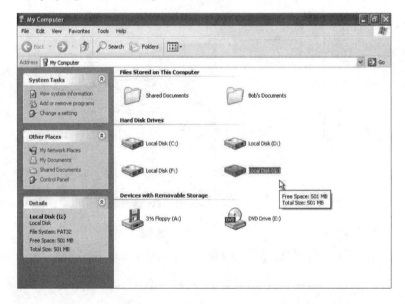

The Details area on the left of the My Computer window displays information about the G: drive.

What is the File System?

How much free space is shown?

Right-click the Local Disk (G:) drive, and choose Properties (see Figure 12-60).

Figure 12-60   Opening the Drive Properties

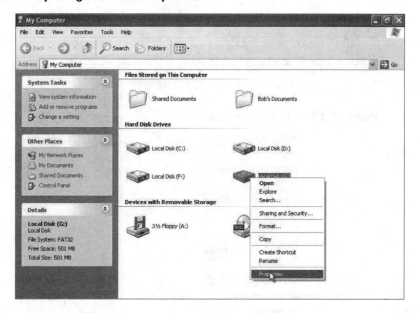

Step 7

The Local Disk (G:) Properties window appears (see Figure 12-61).

Figure 12-61   Drive Properties

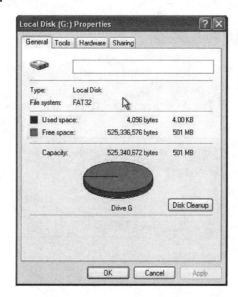

What is the file system of the G: drive?

List the tabs found in the Local Disk (G:) Properties window?

Click OK.

Double-click the Local Disk (G:) drive.

Step 8

Right-click anywhere in the whitespace of the window.

Choose New, Text Document (see Figure 12-62).

Figure 12-62   Creating a New File

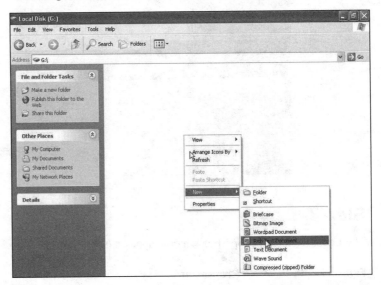

Type **Test** and press Return.

Step 9

Right-click the Test document in the window and choose Properties (see Figure 12-63).

Figure 12-63   Properties of a Text File

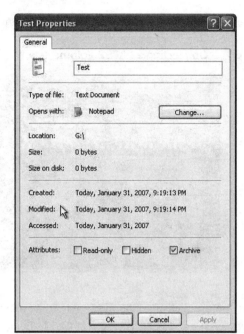

The Test Properties window appears. Notice that there is a tab in the Test Properties window called General.

Click OK.

Step 10

Choose Start, Run.

In the Open field, type **cmd**, and then click OK (see Figure 12-64).

Figure 12-64   Using the Run Option to Open a Command Prompt Window

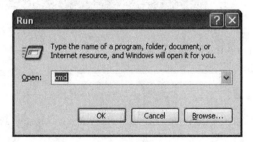

Step 11

The C:\WINDOWS\system32\cmd.exe window appears. Type **convert G: /fs:NTFS** (see Figure 12-65).

Figure 12-65   Converting a FAT32 Volume to a NTFS Volume Using the convert Command

The convert command changes the file system of a volume without losing data.

Press the Enter key (see Figure 12-66).

Figure 12-66   Results Displayed Onscreen After a Drive Is Converted to NTFS

Type **exit**, and then press Return.

Step 12

The C:\WINDOWS\System32\cmd.exe window closes (see Figure 12-67).

Figure 12-67   Partition Now Has an NTFS File System

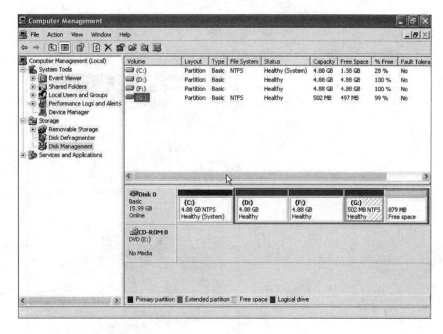

What is the file system of the G: drive?

Step 13

Open My Computer.

Right-click the G: drive, and then click Properties (see Figure 12-68).

Figure 12-68   Opening the Drive Properties

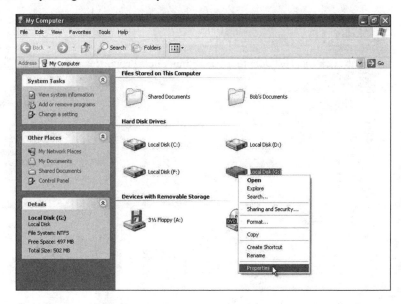

Step 14

The Local Disk (G:) Properties window appears (see Figure 12-69).

Figure 12-69   Drive Properties

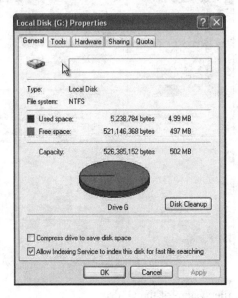

What are the tabs in the Local Disk (G:) Properties window?

_____

When the volume was FAT32, there were four tabs. What is the name of the new tab that was added after the volume was converted to NTFS?

_____

Click Cancel, and then double-click the G: drive.

Step 15

Right-click the Test document, and then click Properties (see Figure 12-70).

Figure 12-70   Properties of Text File

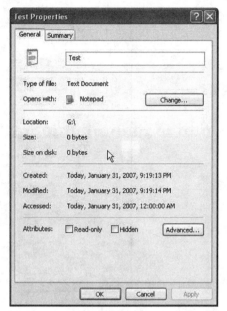

What are the tabs in the Test Properties window?

When the volume was FAT32, there was one tab. What is the name of the new tab that was added after the volume was converted to NTFS?

Click OK.

Step 16

Choose Tools, Folder Options (see Figure 12-71).

Figure 12-71   Opening Folder Options

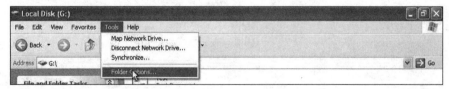

Step 17

The Folder Options window appears. Click the View tab.

Scroll to the bottom of the Advanced Settings area, and then uncheck Use Simple File Sharing (Recommended) (see Figure 12-72).

Click OK.

Figure 12-72   Use Simple File Sharing Is Unchecked

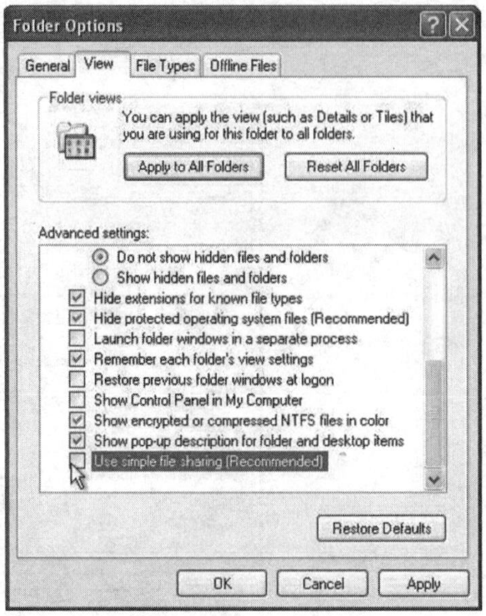

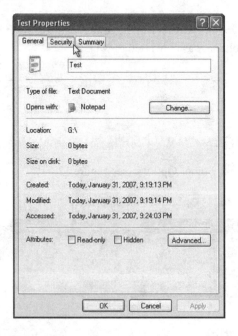

The Folder Options window closes (see Figure 12-73).

Figure 12-73   Properties of a Text File

What are the tabs in the Test Properties window?

_____

When Simple File Sharing was enabled, there were two tabs. What is the name of the new tab that was added after Simple File Sharing was turned off?

_____

Step 18

Right-click the G: drive, and then choose Properties (see Figure 12-74).

Figure 12-74   Drive Properties

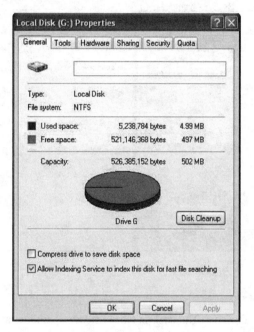

What are the tabs in the Local Disk (G:) Properties window?

When Simple File Sharing was enabled, there were five tabs. What is the name of the new tab that was added after Simple File Sharing was turned off?

Lab 12.2.4: Customize Virtual Memory Settings

In this lab, you will customize Virtual Memory settings. You will customize the Startup folder and RunOnce Key in the Registry. You will change the default Windows Update option.

The following is the recommended equipment for this lab:

- A computer running Windows XP Professional
- Internet access

Step 1

Log on to Windows as an administrator.

Choose Start. Double-click My Computer. The My Computer window appears (see Figure 12-75).

Figure 12-75   My Computer Window

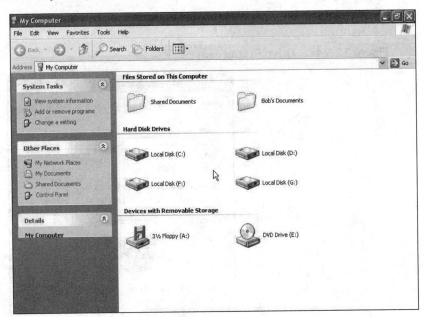

Step 2

Click the D: drive. The Disk Is Not Formatted window appears (see Figure 12-76).

Figure 12-76   Formatting an Unformatted Disk

Click Yes.

Step 3

The Format Local Disk (D:) window appears. Choose NTFS in the File System drop-down menu, and then click Start (see Figure 12-77).

Figure 12-77   Formatting a Partition

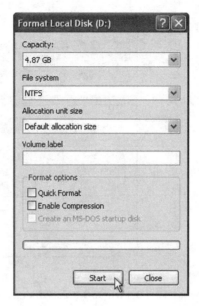

A warning window appears (see Figure 12-78).

Figure 12-78   Warning Specifying That All Data Will Be Erased if You Format a Partition

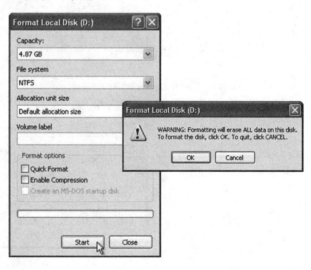

Click OK. The warning window closes, and Windows formats the drive.

When the Format Complete message appears, click OK (see Figure 12-79).

Figure 12-79   Format Complete

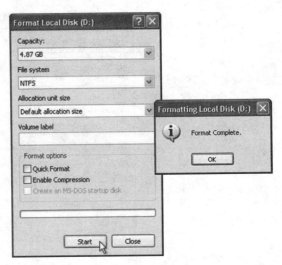

The Format Local Disk (D:) window reappears (see Figure 12-80). Click Close.

Figure 12-80   Format Program

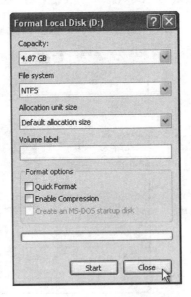

Step 4

Choose Start.

Right-click My Computer, and then click Properties (see Figure 12-81).

Figure 12-81   Opening the System Properties

The System Properties window appears (see Figure 12-82). Click the Advanced tab.

Figure 12-82   System Properties

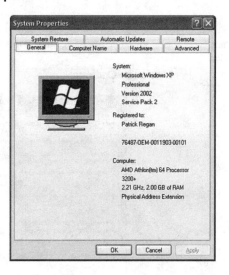

Click Settings in the Performance area (see Figure 12-83).

Figure 12-83   System Properties Advanced Tab

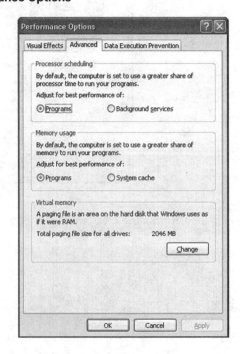

Step 5

The Performance Options window appears. Click the Advanced tab (see Figure 12-84).

Figure 12-84   Performance Options

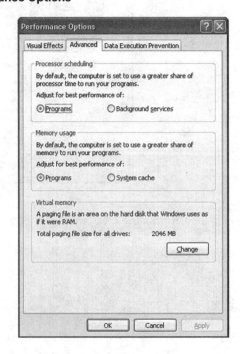

What is the current size of the Virtual Memory (paging file)?

Click Change in the Virtual Memory area (see Figure 12-85).

Figure 12-85   Configuring Virtual Memory

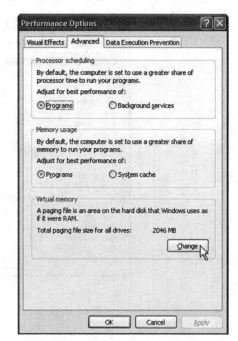

The Virtual Memory window appears (see Figure 12-86).

Figure 12-86   Configuring the Virtual Memory

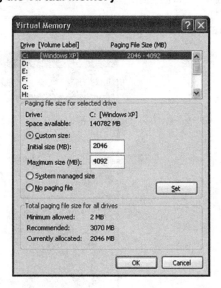

What Drive [Volume Label] contains the paging file?

_____

Choose the D: drive.

Click the Custom Size option button (see Figure 12-87).

Figure 12-87   Specifying the Custom Size

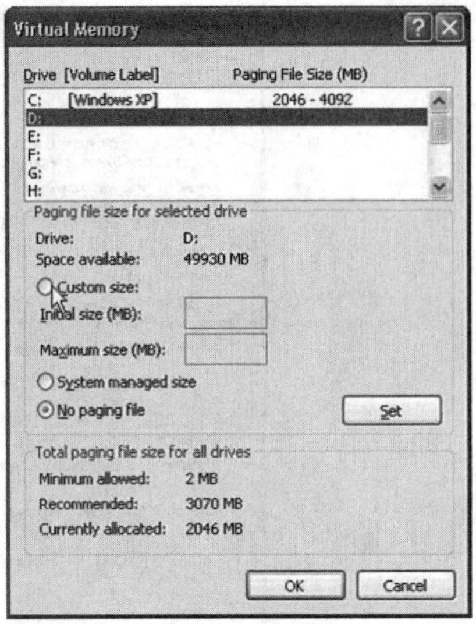

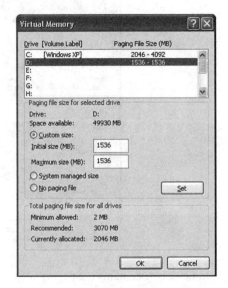

Look at the recommended size in the Total Paging File Size for All Drives section of the Virtual Memory window.

Type the recommended file size into the Initial Size (MB) field.

Type the recommended file size again into the Maximum Size (MB) field.

Click Set (see Figure 12-88).

Figure 12-88   Clicking the Set Button

Choose the C: drive.

Click the No Paging File option button, and then click Set (see Figure 12-89).

Figure 12-89   Changing Virtual Memory Settings

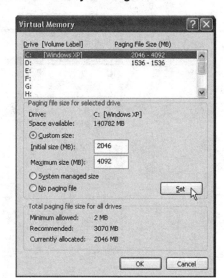

The System Control Panel Applet message window appears (see Figure 12-90).

Figure 12-90   Rebooting Windows After Virtual Memory Changes

Click OK.

The System Settings Change window appears. Click Yes to restart your computer now (see Figure 12-91).

Figure 12-91   Last Warning That the System Has to Be Restarted for the Changes to Take Effect

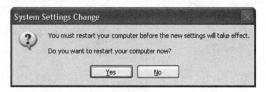

Step 6

Log on to Windows as an administrator.

Open the Virtual Memory window.

What Drive [Volume Label] contains the paging file?

Click Cancel (see Figure 12-92).

Figure 12-92   Closing Virtual Memory Without Changes

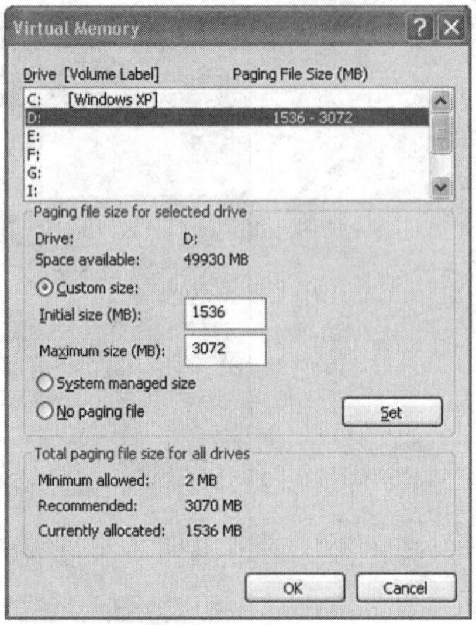

The Virtual Memory window closes (see Figure 12-93).

Figure 12-93   Performance Options

Click Cancel. The Performance Options window closes (see Figure 12-94).

Figure 12-94   System Properties

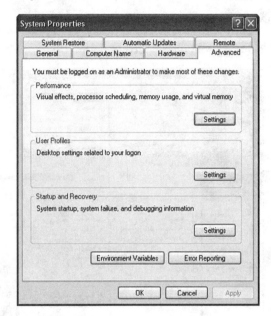

Click Cancel.

Step 7

Choose Start, All Programs, Games.

Right-click FreeCell (see Figure 12-95).

Figure 12-95   FreeCell Is Under the Games Programs

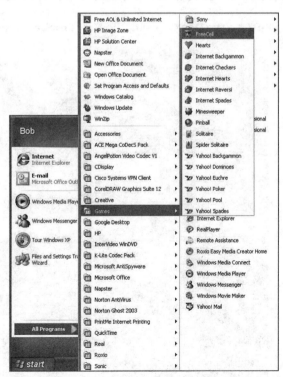

Choose Send To.

Choose Desktop (Create Shortcut) (see Figure 12-96).

Figure 12-96   Creating a Shortcut on the Desktop

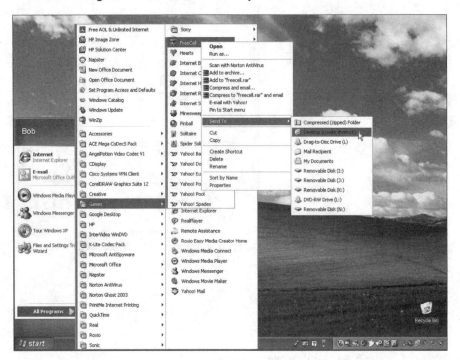

Step 8

Click and drag the Freecell to the Start button (see Figure 12-97).

Figure 12-97   The Desktop with the New FreeCell Shortcut

The Start Menu appears.

Do not release the shortcut icon. Drag the icon to All Programs.

The All Programs menu appears (see Figure 12-98).

Figure 12-98   The All Programs Menu

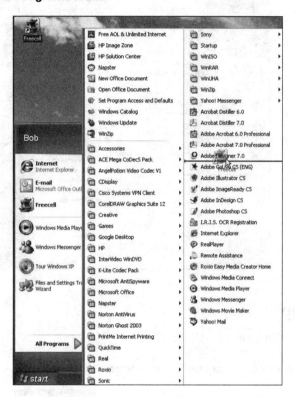

Drag the icon to Startup.

The Startup menu appears. Drag the icon to the Startup menu (see Figure 12-99).

Release the icon.

Figure 12-99 Adding a Program to the Startup Folder

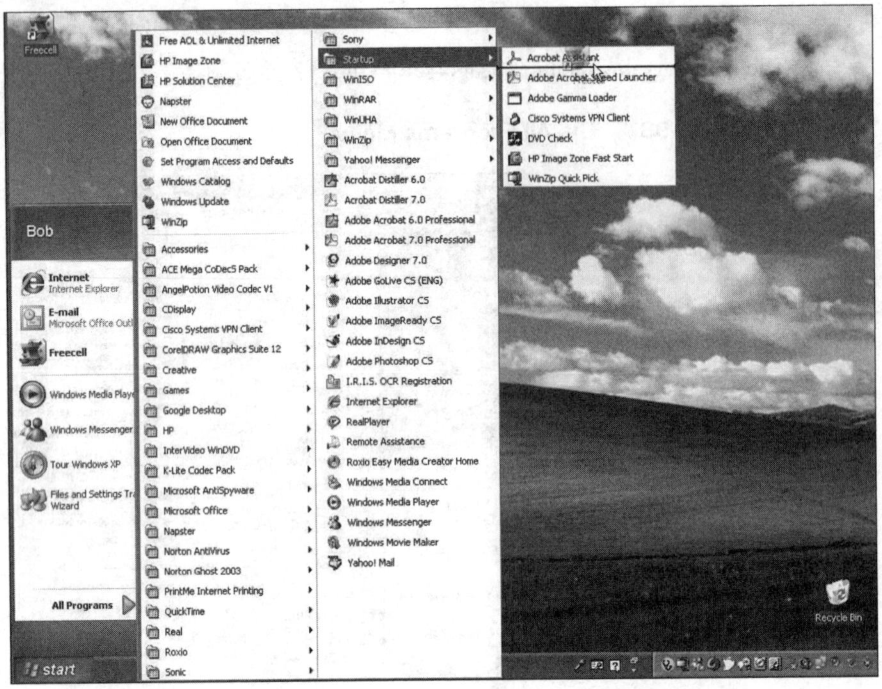

Step 9

Log off Windows (see Figure 12-100).

Figure 12-100 Logging Off Windows XP

Log on to Windows as an administrator.

What happens when you log in?

____

Close the Freecell application.

Step 10

Choose Start, Run.

Type **regedit** into the Open field (see Figure 12-101).

Figure 12-101   Using the Run Option to Start the Registry Editor

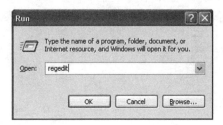

Caution: Incorrect changes to the Registry can cause system errors and/or system instability.

The Registry Editor window appears (see Figure 12-102).

Figure 12-102   Registry Editor

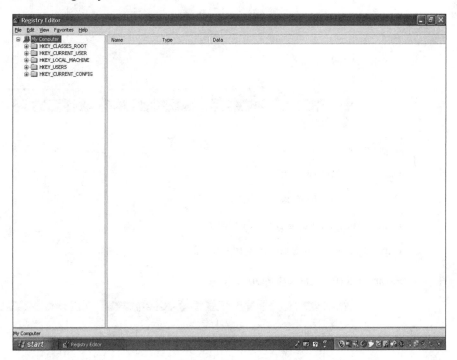

Expand the HKEY_CURRENT_USER key (see Figure 12-103).

Figure 12-103   HKEY_CURRENT_USER Key

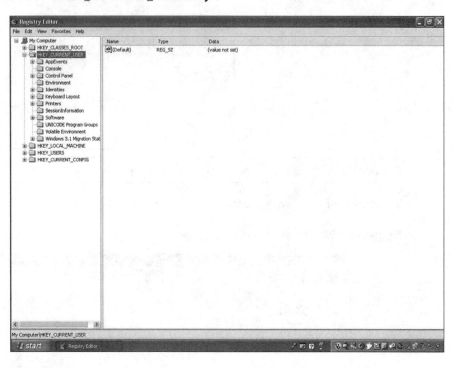

Expand the Software key.

Expand the Microsoft key.

Expand the Windows key.

Expand the CurrentVersion key.

Expand the RunOnce key (see Figure 12-104).

Figure 12-104   The RunOnce Key

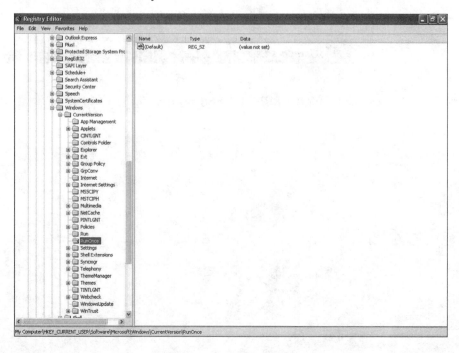

Right-click anywhere in the whitespace of the window.

Hover over New, and then select String Value (see Figure 12-105).

Figure 12-105   Creating a New String Value

Right-click New Value #1, and then choose Rename.

Type **Solitaire**, and then press Enter (see Figure 12-106).

Figure 12-106   Creating a String Key Called Solitaire

Right-click Solitaire, and then choose Modify (see Figure 12-107).

Figure 12-107   Modifying the Solitaire Key

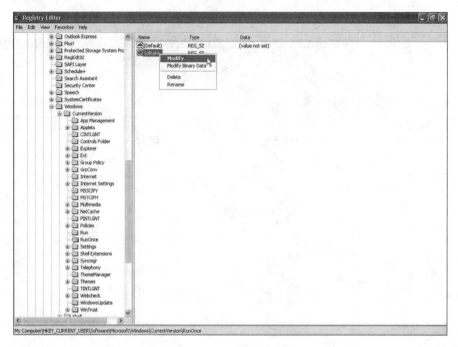

Type **C:\Windows\system32\sol.exe** into the Value Data field (see Figure 12-108).

Click OK.

Figure 12-108   Editing the String of a String Key

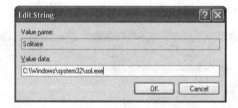

Close the Registry Editor window (see Figure 12-109).

Figure 12-109   Registry Editor

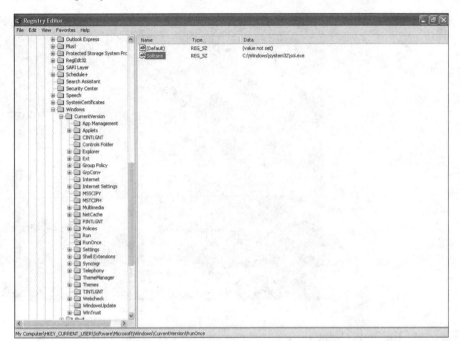

Step 11

Log off the computer (see Figure 12-110).

Figure 12-110   Logging Off Windows XP

Log on to Windows as an administrator (see Figure 12-111).

Figure 12-111 Logging On to Windows XP

The FreeCell and Solitaire windows appear (see Figure 12-112).

Figure 12-112 FreeCell and Solitaire Automatically Started Because of the Startup Folder and Registry Keys

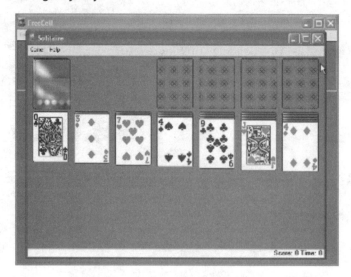

Close the Solitaire and Freecell windows.

Step 12

Choose Start, All Programs.

Right-click My Computer, and then choose Properties (see Figure 12-113).

Figure 12-113   Opening System Properties

Click the Automatic Updates tab.

Click the Download Updates for me, but Let Me Choose When to Install Them option button (see Figure 12-114).

Figure 12-114   Configuring Automatic Updates

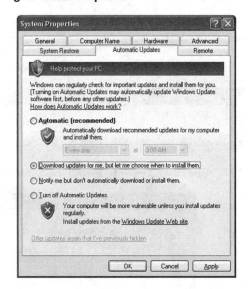

Click Apply, and then click OK (see Figure 12-115).

Figure 12-115   To Save the Changes, Click Apply

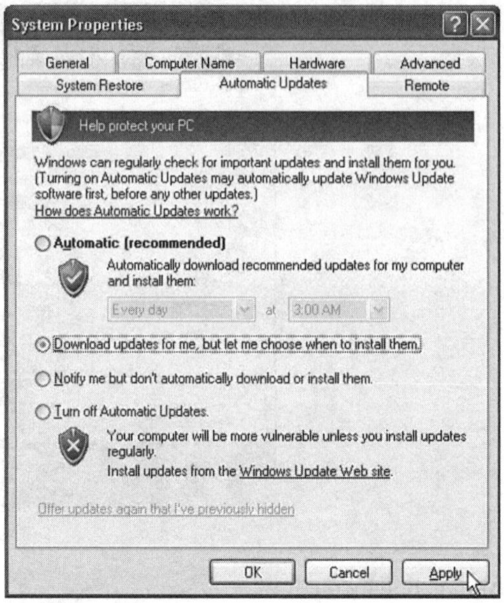

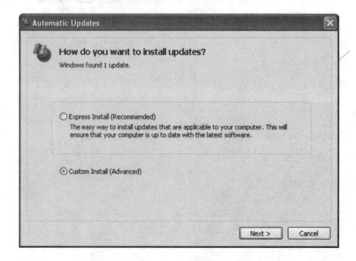

Step 13

Windows checks for updates.

The Updates Are Ready for Your Computer balloon appears. Double-click the shield icon in the system tray (see Figure 12-116).

Figure 12-116   Shield Indicating the Status of Updates

Click Custom Install (Advanced), and then click Next (see Figure 12-117).

Figure 12-117   Specifying How to Install the Updates

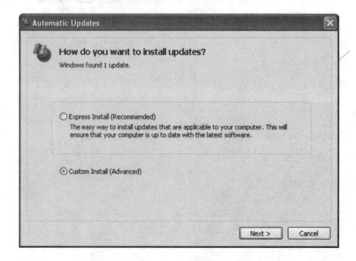

The Choose Updates to Install window appears. Click Install (see Figure 12-118).

Figure 12-118   Choosing Which Updates to Install

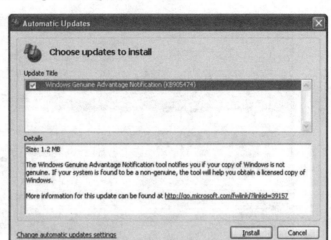

The Installing Updates balloon appears (see Figure 12-119).

Figure 12-119   Updates Are Installing

Lab 12.2.5: Install an Alternate Browser (Optional)

In this lab, you will install the Mozilla Firefox Web Browser.

The following is the recommended equipment for this lab:

- A computer running Windows XP Professional
- Internet access

Step 1

Choose Start, All Programs, Internet Explorer.

In the Address field, type **www.mozilla.com**.

Press Enter (see Figure 12-120).

Figure 12-120   www.mozilla.com Website

Step 2

Click the Download Firefox—Free link.

The File Download—Security Warning window appears (see Figure 12-121). Click Run.

Figure 12-121   Security Warning Verifying That You Want to Run or Download a Remote File

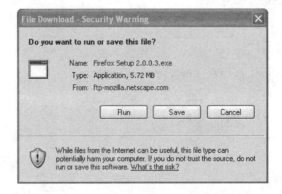

The Internet Explorer download window appears (see Figure 12-122).

Figure 12-122   Firefox Setup File Downloading

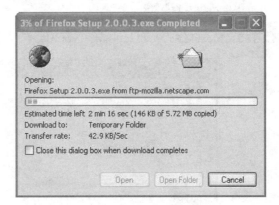

The Internet Explorer—Security Warning window may appear (see Figure 12-123). Click Run.

Figure 12-123   Security Warning Verifying That You Want to Run a Remote File

Step 3

The Mozilla Firefox Setup window appears (see Figure 12-124). Click Next.

Figure 12-124   Starting the Mozilla Firefox Setup Wizard

The License Agreement window appears. Click the I Accept the Terms in the License Agreement option button (see Figure 12-125).

Figure 12-125   Mozilla Firefox License Agreement

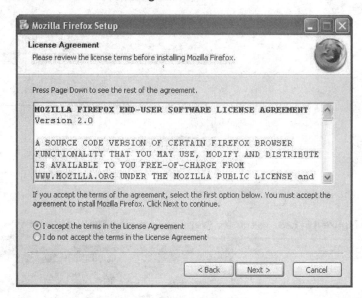

Click Next. The Setup Type window appears. The default is Standard (see Figure 12-126).

Figure 12-126   Mozilla Firefox Setup Type

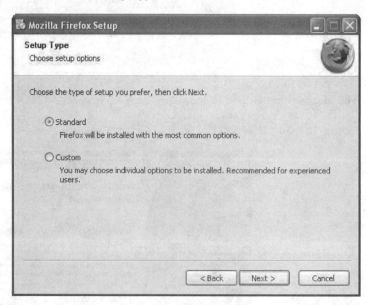

Click Next. The Installing window appears (see Figure 12-127).

Figure 12-127   Mozilla Firefox Installing

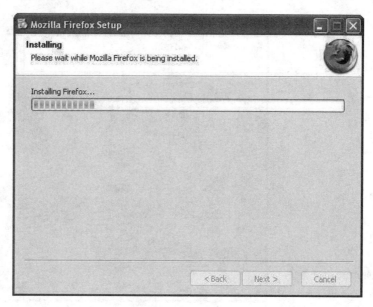

The Completing the Mozilla Firefox Setup Wizard window appears. The default is Launch Mozilla Firefox Now (see Figure 12-128). Click Finish.

Figure 12-128   Completing the Mozilla Firefox Setup Wizard

Step 4

The Import Wizard window appears. The default is Microsoft Internet Explorer (see Figure 12-129).

Figure 12-129   Importing Settings from Internet Explorer

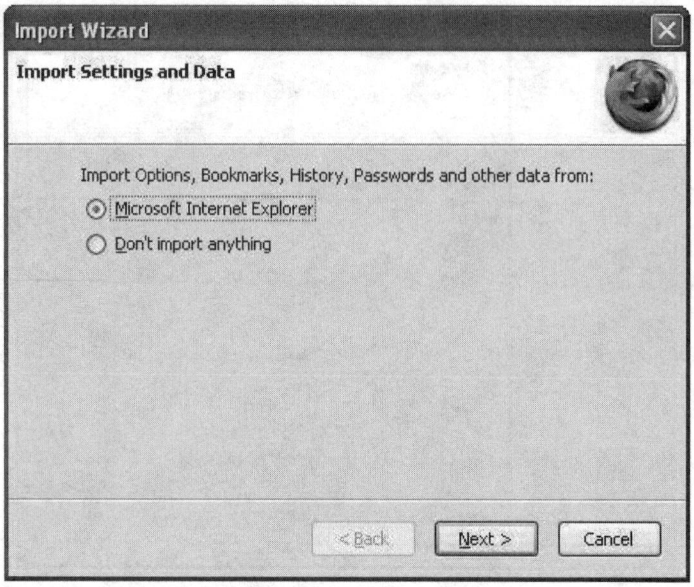

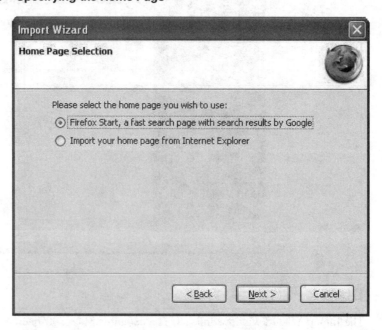

Click Next.

The Home Page Selection window appears. The default is Firefox Start, a Fast Search Page with Search Results by Google (see Figure 12-130).

Figure 12-130   Specifying the Home Page

Click Next. The Import Wizard window appears (see Figure 12-131).

Figure 12-131   Importing IE Settings

Step 5

The Welcome to Firefox—Mozilla Firefox window appears.

The Default Browser window appears. The default is Always Perform This Check When Starting Firefox (see Figure 12-132). Click No.

Figure 12-132   Specifying Whether You Want Firefox to Be the Default Browser

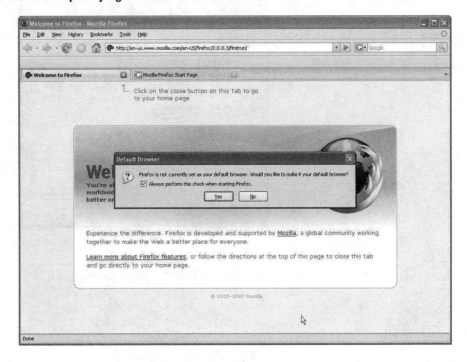

The Options window appears (see Figure 12-133). Click Browse.

Figure 12-133   Mozilla Firefox Options

The Browse for Folder window appears (see Figure 12-134).

Figure 12-134   Specifying Default Download Folder

Choose My Documents, and then click OK.

The Browse For Folder window closes. Click OK. Note the Mozilla Firefox icon on your desktop.

Lab 12.4.1: Schedule Task Using GUI and at Command

In this lab, you will schedule a task using the Windows XP GUI. You will schedule a task in a cmd window using the at command.

The recommended equipment is a computer running Windows XP Professional.

Step 1

Log on to Windows as an administrator.

Choose Start, Control Panel (see Figure 12-135).

Figure 12-135   Opening the Control Panel

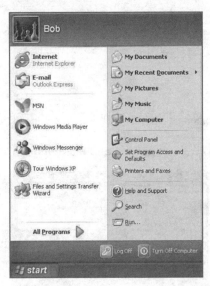

Step 2

The Control Panel window appears. Click Performance and Maintenance (see Figure 12-136).

Figure 12-136   Control Panel

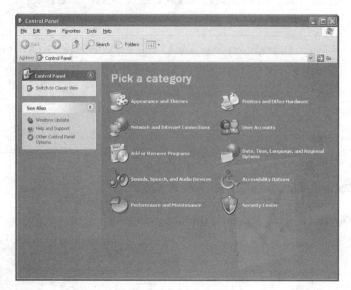

Step 3

The Performance and Maintenance window appears. Click Scheduled Tasks (see Figure 12-137).

Figure 12-137   Performance and Maintenance Window

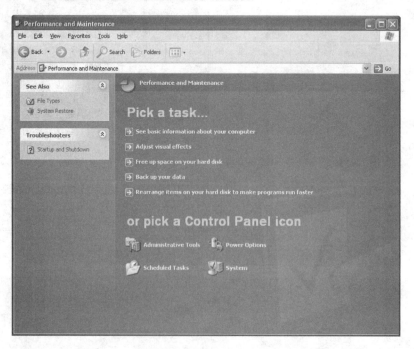

Step 4

The Scheduled Tasks window appears. Double-click Add Scheduled Task (see Figure 12-138).

Figure 12-138   Scheduled Tasks

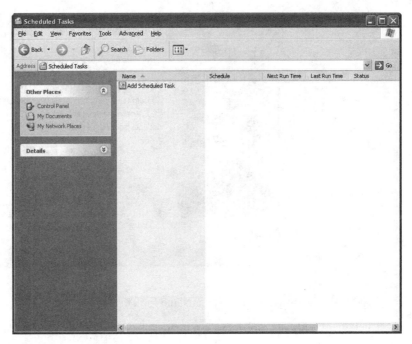

Step 5

The Scheduled Task Wizard appears (see Figure 12-139). Click Next.

Figure 12-139   Starting the Scheduled Task Wizard

Scroll down the Application window, and then select Disk Cleanup (see Figure 12-140).

Click Next.

Figure 12-140 **Selecting the Program to Schedule**

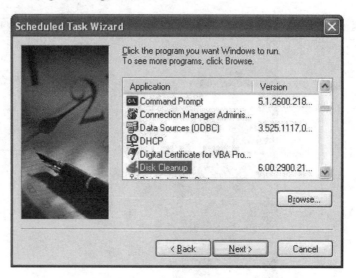

Type **Disk Cleanup** into the Type a Name for This Task field.

Click the Weekly option button, and then click Next (see Figure 12-141).

Figure 12-141 **Specifying How Often to Run the Task**

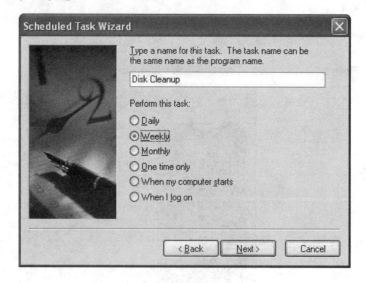

Use the scroll buttons in the Start Time field to select 6:00 PM.

Use the scroll buttons in the Every _ Weeks field to select 1.

Check the Wednesday check box, and then click Next (see Figure 12-142).

Figure 12-142   Specifying When to Run the Task

Enter your username and password into the appropriate fields (see Figure 12-143).

Figure 12-143   User Account and Password to Run the Task Under

Click Next. The You Have Successfully Scheduled the Following Task window appears (see Figure 12-144).

Figure 12-144   Finishing the Scheduled Task Wizard

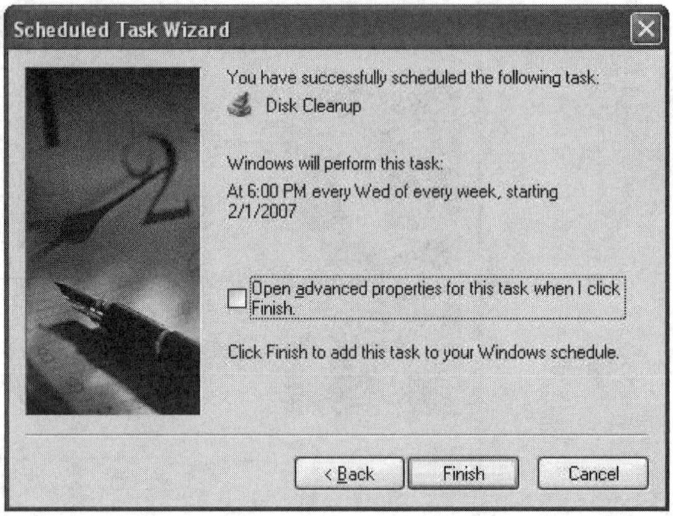

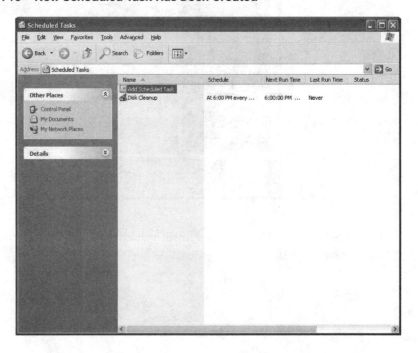

Click Finish.

Step 6

The scheduled task that you created appears in the Scheduled Tasks window (see Figure 12-145).

Figure 12-145   New Scheduled Task Has Been Created

Step 7

Choose Start, Run.

Type **cmd**, and then click OK. The C:\WINDOWS\System32\cmd.exe window appears (see Figure 12-146).

Figure 12-146   Opening a Command Prompt Using the Run Option

Type **at/?**, and then press Enter. The options for the at command are displayed (see Figure 12-147).

Figure 12-147   Looking at the at Command Options

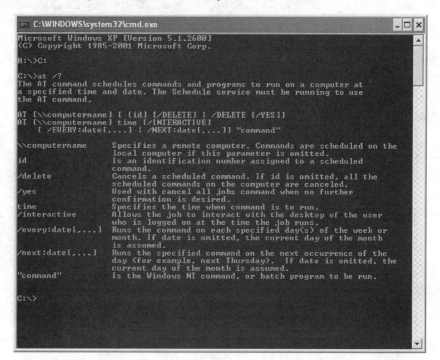

Type **at 20:00 /every:W backup**. Note that the time must be military time.

Added a New Job with Job ID = 1 is displayed (see Figure 12-148).

Figure 12-148   Running the at Command

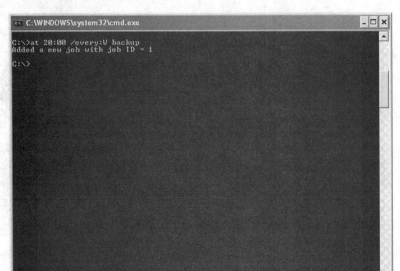

Type **at ***computername*; for example, at \\\\labcomputer. The scheduled job appears (see Figure 12-149).

Figure 12-149   Displaying the at Commands on a Network Computer

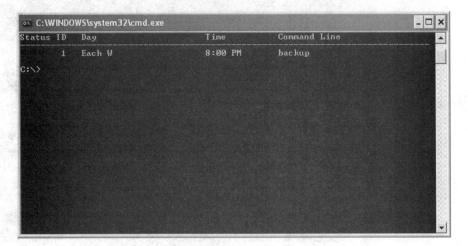

Which command would you enter to get the backup to run every Tuesday and Wednesday at 3:00 PM?

_____

Type **exit**, and then press the Return key.

Step 8

Open the Scheduled Tasks window. The task created using the **at** command is listed in the window (see Figure 12-150).

Figure 12-150   Scheduled Task

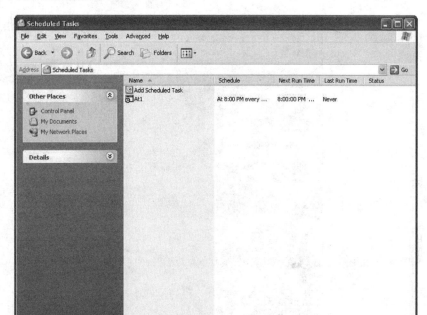

Step 9

Right-click your scheduled task.

Choose File, Delete. The Confirm File Delete window appears (see Figure 12-151).

Figure 12-151   Confirming to Delete a File

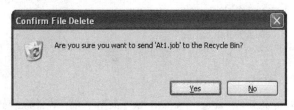

Click Yes. The task created using the **at** command is removed from the Scheduled Tasks window (see Figure 12-152).

Figure 12-152   New Scheduled Task Deleted

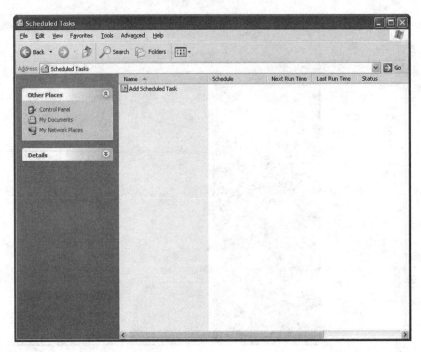

 ## Lab 12.5.3: Fix an Operating System Problem

In this lab, you will troubleshoot and fix a computer that does not connect to the network.

The following is the recommended equipment for this lab:

- A computer running Windows XP Professional
- Linksys 300N wireless router
- Ethernet patch cable

Scenario

The computer will not connect to the Internet, network shares, nor network printers.

Step 1

Open a command line and use command-line tools to determine the IP address, subnet mask, and default gateway of the computer.

Step 2

Use Windows tools to determine the status of the Ethernet NIC.

Step 3

Repair the Ethernet connection by restoring the computer.

Step 4

What steps did you perform to fix the network?

_____

_____

_____

_____

Remote Technician 12.5.3: Fix an Operating System Problem

(Student Technician Sheet)

In this lab, you will gather data from the customer, and then instruct the customer on how to fix a computer that does not connect to the network. Document the customer's problem in the work order that follows.

Company Name: _Main Street Stoneworks_
Contact: _Karin Jones_
Company Address: _4252 W. Main St._
Company Phone: _1-888-555-7744_

| **Work Order** |

Generating a New Ticket

Category _Operating System_   Closure Code _____   Status _Open_

Type _____   Escalated _Yes_   Pending _____

Item _____   Pending Until Date _____

Business Impacting?   ☒ Yes   ○ No

Summary _Customer cannot connect to the network or the Internet._
_____

Case ID# _____   Connection Type _Ethernet_
Priority _2_   Environment _____
User Platform _Windows XP Pro_

Problem Description: _Computer boots correctly. Network cable connected. Link lights_
not working. Network icon not visible in tray.
_____
_____
_____

Problem Solution: _____
_____
_____
_____

(Student Customer Sheet)

Use the contact information and problem description to report the following information to a level-two technician:

Contact Information

Company Name: Main Street Stoneworks

Contact: Karin Jones

Company Address: 4252 W. Main St.

Company Phone: 1-888-555-7744

Problem Description

When I came into the office today, I could not get my e-mail. The Internet does not work either. I tried to restart my computer, but that did not help. None of the files that I need are available to me, either. It is like someone pulled the plug, but the plug is still there. I need to get some files from my folder that I was working on yesterday. It is very important for me to get my files so that I can send them to my client. I do not know how to get the files or send them because my computer cannot find them. What do I do?

Note: After you have given the level-two tech the problem description, use the Additional Information to answer any follow-up questions the technician may ask.

Additional Information

Windows XP Pro.

Computer has not had any new hardware installed recently.

There is no wireless network available at work.

Computer detected new hardware at boot.

Computer could not install new hardware.

CHAPTER 13

Advanced Laptops and Portable Devices

The Study Guide portion of this chapter uses a combination of fill-in-the-blank and open-ended questions to test your introductory knowledge of laptops and portable devices. This portion also includes multiple-choice study questions to help prepare you to take the A+ certification exams and to test your overall understanding of the material.

The Lab Exercises portion of this chapter includes all the online curriculum worksheets to further reinforce your mastery of the laptop and portable devices content.

Study Guide

Processors and RAM

To select the right laptop or notebook computer, you generally will choose the appropriate processor and RAM. Of course, you need to know the differences between processors and RAM that you find in desktop computers and laptop/notebook computers.

Concept Questions

Answer the following questions about processors and RAM:

How do mobile processors conserve power over desktop processors?

They use a technology called CPU Throttling.

What technology do mobile processors use to balance power consumption and performance?

Advanced configuration & Power interface

What type of memory do laptops and notebook computers use?

small outline Dual Inline Memory Modules

Expansion Cards

Much like processors and RAM, the expansion cards used in laptop and notebook computers are different from what you will typically find in desktop computers. Therefore, you need to easily identify them, know the characteristics of these cards, and know how to operate them.

Concept Questions

Answer the following questions about expansion cards:

Today, what are PCMCIA cards called?

Complete the following table with the correct information about PC Cards.

Form Factor	Width (in)	Depth (in)	Height (in)	Application
PC Card Type I	-	3.3mm		SRAM Flash
PC Card Type II		5 mm		NIC, WiFi
PC Card Type III		10.5mm		HDD

What is CardBus?

_____

_____

Mobile Wireless Devices

Over the past few years, wireless technology has become standard in just about every laptop and note-book computer. As the technology matures and new technology is introduced, you will often have to install and configure mobile wireless devices.

Concept Questions

Answer the following questions about mobile wireless devices:

Complete the following table with the correct information about wireless devices.

Class	Maximum Permitted Power (milliwatt mW)	Distance (feet)	Distance (meters)
Class 1	100 mW		100m
Class 2	2.5 mW		10m
Class 3	1 mW		1m

What class are most wireless Bluetooth network devices?

Class 2

When connecting to a Bluetooth device, what do you need to authenticate?

_____

On what wireless frequency do Bluetooth devices operate?

2.45GHz

What are some of the limitations of using infrared wireless devices?

- _Speed of data transfer_
- _Short ranges_

_____

- _Need a clear unobstructed view between devices._

_____

On what IEEE standard is Wi-Fi based?

_802.11_

Complete the following table with the correct information about wireless technology standards.

Standard	Data Rate (Max)	Range (in feet)	Range (in meters)
802.11a	54 Mbps		45.7m
802.11b	11 Mbps		91m
802.11g	54 Mbps		91m
802.11n	540 Mbps		250 m

What popular standards are used to actually secure Wi-Fi networks?

Wired Equivalent Privacy WEP

Wi-Fi Protected Access WPA

If your wireless device is configured to operate at 2.4 GHz and your wireless phone operates at 2.4 GHz, what would happen?

There would be radio interference

Batteries

Because laptop and notebook computers are meant to be portable, you often need to use batteries to power them. Therefore, you need to understand how batteries are being used in a laptop or notebook computer and know how to differentiate between the types of batteries.

Vocabulary Exercise: Completion

Fill in the blanks with the appropriate terms about batteries:

Nickel-Cadmium (NiCad) batteries suffer from memory effect; if they are partially drained and then recharged, they lose about 40% of their charge.

Nickel Metal-Hydride (NiMh) batteries store about 50% more power than _____ batteries.

Lithium-Ion (Li-Ion) batteries offer the _____ electrochemical potential.

Lithium-Ion Polymer (Li-Poly) batteries are usually found in _PDA's_ and _Laptops_

Concept Questions

Answer the following questions about batteries.

What should you occasionally do with NiCad and NiMH rechargeable batteries to maintain the best charge?

Totally discharge to remove the battery memory when the battery is completely discharged, it should then be charged to maximum capacity.

What could happen if you mishandle batteries, including inserting Li-Ion batteries into a system designed for a NiCad or NiMH battery?

If the battery does not fully charge, what are the steps to overcome the problem?

_____

_____

_____

_____

_____

_____

Mobile Video Systems

Like other mobile components found in laptop and notebook computers, the video systems are different from their desktop counterparts. Therefore, you need to understand these differences to successfully configure and troubleshoot mobile video systems.

Concept Questions

Answer the following questions about mobile video systems:

If you have a laptop computer that has 1 GB of RAM, and you are using 64 MB of shared video memory, how much memory is available for Windows?

936 MB

If nothing is displayed on a notebook computer LCD monitor, what are some of the things you should check to troubleshoot the problem?

- Toggle the Function key in case laptop is set to use external monitor
- Check power to laptop
- Laptop may be in hibernation/standby power-saving modes
- _____
- _____
- _____

If the image on your LCD panel is very dim, what should you do to troubleshoot this problem?

- Swap the laptop to AC power
- Adjust brightness controls
- _____

Study Questions

Choose the best answer for each of the questions that follow.

1. What technology will users most likely use on today's laptop or notebook computer if they want to directly print to a printer, assuming that the mobile computer and printer have such equipment?

    A. SCSI

    B. 802.11b

    C. IEEE 1396

    D. Bluetooth

2. What is used to connect a wireless keyboard and mouse to a laptop computer?

    A. Bluetooth

    B. 802.11b

    C. IEEE 1396

    D. Microwaves

3. How would a user check to make sure that the AC power pack is supplying the correct DC voltage?

    A. Use a multimeter to measure the voltage.

    B. Use the LED lights on the AC adapter.

    C. Use the LED lights on the DC adapter.

    D. You cannot tell.

4. Which of the following batteries are not recommended for mobile computers because of short battery life and memory effect?

    A. Nickel Metal-Hydride (NiMH)

    B. Nickel Cadmium (NiCD)

    C. Nickel-Lithium (Ni-Li)

    D. Lithium-Ion (Li-Ion)

5. Which two devices are considered hot swappable on a mobile computer?

    A. A hard drive.

    B. Processor

    C. Memory.

    D. USB device

    E. A modular DVD drive.

6. What is the thickness of a Type II PC card?

    A. 0.13 inches (3.3 millimeters)

    B. 0.40 inches (10 millimeters)

    C. 0.20 inches (5 millimeters)

    D. 0.50 inches (12 millimeters)

7. Today, PCMCIA cards are known as _____.

   A. PC cards

   B. Smart cards

   C. Mini-PCI cards

   D. Mini-PCX cards

8. If you are to perform hardware maintenance on a mobile computer, what should you do before opening the system?

   A. Remove the keyboard.

   B. Remove the power supply cable and battery pack.

   C. Close the LCD panel.

   D. Remove the CMOS battery.

9. If you install 768 MB of RAM and you have 64 MB of shared video memory, how much memory is available for the operating system?

   A. 256 MB

   B. 448 MB

   C. 512 MB

   D. 704 MB

10. How do you toggle between your LCD panel and an external monitor?

    A. Device Manager.

    B. Use the Fn keys on the keyboard.

    C. Press the Ctrl+Tab keys.

    D. Use the Mobile Management console.

11. What is the problem when the images on the LCD panel are so dim that you can barely see that they are there?

    A. The power adapter is faulty.

    B. The inverter board is faulty.

    C. The video adapter is faulty.

    D. The laptop has overheated.

Lab Exercises

Worksheet 13.2.0: Investigating Repair Centers

For this worksheet, you will investigate the services provided by a computer repair center. Use the Internet or a local phone directory to locate a repair center. After you have found a repair center, use the center's website to obtain information and answer the following questions. If a website is not available, contact the local repair center.

1. What laptop and desktop computers can be repaired at this repair center?

_____

2. What type of warranty is offered at this repair center?

_____

_____

_____

3. Does the staff have industry certifications? If so, what are the certifications?

_____

_____

4. Is there a guaranteed completion time for repairs? If so, what are the details?

_____

_____

5. Does the repair center offer remote technical services?

_____

Worksheet 13.3.1: Laptop Batteries

In this activity, you will use the Internet, a newspaper, or a local store to gather information and then enter the specifications for a laptop battery onto this worksheet.

1. List the specifications for a(n) _____ laptop battery. (Please ask your instructor for the laptop model to research.)

_____

_____

_____

_____

2. Shop around, and in the following table list the features and cost for a generic and a(n) _____ laptop battery.

Battery Specifications	Generic
Voltage requirements	
Battery cell configuration For example: 6-Cell, 9-Cell	
Compatibility	
Dimensions	
Hours of life	
Approximate cost	

3. Based on your research, which battery would you select? Be prepared to discuss your decisions regarding the battery you select.

Worksheet 13.3.2: Docking Station

In this activity, you will use the Internet, a newspaper, or a local store to gather information and then enter the specifications for a laptop docking station onto this worksheet. Be prepared to discuss your decisions regarding the docking station you select.

1. Research a docking station compatible with a(n) _____ laptop. (Please ask your instructor for the laptop model to research.) What is the model number of the docking station?

2. What is the approximate cost?

3. What are the dimensions of the docking station?

4. How does the laptop connect to the docking station?

5. List the features available with this docking station.

_____

_____

_____

_____

_____

_____

_____

_____

6. Is this docking station compatible with other laptop models?

_____

Worksheet 13.3.3: Research DVD Drive

In this activity, you will use the Internet, a newspaper, or a local store to gather information about DVD rewritable (DVD/RW) drives for a(n) _____ laptop. (Please ask your instructor for the laptop model to research.)

Shop around, and in the following table list the features and costs for an internal DVD/RW drive and an external DVD/RW drive.

	Internal DVD/RW Drive	External DVD/RW Drive
Connection Type		
Write Speed		
Cost		

1. List the advantages of an internal drive.

_____

_____

2. List the advantages of an external drive.

_____

3. Which DVD drive would you purchase based on your research? Write a brief explanation supporting your answer.

_____

Worksheet 13.3.4: Laptop RAM

In this activity, you will use the Internet, a newspaper, or a local store to gather information about expansion memory for a(n) _____ laptop. (Please ask your instructor for the laptop model to research.)

1. Research the manufacturer specifications for the memory in the _____. List the specifications in the following table:

Memory Specifications	Laptop Expansion Memory
Form Factor	
Type	
Size (MB)	
Manufacturer	
Speed	
Slots	

2. Shop around, and in the following table list the features and costs for expansion memory for a(n) _____.

Memory Specifications	Expansion Memory
Form Factor	
Type	
Size (MB)	
Manufacturer	
Speed	
Retail Cost	

3. In your research, did you find any reason to select a particular type of expansion memory over another?

_____

4. Is the new expansion memory compatible with the existing memory installed in the laptop? Why is this important?

_____

_____

Worksheet 13.5.3: Verify Work Order Information

In this worksheet, a level-two call center technician will find creative ways to verify information that the level-one tech has documented in the work order.

A customer complains that the network connection on the laptop is intermittent. The customer states that he is using a wireless PC card for network connectivity. The customer believes that the laptop may be too far from the wireless access point; however, he does not know where the wireless access point is located.

As a level-two technician, you need to be able to verify information from the work order without repeating the same questions previously asked by the level-one technician. In the following table, reword the level-one technician's question with a new question or direction for the customer.

Level-One Tech	Level-Two Tech
What are the problems that you are experiencing with the laptop?	
What is the manufacturer and model of the laptop?	
Which operating system is installed on the laptop?	
How is the laptop getting power?	
What were you doing when the problem occurred?	
Were there any system changes on the laptop recently?	
Does your laptop have a wireless network connection?	
Is your PC Card installed securely?	
How much RAM does your laptop have?	

CHAPTER 14

Advanced Printers and Scanners

The Study Guide portion of this chapter uses short-answer questions to test your knowledge of printers and scanners. This portion also includes multiple-choice study questions to help prepare you to take the A+ certification exams and to test your overall understanding of the material.

The Lab Exercises portion of this chapter includes all the online curriculum hands-on labs, worksheets, and remote technician exercises to further reinforce your mastery of the advanced printer and scanner content.

Study Guide

Printer Technology and Interfaces

Before you can learn how to install, configure, and troubleshoot printers, you must understand the different types of printers and how they work. You also need to understand the interfaces that you use to connect printers to a local PC or network and their limitations.

Concept Questions

Answer the following printer questions:

Which interface is the slowest interface used by older printers?

Serial Data Transfer

What is the maximum length of an IEEE 1284 parallel cable?

15 feet

What is the most common interface used in today's modern small office/home office printers?

USB

Which type of printers use a print head?

Dot Matrix

What is the central part of the laser printer?

Fuser Assembly

For which printer do you need special paper to print?

Thermal Printer

Page Description Languages (PDL) are the languages that printers use to format and print text and graphics. What are the three primary PDLs used?

Printer Command language (PCL)

Post Script (PS)

Graphics Device interface (GDI)

How can you increase the performance of a color laser printer?

Install more memory

Troubleshooting Printers

Although printers are easy to install, they can cause all sorts of headaches. Any problem that occurs with a printer has one of four sources: the printer, the print cable, the interface, or the software (including drivers).

Concept Questions

Answer the following questions about troubleshooting printers.

What are the different ways that you can print a test page?

Using the Print Test Page option from the Printer

Using the Print Test Page option from Windows

Using the print function of an application

Sending a file directly to a parallel port printer using the command line.

A paper jam is a sheet of paper catching or refusing to pass through the printer mechanism. What are the causes of a paper jam?

Paper dust caued 'paper dander' tends to build up where paper is bent around rollers which can cause the rollers to slip or jam.

When turning knobs and wheels within the printer, what do you need to do?

Turn printer off and unplug it

If you print and nothing happens, what should you do?

- check printer is on
- Check printer is connected
- Check printer is online
- Check printer has paper & that it is correct size

If printer still does not print check spooler status and delete pending job & try again

What do you do if the printer prints garbage (strange characters or many pages of what appears to be programming code)?

Check that the correct driver is being used.
Uninstall & re-install driver.

What do you do if you print and the document print is light?

Check ink levels
Alter the quality of print

Printing in Windows

So far, the emphasis has been on the three sources of problems: the printer, the printer cable, and the interface. This section deals with the software that provides an interface to interact with and as a translator between the documents you create on the computer and the language that the printer understands.

Concept Questions

Answer the following questions about printing in Windows.

What technology automatically loads the driver when a printer is connected to a Windows XP computer?

PnP utility

When connecting to a network printer, where can Windows 2000 or Windows XP get the driver?

Network Print Server Device

If documents become stuck in the print queue, what should you do?

Delete affected job and try again

What command do you use to restart the print spooler service for Windows 2000 and Windows XP computers?

What is the process to install print drivers in Windows XP?

1. *Determine the current version of the installed printer driver. Seek newer version to increase functionality*

2. *Search Internet to locate the most recent version of the driver.*

3. *Download the driver*

4. *Install the driver*

5. *Test the driver Start > Settings > Printers and Faxes Right Click the printer and choose properties. Then choose Print Test Page.*

Scanners

Earlier in this book, you looked at what a scanner is and how you connect a scanner to the computer. Because scanners are not as popular as printers, there is a little bit more mystery when troubleshooting scanners. Yet, if you understand how they work, you will apply a lot of the same troubleshooting techniques that you used in other devices that you connect to a computer.

Concept Questions

Answer the following questions about scanners.

What is the most common standard for scanners?

USB

If a scanner is not being detected, what should you check?

Check that the Scanner is switched on and that the USB port supports the speed you need for the Scanner

What happens if the glass on the scanner becomes dirty or scratched?

use a glass cleaner and soft cloth to clean the glass.

Study Questions

Choose the best answer for each of the questions that follow:

1. What type of printer uses a toner and drum?

    A. Laser printers ✓
    B. Inkjet printers
    C. Thermal printers
    D. Dot-matrix printers

2. What is the most common standard for scanners?

    A. RAW
    B. JPG
    C. TWAIN
    D. PNG

3. What type of cable is used in parallel ports?

    A. RS-232c
    B. IEEE 1284 ✓
    C. IEEE 1394
    D. IEEE 802.11g

4. What do you need to do if documents seemed to be stuck in the Windows print queue?

    A. Restart the print spooler service.
    B. Delete the oldest print job. ✓
    C. Delete files on the C drive.
    D. Reboot the computer.

5. What are ECP and EPP printers associated with?

    A. Parallel ports
    B. Serial ports
    C. FireWire
    D. 802.11b

6. What will adding memory to your laser printer do?

    A. It will usually increase performance. ✓
    B. It will allow you to print graphics.
    C. It will allow you to print color.
    D. It will allow you to print PostScript documents.

7. If the images on a freshly printed document seem to rub off or flake off, what do you need to check?

    A. The pickup rollers
    B. The fuser assembly
    C. The paper that is being used
    D. The corona wire
    E. The toner cartridge

8. You install a second printer on a user's Windows XP computer. However, every time the user prints, it prints to the first printer. What do you need to do to make it print to the second printer?

    A. Remove the old printer.
    B. Set the new printer as the default printer. ✓
    C. Reinstall the new print driver.
    D. Remove and reinstall the new printer. When you run the wizard, select the printer as the default printer.

9. When troubleshooting a scanner problem, what should you do first?

    A. Check to see whether the scanner has ever worked.
    B. Check all cables to the scanner.
    C. Make sure that the scanner is turned on.
    D. Make sure that the drivers are loaded.

10. When you print a document, you get a lot of strange characters. What do you need to check first?

    A. Check for a loose cable.
    B. Check to see if the printer is running in the right mode.
    C. Make sure that the correct printer driver is loaded. ✓
    D. Make sure that the toner cartridge is full.

Lab Exercises

 Lab 14.2.4: Install an All-in-One Printer/Scanner

In this lab, you will check the Windows XP Hardware Compatibility List (HCL) for the Epson Stylus CX7800, install the all-in-one printer/scanner, upgrade the driver and any associated software, and test the printer and scanner.

The following is the recommended equipment for this lab:

- A computer with the Windows XP Professional operating system
- An available USB port on the computer
- An Epson Stylus CX7800 printer/scanner
- Printer/scanner installation CD
- An Internet connection

Step 1

Open Internet Explorer.

Search the Microsoft website for "windows xp professional hcl."

Choose Windows XP.

Choose Devices.

Choose the processor type used by the computer.

Select Printers & Scanners.

Choose Start.

Search the HCL for Epson Stylus CX7800.

What company manufactures this component?

_____

For what operating system(s) was this component designed?

_____

For what operating system(s) has this component been certified?

_____

_____

_____

Step 2

Carefully unpack and assemble the printer/scanner if necessary. Follow the manufacturer's instructions.

Plug in the printer/scanner to a grounded wall outlet and turn on the unit. Do not attach the USB cable to the computer until instructed to do so.

Step 3

Insert the manufacturer's software CD into the optical drive. If the installation program does not start automatically, select Start, My Computer, and then double-click the Epson CD-ROM icon.

The Install Menu window appears (see Figure 14-1).

Figure 14-1   Epson Stylus CX7800 Series Install Menu

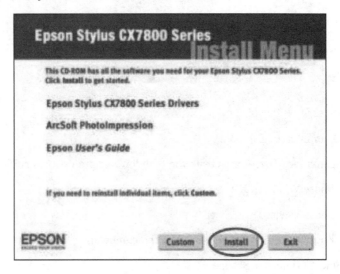

Click Install.

Connect the USB cable when instructed (see Figure 14-2).

Figure 14-2   Prompting to Connect the USB Cable to the Computer

The License Agreement window appears (see Figure 14-3).

Figure 14-3   ArcSoft License Agreement

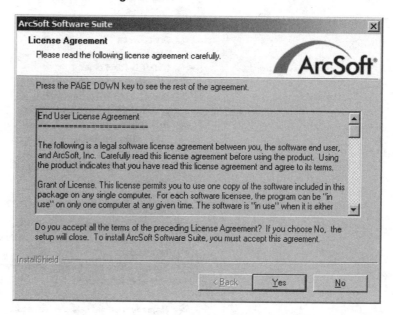

Click Yes. The Epson Product Registration window appears (see Figure 14-4).

Click Cancel.

Figure 14-4   Epson Product Registration

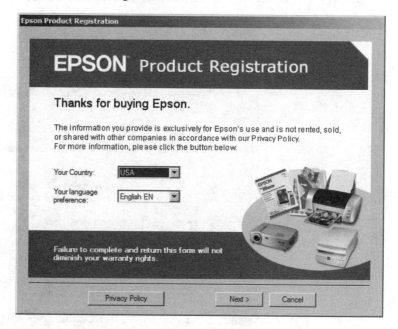

Step 4

Go to the Epson website and download the newest drivers for the Epson Stylus CX 7800.

Click Start, and then right-click My Computer. Choose Manage, Device Manager. The Device Manager appears in the right column (see Figure 14-5).

Figure 14-5   Device Manager Tree

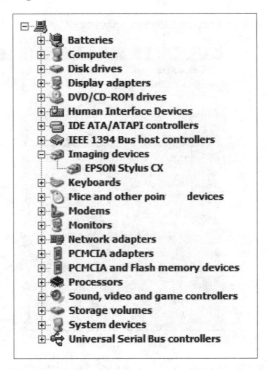

Double-click the Epson Stylus CX, and then select the Driver tab (see Figure 14-6).

Figure 14-6   Driver Tab for the Epson Stylus CX Found in Device Manager

Choose Update Driver.

Follow the instructions to install the driver that was downloaded.

Choose Start, Printers and Faxes (see Figure 14-7).

Figure 14-7   Printer and Faxes Window Showing the Available Configured Printers

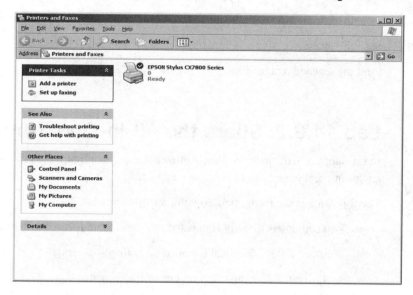

Right-click Epson Stylus and then click Properties (see Figure 14-8).

Figure 14-8   Epson Stylus CX7800 Series Properties

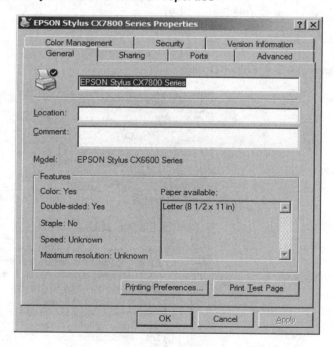

Click the Print Test Page button.

Step 5

Place a picture or document face down in the upper-left corner of the scanner.

Double-click the Epson Scan icon on the desktop or open the Epson SmartPanel using the Start menu.

Scan the image.

Print the scanned image.

Lab 14.3.2: Share the All-in-One Printer/Scanner

In this lab, you will share the Epson printer/scanner, configure the printer on a networked computer, and print a test page from the remote computer.

The following is the recommended equipment for this lab:

- Two computers directly connected or connected through a hub or switch
- Windows XP Professional installed on both computers
- An Epson CX7800 installed on one of the computers

Step 1

Click My Computer, Tools, Folder Options, View, and then uncheck Use Simple File Sharing (Recommended) (see Figure 14-9).

Click OK.

Figure 14-9   Folder Options

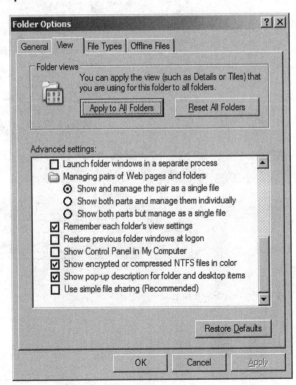

Step 2

Choose Start, Printers and Faxes.

Right-click Epson CX7800, and then choose Properties.

Click the Sharing tab (see Figure 14-10).

Figure 14-10   Printer Sharing Tab

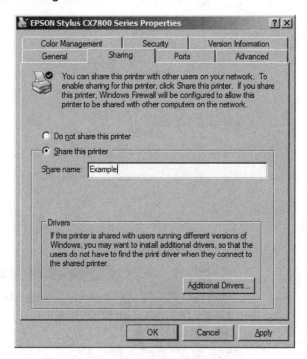

Choose Share This Printer. Name the new share Example, and then click Apply.

Click OK.

Step 3

Log on to the computer without the printer/scanner connected, and then choose Start, Printers and Faxes (see Figure 14-11).

Figure 14-11   Empty Printers and Faxes Folder

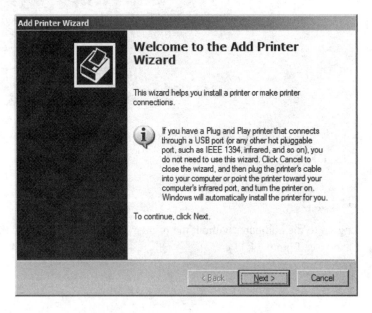

Click Add a Printer. The Add Printer Wizard window appears (see Figure 14-12).

Figure 14-12   Welcome to the Add Printer Wizard

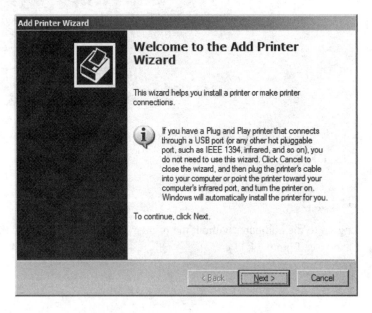

Click Next. The Local or Network Printer window appears (see Figure 14-13).

Figure 14-13   Specifying Whether the Printer Is a Local Printer or a Network Printer

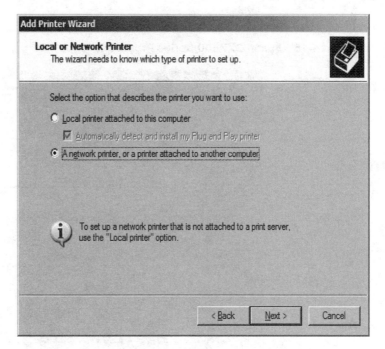

Click the A Network Printer, or a Printer Attached to Another Computer option button, and then click Next.

Type ***computername**printer*** into the Connect to This Printer (or to Browse for a Printer, Select This Option and click Next) option button, where *computername* is the name of the computer with the connected printer/scanner and *printer* is the name of the printer/scanner (see Figure 14-14).

Figure 14-14   Connecting to a Networked Shared Printer

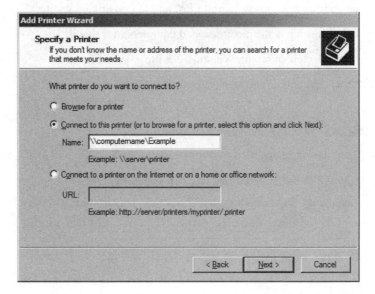

Step 4

Choose Start, Printers and Faxes.

Right-click Epson Stylus, and then choose Properties (see Figure 14-15).

Click the Print Test Page button.

Figure 14-15   Epson CX7800 Series Properties

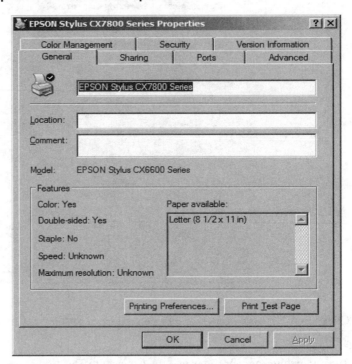

 # Lab 14.4.2: Optimize Scanner Output

In this lab, you will scan a picture at two levels of DPI. The results will be displayed and compared on your monitor, as two saved files, and as two printed images.

The following is the recommended equipment for this lab:

- A computer with Windows XP Professional installed
- Epson CX7800 printer/scanner installed

Step 1

Scan the image supplied by your instructor at 300 DPI, and then save it as a file named SCAN1.

Right-click the SCAN1 file, and then select Properties.

What is the size of the image?

_____

Print the image.

Step 2

Scan the same image at 72 DPI, and then save it as a file named SCAN2.

Right-click the SCAN2 file, and then select Properties.

What is the size of the image?

_____

Print the image.

Step 3

Did it take longer to scan SCAN2 than it did to scan SCAN1?

_____

Why?

_____

Step 4

Is there a difference between the sizes of the image files?

_____

Why?

_____

Step 5

Open both image files.

Which image, in your opinion, looks better?

_____

Which of the printed images, in your opinion, looks better?

_____

Step 6

What DPI setting would work best when scanning an image to be used on a website?

_____

Why did you choose this DPI setting?

_____

Which DPI setting would work best when printing an image?

_____

Why did you choose this DPI setting?

_____

_____

Worksheet 14.5.1: Search for Certified Printer Technician Jobs

In this activity, you will use the Internet to gather information about becoming a certified printer technician.

In the following table, list the name of three printer manufacturers, any certification programs available, the required skills of the certification, and the make and model of the printers that require a certified technician. An example has been provided for you. Be prepared to discuss your answers.

Printer Manufacturer	Certification Programs	Required Skills	Printer Make/Model
HP	Accredited Platform Specialist (APS): HP LaserJet Solutions HP Designjet Solutions	Fundamental architectures and technologies of electro photographic printers. Troubleshooting of LaserJet products and solutions. Drivers. LaserJet components fundamentals.	All

Lab 14.6.3: Fix a Printer

In this lab, you will troubleshoot and fix a printer that does not print documents for a user.

The following is the recommended equipment for this lab:

- At least two computers running Windows XP Professional

- All-in-one printer connected and installed on one of the computers

- All-in-one printer installed as a network printer on other computer(s)

- Computers networked using switch, hub, or wireless router

Scenario

The printer will not print documents for a user.

Step 1

Verify printer hardware.

Step 2

Verify network printer installation on client computer(s).

Step 3

Verify network connectivity for computer that will not print.

Step 4

Verify installation of printer on directly connected computer.

Step 5

What steps did you perform to fix the printer?

_____

_____

_____

_____

_____

Remote Technician 14.6.3: Fix a Printer Problem

(Student Technician Sheet)

In this lab, you will gather data from the customer and then instruct the customer on how to fix a printer that does not print documents for a user. Document the customer's problem in the work order that follows:

Company Name: _Don's Delivery_

Contact: _Don Marley_

Company Address: _11 E. Main Street_

Company Phone: _1-866-555-0032_

Work Order

Generating a New Ticket

Category _Printer_   Closure Code _____   Status _Open_

Type _____   Escalated _Yes_   Pending _____

Item _____   Pending Until Date _____

Business Impacting? ☒ Yes ○ No

Summary _____

Case ID# _____   Connection Type _Ethernet_

Priority _2_   Environment _____

User Platform _Windows XP Pro_

Problem Description: _Printer is powered on. Cables are securely connected. Printer has_
ink and paper. Printer is installed as network printer on all client computers. Other users are able
to print to the printer.

Problem Solution: _____

(Student Customer Sheet)

Use the contact information and problem description to report the following information to a level-two technician:

Contact Information

Company Name: Don's Delivery

Contact: Don Marley

Company Address: 11 E. Main Street

Company Phone: 1-800-555-0032

Problem Description

I am not able to print documents on our printer. I tried turning the printer off and then back on, but I am still unable to print. The printer worked fine yesterday, but now, no documents print. Nobody has touched the printer since yesterday, and I do not understand why it will not print. What can I do to make my documents print?

Note: After you have given the level-two tech the problem description, use the Additional Information section to answer any follow-up questions the technician may ask.

Additional Information

Printer is hosted by dedicated computer on the network.

Printer is an all-in-one device.

Tech support fixed a similar problem for a user yesterday.

CHAPTER 15

Advanced Networks

The Study Guide portion of this chapter uses a combination of matching, fill-in-the-blank, and open-ended questions to test your knowledge of computer networks. This portion also includes multiple-choice study questions to help prepare you to take the A+ certification exams and to test your overall understanding of the material.

The Lab Exercises portion of this chapter includes all the online curriculum hands-on labs, worksheets, and remote technician exercises to further reinforce your mastery of the computer networks content.

Study Guide

OSI Model

With the goal of standardizing the network world, the International Organization for Standardization (ISO) began development of the Open Systems Interconnection (OSI) reference model. Today, the OSI reference model is the world's prominent networking architecture model. It is a popular tool for learning about networks.

Identify the OSI Layers

Complete the following table with the correct OSI layer names:

	OSI Layer	Devices and Addresses	Protocols
7.	Application	Host/Domain names	HTTP, Telnet, SMTP, POP3, DNS, DHCP, SMB
6.	Presentation		
5.	Session		
4.	Transport	Port numbers	TCP, UDP
3.	Network	Routers, IP addresses	IP, RIP, OSPF, ARP, ICMP
2.	Data Link	Bridges, switches, MAC addresses	Ethernet
1.	Physical	Cables, repeaters, hubs	

TCP/IP Protocol Suite

By far, the most popular protocol suite in use today is the TCP/IP protocol suite, which is the same protocol suite that is used by the Internet. Because most PCs need to connect to the Internet, you will need to be familiar with the TCP/IP protocol.

Vocabulary Exercise: Matching

Match the definition on the left with a term on the right.

Definitions

a. A connectionless protocol primarily responsible for addressing and routing packets between hosts.

b. Used to obtain hardware addresses (MAC addresses) of hosts located on the same physical network.

c. Sends messages and reports errors regarding the delivery of a packet.

d. Used by IP hosts to report host group membership to local multicast routers.

e. Provides connection-oriented, reliable communications for applications that typically transfer large amounts of data at one time or that require an acknowledgement for data received.

f. Provides connectionless communications and does not guarantee that packets will be delivered. Applications that use this typically transfer small amounts of data as one packet.

Terms

_b_ Address Resolution Protocol (ARP)

_c_ Internet Control Message Protocol (ICMP)

_d_ Internet Group Management Protocol (IGMP)

_a_ Internet Protocol (IP)

_e_ Transmission Control Protocol (TCP)

_f_ User Datagram Protocol (UDP)

Vocabulary Exercise: Matching

Match the definition on the left with a term on the right.

Definitions

a. Allows a user to transfer files between local and remote host computers.

b. A virtual terminal protocol (terminal emulation) allowing a user to log on to another TCP/IP host to access network resources.

c. The standard protocol for the exchange of electronic mail over the Internet.

d. A simple interface between a user's mail client software and e-mail user, used to download mail from the server to the client; it allows users to manage their mailboxes.

e. The basis for exchange over the World Wide Web (WWW) pages.

f. Defines the structure of Internet names and their association with IP addresses.

g. Used to automatically assign TCP/IP addresses and other related information to clients.

h. Allows users to share a file or printer.

Terms

_f_ Domain Name System (DNS)

_g_ Dynamic Host Configuration Protocol (DHCP)

_a_ File Transfer Protocol (FTP)

_e_ Hypertext Transfer Protocol (HTTP)

_c_ Post Office Protocol (POP)

_d_ Simple Mail Transfer Protocol (SMTP)

_b_ Telecommunication Network (Telnet)

_h_ Server Message Block (SMB)

Identify the TCP/IP Ports

TCP/IP ports are used to identify the upper-layer protocols and act as a switchboard to make sure that packets find their way to the right process. Therefore, it is important that you identify common application layer protocols and the well-known port numbers they use.

Identify the following TCP/IP ports:

Domain Name System (DNS): _____53_____

File Transfer Protocol (FTP): _____20 or 21_____

Hypertext Transfer Protocol (HTTP): _____80_____

Secure Socket Layer (SSL): _____

Simple Mail Transfer Protocol (SMTP): _25_____

Telecommunication Network (Telnet): _23/22_____

Dynamic Host Configuration Protocol (DHCP): _67_____

IP Addressing

The traditional version of the IP protocol is version 4: IPv4. Each connection on a TCP/IP network is assigned a unique IP address (logical address).

Concept Questions

Answer the following IP addressing questions.

How many bits is each IPv4 address?

32 bits

What is the format of each IP address?

Four sets of eight binary numbers (octets) each separated by a period

How are addresses assigned to a host?

Dynamic Host Configuration Protocol (DHCP)

What if two host are assigned the same address?

What is the function of the subnet mask?

To block out the network portions of an IP address.

What is the format of the subnet mask?

_____

_____

_____

If you want a computer to communicate with another computer on another network, what must you also specify?

___MAC Address_____

In traditional IPv4 addresses, the first octet will define which class the address is in. What are the ranges of the first octet that define each class, and what is the default subnet mask for each class?

Class A: _1- 126_____

Class B: _128 - 191_____

Class C: _192- 223_____

Because TCP/IP addresses are scarce for the Internet (based on the IPv4 and its 32-bit addressing structure), a series of addresses have been reserved to be used by the private networks. These addresses can be used by many organizations because these addresses are not seen from outside the local network. What are the ranges of these private addresses?

_____

_____

_____

How does a private address communicate over the Internet?

_____

_____

What is the limitation of NAT working with IPsec?

_____

Besides the IP address, subnet mask, and default gateway, what do you need to configure for an IP host to translate hostnames or domain names to IP addresses?

_____

Configuring Windows

Because Windows is the most popular operating system, it will not be long before you will have to configure Windows so that it can communicate with a network and to communicate over the Internet.

Concept Questions

Answer the following questions about configuring Windows.

Where can you enable or disable a network interface?

_____

_____

How do you share a folder in Windows XP?

_____

What is simple file sharing in Windows XP?

_____

How can you specify which users can access a shared folder on a newly installed computer running Windows XP?

_____

How do you map a network shared folder to a network drive letter that you can see under My Computer?

_____

_____

Troubleshooting Tools

Eventually, when connecting to a computer, you are going to encounter certain problems. Therefore, you will need to be familiar with the tools that are available.

Concept Questions

Answer the following questions about troubleshooting networks.

What command would you use to display all the IP address information, including the DNS servers being used and the MAC address on a Windows-based TCP/IP host?

_____

What command would you use to release the IPv4 address assigned to a client by a DHCP server?

_____

What command would you use to purge the DNS information that has already been cached by a Windows computer?

_____

What command can you use to test connectivity to PC.ACME.COM?

_____

If you suspect a bad cable, what can you do to test the cable? (Name three devices.)

_____

_____

Study Questions

Choose the best answer for each of the following questions:

1. Which protocol provides name resolution for host and domain names for a TCP/IP network?

   A. HTTP

   B. SNMP

   C. DNS

   D. Telnet

2. What protocol do you use to remotely connect to a TCP/IP host to execute commands at a command prompt?

   A. HTTP

   B. SNMP

   C. Telnet

   D. SNMP

3. What protocol in a TCP/IP network is used to send e-mail to another e-mail server?

   A. POP3

   B. SMTP

   C. SNMP

   D. IMAP

4. Which protocol is used to display web pages?

   A. HTTP

   B. SNMP

   C. SMPT

   D. Telnet

5. Which protocol is used to identify hosts using IP addresses?

   A. TCP

   B. SMTP

   C. IP

   D. DNS

6. What protocol allows you to share a folder or printer in Windows and other operating systems?

   A. ICMP

   B. TCP

   C. SMB

   D. RIP

7. What physical address that is assigned to a network interface is used to identify a PC with a 48-bit address?

   A. IPv4 address

   B. MAC address

   C. Host address

   D. Network address

8. What protocol is used to translate the IP address to the MAC address?

   A. ICMP

   B. IP

   C. TCP

   D. ARP

9. What is the default subnet mask of the IP address 199.160.3.250?

   A. 255.0.0.0

   B. 255.255.0.0

   C. 255.255.255.0

   D. 255.255.255.255

10. How many bits does an IPv4 address consist of?

    A. 24 bits

    B. 32 bits

    C. 48 bits

    D. 64 bits

11. Which address is referred to as loopback?

    A. 192.168.1.1

    B. 169.254.1.1

    C. 255.255.255.0

    D. 127.0.0.1

12. What feature simplifies the sharing of a folder that makes it available for everyone?

    A. ICMP

    B. Simple File Sharing

    C. NetBIOS

    D. Network Browser Service

13. What protocol assigns IP addresses as a host comes online and may give different addresses as the host goes online each time?

    A. DHCP

    B. Static

    C. DNS

    D. WINS

14. What tool is used to attach a RJ-45 connector to a UTP cable?

    A. UTP wire crimper

    B. Punch down tool

    C. Wire attachment kit

    D. DMM

15. What tool can you use to check for a break in a wire or cable?

    A. Punch down tool

    B. Optical tester

    C. Flashback analyzer

    D. Multimeter

16. What OSI layer does the IP address belong to?

    A. Physical

    B. Data link

    C. Network

    D. Transport

17. How fast is Fast Ethernet?

    A. 10 Mbps

    B. 100 Mbps

    C. 1 Gbps

    D. 10 Gbps

18. How fast is the 802.11g wireless solution?

    A. 10 Mbps

    B. 11 Mbps

    C. 54 Mbps

    D. 280 Mbps

19. You have a network card with an amber lighting continually flashing. What does the continually flashing amber light indicate?

    A. Data is being received by the computer.

    B. Transmission collisions are occurring.

    C. There is no network connection.

    D. The computer is communicating at 10 Mbps

20. What should you first check if a computer cannot connect to the network?

    A. Check for a link light on the network adapter.

    B. Check the TCP/IP settings on the computer.

    C. Verify that the network cable is good.

    D. Make sure that the switch is turned on and the PC is connected to the switch.

Lab Exercises

Worksheet 15.2.2: Protocols

In this activity, you will write the name of the protocol and the default port(s) for each protocol definition in the table.

Be prepared to discuss your answers.

Protocol Definition	Protocol	Default Port(s)
Provides connections to computers over a TCP/IP network		
Sends e-mail over a TCP/IP network		
Translates URLs to IP address		
Transports web pages over a TCP/IP network		
Automates assignment of IP address on a network		
Securely transports web pages over a TCP/IP network		
Transports files over a TCP/IP network		

Worksheet 15.3.2: ISP Connection Types

In this activity, you will determine the best ISP type for your customer.

Be prepared to discuss your answers.

Scenario 1

The customer lives in a remote area deep in a valley and cannot afford broadband.

Scenario 2

The customer can receive television only using satellite but lives in an area where high-speed Internet access is available.

Scenario 3

The customer is a salesperson who travels most of the time. A connection to the main office is required almost 24 hours a day.

Scenario 4

The customer works from home, needs the fastest possible upload and download speeds to access the company's FTP server, and lives in a very remote area where DSL and cable are not available.

Scenario 5

The customer wants to bundle television, Internet access and phone all through the same company, but the local phone company does not offer all the services.

Lab 15.4.2a: Configure Browser Settings

In this lab, you will configure browser settings in Microsoft Internet Explorer. You will select Internet Explorer as the default browser.

The following is the recommended equipment for this lab:

- A computer with Windows XP Professional installed

- An Internet connection

- Mozilla Firefox browser installed (from lab in Chapter 12)

Step 1

Choose Start, Run. Type **www.cisco.com** and press Return (see Figure 15-1).

Figure 15-1   Using the Run Option to Open the www.cisco.com Website

Which browser was used to open the web page?

_____

If you answered Internet Explorer:

Choose Start, All Programs, Mozilla Firefox, Mozilla Firefox.

Choose Tools, Options, and click the Main tab.

Click the Always Check to See if Firefox Is the Default Browser on Startup check box, and then click OK.

Restart your computer.

Choose Start, All Programs, Mozilla Firefox, Mozilla Firefox.

Click Yes to make Firefox the new default browser.

If you answered Firefox:

Choose Start, All Programs, Internet Explorer.

Choose Tools, Internet Options, and then click the Programs tab.

Click Internet Explorer Should Check to See Whether It Is the Default Browser, and then click OK.

Restart your computer.

Choose Start, All Programs, Internet Explorer.

Click Yes to make Internet Explorer the new default browser.

Step 2

Choose Start, Run. Type **www.cisco.com** and press Enter (see Figure 15-2).

Figure 15-2   Using the Run Option to Open the www.cisco.com Website

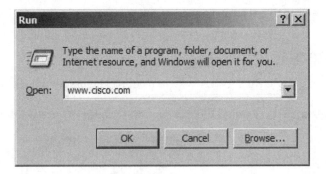

Which browser was used to open the web page this time?

_____

_____

Make Internet Explorer your default browser.

Open Internet Explorer, and then choose Help, About Internet Explorer (see Figure 15-3).

Figure 15-3   Opening the About Internet Explorer Window

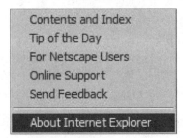

Which version of Internet Explorer is installed on your computer?

_____

Step 3

Choose Tools, Internet Options. The Internet Options window appears (see Figure 15-4).

Figure 15-4   The Internet Options Dialog Box

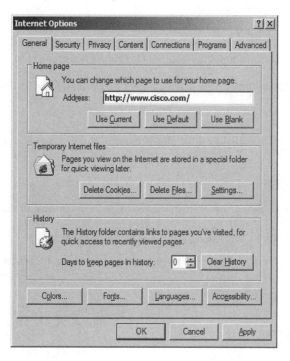

Click the Settings button, and then click the View Files button (see Figure 15-5).

Figure 15-5   Modifying the Temporary File Settings

How many temporary Internet files were listed?

_____

Close the Temporary Internet Files window.

Close the Settings window.

Choose Delete Files.

A confirmation window appears. Click the OK button.

Click the Settings button, and then click the View Files button.

How many temporary Internet files were listed?

_____

Step 4

Click the down arrow at the right end of the Address field to view previously visited sites (see Figure 15-6).

Figure 15-6   Viewing Previously Visited Sites

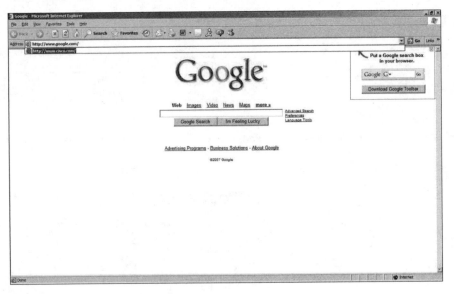

How many sites are listed in the drop-down box?

_____

To clear the browser history, choose Tools, Internet Options, and then click the Clear History button (see Figure 15-7).

Figure 15-7   Clearing Browser History

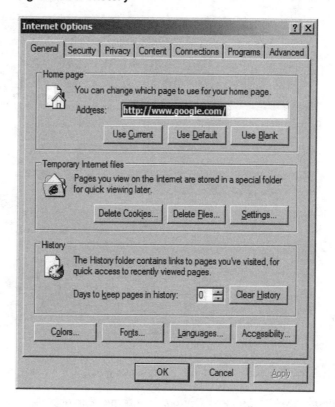

A confirmation window appears. Click Yes.

Click the down arrow at the right end of the Address field to view previously visited sites.

How many sites are now found in the drop-down box?

Step 5

Use this path to change Security settings:

Choose Tools, Internet Options, and then click the Security tab (see Figure 15-8).

Figure 15-8   Security Tab in Internet Explorer Options

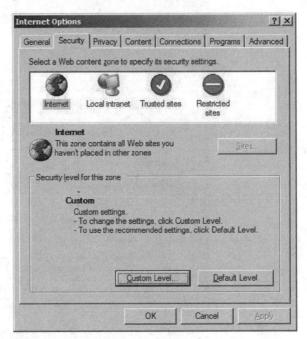

Click the Custom Level button. The Security Settings window appears (see Figure 15-9).

Figure 15-9   Security Options in Internet Explorer

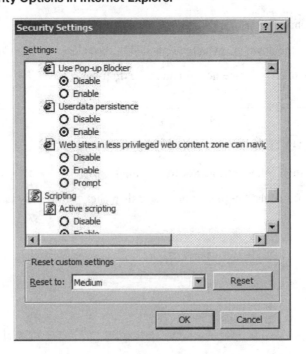

Select the options in the list that you want to change, and then click OK.

Lab 15.4.2b: Share a Folder, Share a Printer, and Set Share Permissions

In this lab, you will create and share a folder, share a printer, and set permissions for the shares.

The following is the recommended equipment for this lab:

- Two computers running Windows XP Professional that are directly connected to each other or through a switch or hub.

- A printer installed on one of the two computers.

Step 1

Choose My Computer, Tools, Folder Options.

Click the View tab (see Figure 15-10).

Figure 15-10   Folder Options in Windows Explorer

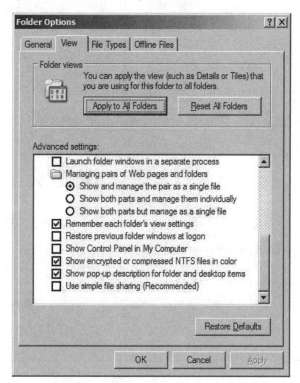

Uncheck the Use Simple File Sharing (Recommended) check box, and then click OK.

Step 2

Right-click the desktop, and then choose New, Folder.

Type **Example**, and then press Enter.

Open WordPad. Type **This Is an Example Document**.

Save the file in the Example folder with the name Brief.doc, and then close WordPad.

Step 3

Right-click the Example folder, and then choose Sharing and Security (see Figure 15-11).

Figure 15-11   The Sharing Tab in Internet Explorer Options

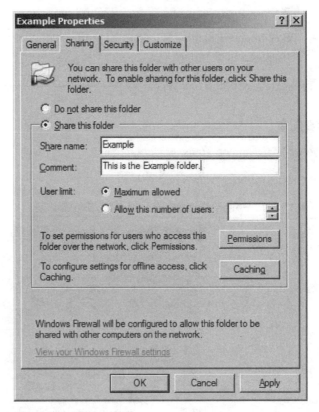

Click the Share This Folder option button, and then click OK.

What is the icon of the Example folder?

_____

On the computer with the shared folder, right-click My Computer, and then click the Computer Name tab.

What is the name of the computer?

_____

Step 4

On the other computer, choose Start, Run.

Type ***computername*\Example**, where *computername* is the name of the computer with the Example folder, and then press the Enter key.

Open the Brief.doc file.

Delete the text in the Brief.doc file and then choose File, Save.

What happens?

_____

Click OK.

Close WordPad, and then choose No when prompted to save changes to the file.

Step 5

Return to the computer with the shared folder.

Right-click Example folder, Sharing and Security, and then click Permissions.

What are the default permissions?

Step 6

Open the Control Panel on the computer with the attached printer.

Choose Printers and Other Hardware, Printers and Faxes.

Right-click the icon of the installed printer, and then choose Sharing (see Figure 15-12).

Figure 15-12   Sharing a Printer

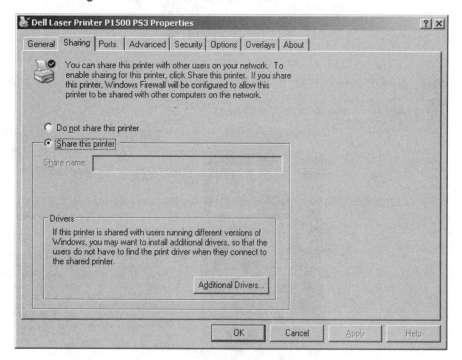

Click the Share This Printer option button, and then click OK.

Step 7

Return to the computer that is not directly connected to a printer.

Open the Control Panel. Choose Printers and Other Hardware, Printers and Faxes (see Figure 15-13).

Figure 15-13   Printer and Faxes Dialog Box with a Shared Printer as Marked by the Check Mark

Choose File, Add Printer. The Add Printer Wizard window appears (see Figure 15-14).

Figure 15-14   Add Printer Wizard

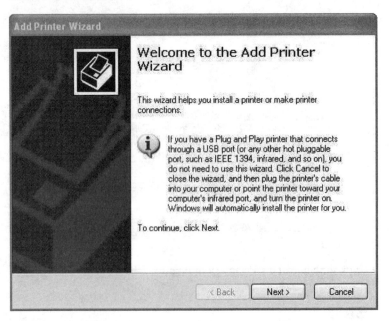

Click Next.

The Local or Network Printer of the Add Printer Wizard window appears. Click the A Network Printer, or a Printer Attached to Another Computer option button, and then click Next (see Figure 15-15).

Figure 15-15   Select Local or Network Printer in the Add Network Printer Wizard

The Specify a Printer window appears. Click the Connect to This Printer option button, and then click Next (see Figure 15-16).

Figure 15-16   Connecting to a Shared Printer Using the Add Printer Wizard

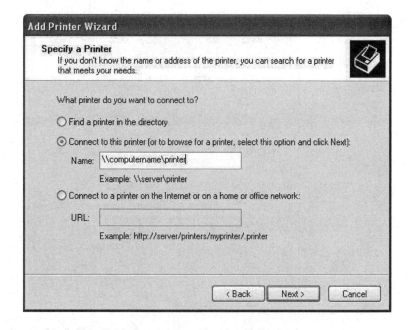

The Browse for a Printer window appears (see Figure 15-17).

Figure 15-17   Browsing to a Shared Printer in the Add Printer Wizard

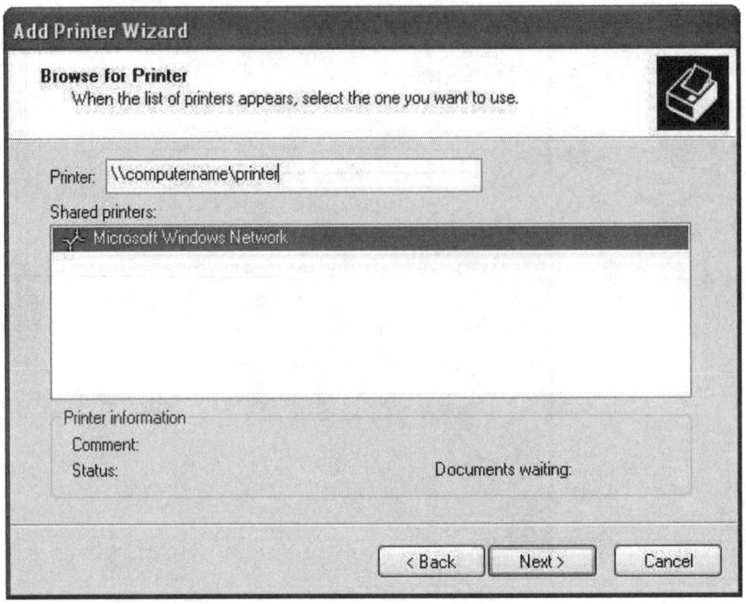

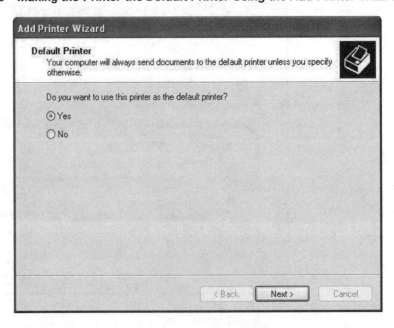

Expand Shared printers.

Choose the printer from the list, and then click Next. The Default Printer screen of the Add Printer Wizard appears (see Figure 15-18).

Figure 15-18   Making the Printer the Default Printer Using the Add Printer Wizard

Click Next. The Completing the Add Printer Wizard window appears.

Click Finish (see Figure 15-19).

Figure 15-19   Finishing the Add Printer Wizard

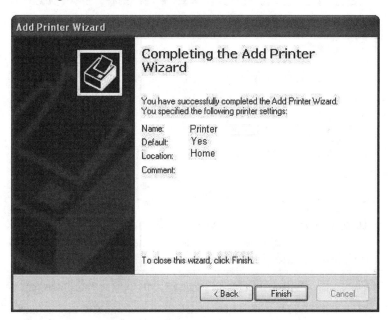

Step 8

Choose Start, Printers and Faxes.

Right-click the printer you installed, and then choose Properties. The Printer Properties window appears (see Figure 15-20).

Figure 15-20   Printer Options

Choose the General tab, and then click Print Test Page.

Click OK in the confirmation dialog box, and then click OK to close the printer properties window.

Lab 15.5.1: Install a Wireless NIC

In this lab, you will install and configure a wireless NIC.

The following is the recommended equipment for this lab:

- A computer with Windows XP Professional installed

- Empty PCI slot on the motherboard

- A wireless access point or router

- A wireless PCI NIC

Step 1

Turn off your computer. If a switch is present on the power supply, set the switch to 0 or Off. Unplug the computer from the AC outlet. Remove the side panels from the case. Put on the antistatic wrist strap and clip it to the case.

Choose an appropriate slot on the motherboard to install the new wireless NIC.

You might need to remove the metal cover near the slot on the back of the case (see Figure 15-21).

Figure 15-21 Removing the Metal Cover Near the Slot on the Back of the Case

Make sure the wireless NIC is properly lined up with the slot. Push down gently on the wireless NIC (see Figure 15-22).

Figure 15-22   Inserting the Wireless Network Card into the Slot

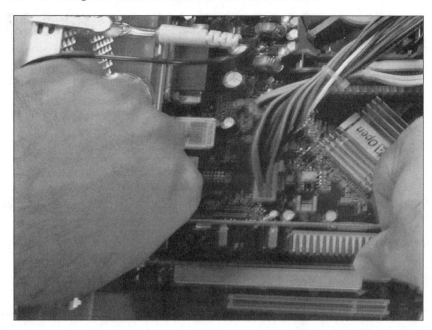

Secure the wireless NIC mounting bracket to the case with a screw (see Figure 15-23).

Figure 15-23   Securing the Wireless NIC

Attach the antenna to the antenna connector on the back of the computer.

Disconnect the antistatic wrist strap. Replace the case panels. Plug the power cable into an AC outlet. If a switch is present on the power supply, set the switch to 1 or On.

Step 2

Boot your computer, and then log on as an administrator.

The wireless NIC will be detected by Windows. The Found New Hardware Wizard window will appear (see Figure 15-24).

Figure 15-24   Starting the New Hardware Wizard

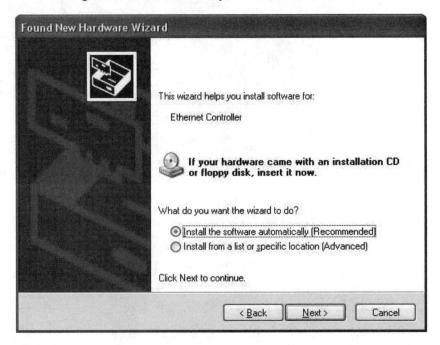

Click the Yes, This Time Only option button, and then click Next.

Insert the manufacturer's CD.

Click the Install the Software Automatically (Recommended) option button, and then click Next (see Figure 15-25).

Figure 15-25   Installing Software Automatically for a New Hardware Device

Step 3

Right-click My Computer and choose Manage.

Choose Device Manager, and then expand Network Adapters (see Figure 15-26).

Figure 15-26   Device Manager in Computer Management Console

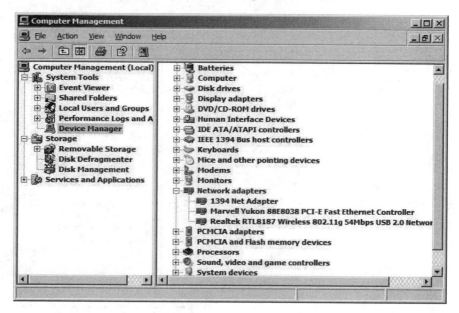

What network adapters are installed in the computer?

_____

Close the Computer Management window.

Step 4

Choose Start.

Right-click My Network Places, and then choose Properties.

Double-click the wireless NIC, and then click the Properties button.

Choose Internet Protocol (TCP/IP), and then click the Properties button (see Figure 15-27).

Figure 15-27   TCP/IP Properties

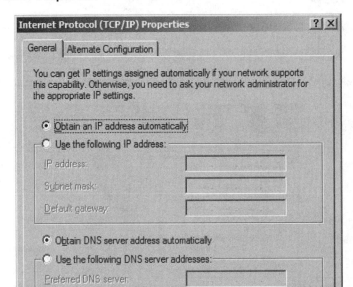

Click the Obtain an IP Address Automatically option button.

Click the Obtain DNS server address automatically option button.

Step 5

Choose Start, Run.

Type **cmd**, and then press the Enter key.

Type **ipconfig /all**, and then press the Enter key.

What is the IP address of the computer?

_____

What is the subnet mask of the computer?

_____

What is the default gateway of the computer?

_____

What are the DNS servers for the computer?

_____

What is the MAC address of the computer?

_____

Is DHCP Enabled?

_____

What is the IP address of the DHCP server?

_____

 # Lab 15.5.2: Configure a Wireless Router

In this lab, you will configure and test the wireless settings on the Linksys WRT300N.

The following is the recommended equipment for this lab:

- A computer with Windows XP Professional
- A Wireless NIC installed
- An Ethernet NIC installed
- Linksys WRT300N Wireless Router
- Ethernet patch cable

Step 1

Connect the computer to one of the Ethernet ports on the wireless router with an Ethernet patch cable.

Plug in the power of the wireless router. Boot the computer and log in as an administrator.

Step 2

Choose Start, Run, and type **cmd**. Press the Enter key.

Type **ipconfig**.

What is the default gateway for the computer?

_____

Step 3

Open Internet Explorer. Type **192.168.1.1** into the Address field, and then press Enter (see Figure 15-28).

Figure 15-28 Opening a URL Using Internet Explorer

The Connect to 192.168.1.1 window appears (see Figure 15-29).

Figure 15-29 Login Screen to a Wireless Switch

Type **admin** into the Password field.

The Setup screen appears.

Step 4

Click the Wireless tab.

Choose Mixed in the Network Mode drop-down box (see Figure 15-30).

Figure 15-30   Selecting the Network Mode for a Wireless Switch

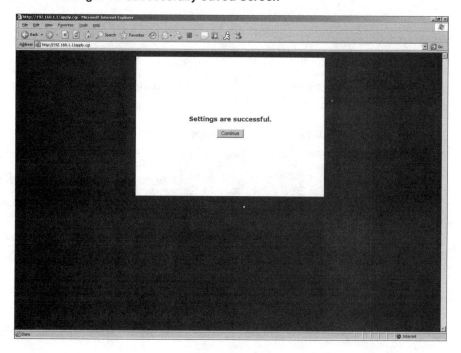

What is the default SSID for the wireless router?

_____

Type **cisco#** into the Network Name (SSID) field, where # is the number assigned by your instructor.

Click Save Settings. The Settings Are Successful screen appears (see Figure 15-31).

Figure 15-31   Settings Are Successfully Saved Screen

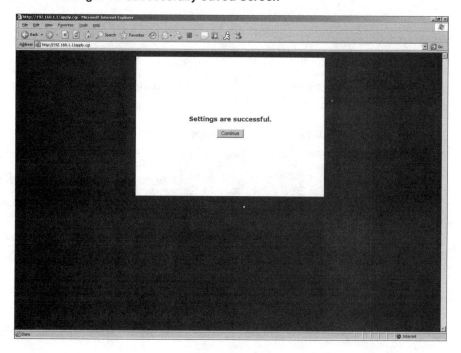

Click Continue, and then close the browser window.

Step 5

Unplug the Ethernet patch cable from the rear of the computer.

Choose Start, and then right-click My Network Places. Choose Properties.

Double-click the wireless adapter, and then select View Wireless Networks.

What wireless network(s) are available?

Choose cisco#, and then click the Connect button.

Open Internet Explorer, and then connect to the wireless router.

Log in to the wireless router.

Close Internet Explorer.

Lab 15.5.3: Test the Wireless NIC

In this lab, you will check the status of your wireless connection, investigate the availability of wireless networks, and test connectivity.

The following is the recommended equipment for this lab:

- A computer with Windows XP Professional installed
- A wireless NIC installed
- An Ethernet NIC installed
- Linksys WRT300N Wireless Router
- Internet connectivity

Step 1

Disconnect the Ethernet patch cable from your computer. A red X appears over the Local Area Connection icon (see Figure 15-32).

Figure 15-32   Disconnected Network Connection

Hover over the Wireless Network Connection icon in the tray (see Figure 15-33).

Figure 15-33   Pop-up Box Specifying the Speed of the Wireless Connection

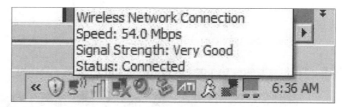

What is the speed and signal strength?

Open a command window. Ping 127.0.0.1 (see Figure 15-34).

Figure 15-34   Using the Ping Command to Test Network Connectivity

```
C:\WINDOWS\system32\cmd.exe                                        _ □ ×

C:\>ping 127.0.0.1

Pinging 127.0.0.1 with 32 bytes of data:

Reply from 127.0.0.1: bytes=32 time<1ms TTL=128
Reply from 127.0.0.1: bytes=32 time<1ms TTL=128
Reply from 127.0.0.1: bytes=32 time<1ms TTL=128
Reply from 127.0.0.1: bytes=32 time<1ms TTL=128

Ping statistics for 127.0.0.1:
    Packets: Sent = 4, Received = 4, Lost = 0 (0% loss),
Approximate round trip times in milli-seconds:
    Minimum = 0ms, Maximum = 0ms, Average = 0ms

C:\>
```

How many replies did you receive?

Use the **ipconfig** command (see Figure 15-35).

Figure 15-35   Using the ipconfig command to display the TCP/IP configuration.

```
C:\WINDOWS\system32\cmd.exe                                        _ □ ×

C:\>ipconfig

Windows IP Configuration


Ethernet adapter Local Area Connection:

        Media State . . . . . . . . . . . : Media disconnected

Ethernet adapter Wireless Network Connection:

        Connection-specific DNS Suffix  . :
        IP Address. . . . . . . . . . . . : 192.168.2.3
        Subnet Mask . . . . . . . . . . . : 255.255.255.0
        Default Gateway . . . . . . . . . : 192.168.2.1

C:\>
```

What is the IP address of the default gateway?

_____

Ping the default gateway (see Figure 15-36).

Figure 15-36   Using the ping Command to Ping the Default Gateway Address

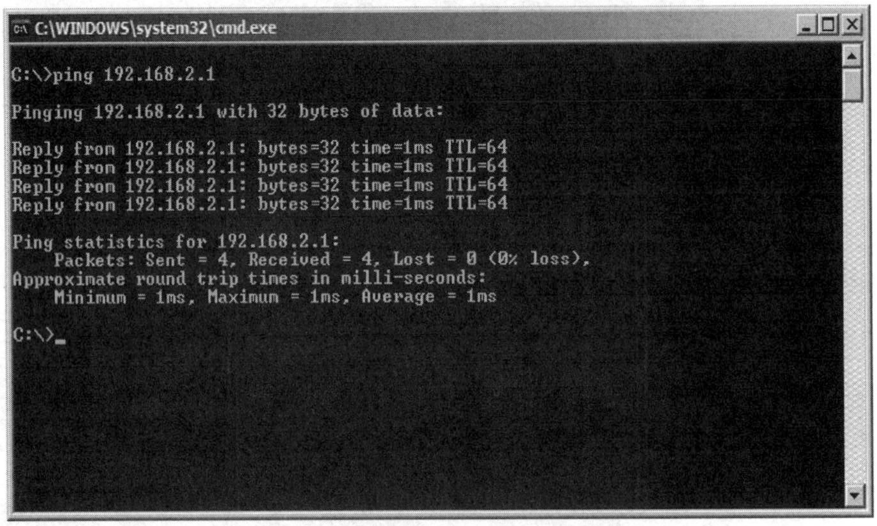

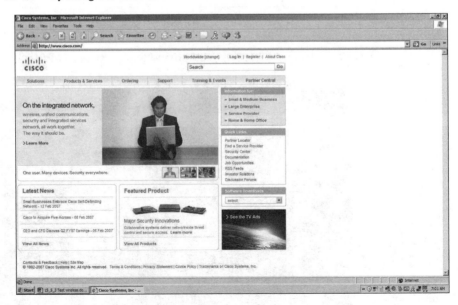

A successful ping indicates that there is a connection between the computer and the default gateway.

Step 2

Open a web browser.

Type **www.cisco.com** into the Address field, and then press Enter (see Figure 15-37).

Figure 15-37   Opening the www.cisco.com Website

Step 3

Open the Network Connections window (see Figure 15-38).

Figure 15-38   The Network Connections Window

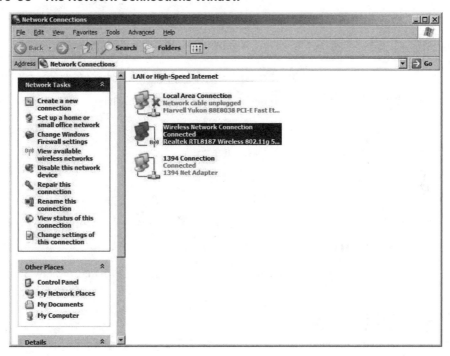

Right-click the wireless connection and choose Properties.

Click the Wireless Networks tab (see Figure 15-39).

Figure 15-39   Wireless Network Connection Properties Dialog Box

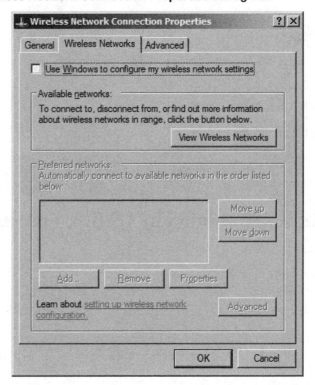

Click the View Wireless Networks button.

What are the names of the wireless networks that are available?

 # Lab 15.8.3: Fix Network Problem

In this lab, you will troubleshoot and fix a computer that does not connect to the network.

The following is the recommended equipment for this lab:

- A computer running Windows XP Professional
- Linksys 300N wireless router
- Ethernet patch cable

Scenario

The computer will not connect to the Internet, network shares, or network printers.

Step 1

Open a command line and use command-line tools to determine the IP address, subnet mask, and default gateway of the computer.

Step 2

Use command-line tools to attempt to fix the network connection problem.

Step 3

Verify the settings in the wireless router configuration screens.

Step 4

What steps did you perform to fix the network?

Remote Technician 15.8.3: Fix Network Problem

(Student Technician Sheet)

In this lab, you will gather data from the customer and then instruct the customer on how to fix a computer that does not connect to the network. Document the customer's problem in the work order that follows.

Company Name: __JH Paint Supply__
Contact: __Jill Henderson__
Company Address: __114 W. Main Street__
Company Phone: __1-866-555-2143__

Work Order

Generating a New Ticket

Category __Network__   Closure Code _____   Status __Open_____

Type _____   Escalated __Yes_____   Pending _____

Item _____   Pending Until Date _____

Business Impacting? ☒ Yes ○ No

Summary __One computer cannot connect to the Internet, network shares, or network printers.__

Case ID# _____   Connection Type __Wireless_____
Priority __2_____   Environment _____
User Platform __Windows XP Pro_____

Problem Description: __All computers boot up properly. Computer does not connect to shares or the__
__Internet. Computer has not been moved. Cables are securely connected. Link lights are blinking.__

Problem Solution: _____

(Student Customer Sheet)

Use the following contact information and problem description to report the following information to a level-two technician:

Contact Information

Company Name: JH Paint Supply

Contact: Jill Henderson

Company Address: 114 W. Main Street

Company Phone: 1-866-555-2143

Problem Description

Well, the problem does not always seem to be there. Typically, not all computers on the network are used all of the time, so everything seems to be fine. On some busy days, every computer is being used and there is always one computer that cannot connect. I cannot figure out what the problem is because it is not usually on the same computer. When a computer cannot make connectivity, I check to make sure all cables and connections are fine.

Note: After you have given the level-two tech the problem description, use the Additional Information to answer any follow-up questions the technician may ask.

Additional Information

Windows XP Pro.

Computer has no new hardware.

Computer has not been moved recently.

An extra computer was added to the network recently.

Computer looks the same as it did yesterday.

CHAPTER 16

Advanced Security

The Study Guide portion of this chapter uses short-answer questions to test your knowledge of advanced computer security. This portion also includes multiple-choice study questions to help prepare you to take the A+ certification exams and to test your overall understanding of the material.

The Lab Exercises portion of this chapter includes all the online curriculum hands-on labs, worksheets, remote technician exercises, and class discussions to further reinforce your mastery of advanced computer security.

Study Guide

Access Control

Access control is the process by which you restrict access to computing resources. It is a combination of authentication (proving who you claim to be) and authorization (what are you allowed to see, presuming you are whom you claim you are). It defines how users and systems communicate and in what manner. Access control allows you to enforce the security principle of least privilege, which states that individuals authorized to access resources are permitted access to them. In other words, access control protects information from unauthorized access.

The following are the three basic models for access control:

- *Discretionary access control (DAC):* Owners of objects (such as programs, processes, files, or folders) manage access control at their own discretion.

- *Mandatory access control (MAC):* Access to an object is restricted based on the sensitivity of the object (defined by the label or level that is assigned) and granted through authorization (clearance) to access that level of data.

- *Role-based access control (RBAC):* Access is based on the role a user plays in the organization.

Concept Questions

Answer the following access control questions.

Which of the basic models does Microsoft Windows 2000 and XP use?

_____

In Windows, what is used to enable a user to log on to a computer and domain with an identity that can be authenticated and authorized for access to domain resources?

_____

What is a collection of user accounts that can simplify administration by assigning rights and permissions to a set of users?

_____

The default installation of Windows 2000 has two user accounts. What are the two accounts?

_____

_____

Of the two accounts, what can you say about the initial availability of the guest account?

_____

What are the two types of user accounts available on your computer?

_____

_____

Explain the capability of the computer administrator account.

_____

_____

_____

Explain the capabilities of the Windows XP limited account.

_____

_____

NTFS and Share Permissions

A primary advantage of NTFS over FAT and FAT32 is that NTFS volumes have the capability to apply NTFS permissions to secure folders and files, no matter whether the files and folders are accessed directly or through a share.

Concept Questions

Answer the following questions about NTFS and share permissions.

List the standard NTFS folder permissions and describe what they can do.

- _____

- _____

  _____

- _____

- _____

  _____

- _____

  _____

- _____

  _____

  _____

Share permissions apply only when the folder is accessed as a shared folder. What are the shares permissions available in Windows and describe what they can do?

- _____

  _____

- _____

  _____

■ _____

_____

When you share a folder, Microsoft recommends that you give everyone Full Control permission and then use the NTFS permissions to specify who can access the folders and files and what can be done with the files and folders.

Auditing

Trying to detect intruders can be a very daunting task; it often requires a lot of hard work and a thorough knowledge of the operating system and the network. To detect these intruders, you have to establish auditing, which is the process that tracks the activities of users by recording selected types of events in the security log of a server or workstation.

Concept Questions

Answer the following questions about auditing.

If you enable auditing, where do you view the security logs in Windows?

_____

In Windows XP, how do you enable auditing?

_____

_____

Depending on how the logs in the Event Viewer are configured, you may fill up the logs. How do you clear the logs?

_____

Wireless Security

Wireless technologies bring with them special security concerns. You should be familiar with how to secure wireless devices.

Concept Questions

Answer the following questions about wireless security.

What is required to set up a secure wireless connection?

_____

If you are implementing WEP, what do you need to connect to an access point?

_____

Why are WPA and WPA2 recommended over WEP?

_____

What is the difference between WPA and WPA2?

_____

_____

_____

What is the difference between Personal and Enterprise modes?

_____

_____

How do you prevent a wireless network from being displayed when you view wireless networks in Windows?

_____

_____

Social Engineering

When it comes to your organization, you will find that people and knowledge are the organization's greatest assets. However, they can also be the greatest risks, often making them the weakest link when it comes to security. Even at their best, people make mistakes. They fail to see the issues or do not appreciate the consequences. Sometimes, bad judgment or failure to communicate clearly can be the root of the problem.

To minimize the problems caused by people, established systems procedures and rules can be accepted by the user without causing too much hindrance. You must establish a security awareness program. Security must be sold to your users; they must understand and accept the need for security. In addition, you have to train your users about security and give them constant reminders.

One of the simplest, yet often the most effective, attacks is *social engineering*. Social engineering is the process whereby an attacker attempts to acquire information about your network and system by talking to people in the organization. A social engineering attack may occur over the phone, by e-mail, or by a visit. The intent is to acquire access information, such as user IDs and passwords, or physical access to a secure area. These types of attacks are relatively low tech, very similar to a con done by a con artist, and the hardest attacks to defend against.

Concept Questions

Answer the following question about social engineering.

What are preventive measures in dealing with social engineering attacks?

_____

_____

_____

_____

Denial of Services Attacks and Other Forms of Attacks

An attacker does not necessarily have to gain access to cause significant problems. Denial of Services (DoS) is a type of attack on a network that is designed to bring the network to its knees either by disabling or crippling a server or by flooding it with useless traffic. Many DoS attacks, such as the Ping of Death and Teardrop attacks, exploit limitations in the TCP/IP protocols. Other attacks are application specific, which strike at specific flaws within the program.

A Denial of Service attack can also destroy programming and files in a computer. Although usually intentional and malicious, a Denial of Service attack can sometimes happen accidentally. For all known DoS attacks, system administrators can install software fixes to limit the damage caused by the attacks. But, like viruses, new DoS attacks are constantly being dreamed up by hackers.

Distributed Denial of Services (DDoS) attacks involve installing programs known as zombies on various computers in advance of the attack. A command is issued to these zombies, which then launch the attack on behalf of the attacker, thus hiding their tracks. The zombies themselves are often installed using worms. The real danger from a DDoS attack is that the attacker uses many victim computers as host computers to control other zombies that initiate the attack, which results in overwhelming the attacked system.

Concept Questions

Answer the following questions about attacks.

Define the following forms of attacks:

- *Hijacking:* _____

    _____

- *Man-in-the-middle attack:* _____

    _____

    _____

    _____

- *Replay attack:* _____

    _____

    _____

    _____

- *Spoofing attack* _____

    _____

    _____

To crack passwords and keys, some people will try different combinations of characters until the password or key is found. What is this type of attack called?

_____

Another common form of attack is malicious software. Describe the following:

- *Virus:* _____

  _____

  _____

- *Trojan horse* _____

  _____

  _____

How do you protect your system against DoS attacks and malicious software?

- _____

- _____

- _____

- _____

Study Questions

Choose the best answer for each of the questions that follow:

1. Which file system allows the user to assign permissions to files and folders?

   A. FAT

   B. FAT32

   C. NTFS

   D. CDFS

2. What is a task that limited accounts cannot perform in Windows XP?

   A. Cannot connect to the Internet

   B. Cannot install software

   C. Cannot run programs

   D. Cannot access their e-mail

3. Where would you find the security logs for a Windows 2000 or Windows XP machine?

   A. In the security logs in the Event Viewer

   B. In the security.log file found in the C:\WINDOWS folder

   C. In the security.log file found in the C:\ folder

   D. In the Login.log file found in the C:\WINNT folder

4. When connecting to a wireless access point that is using WEP, what do you need to connect to the access point?

   A. The WEP key and the SSID

   B. The IP address of the access point

   C. The Admin password of the access point

   D. The encrypted key

5. If you want to connect to a wireless access point, what two items do you need to know?

    A.   The brand and model of the access point

    B.   The frequency of the access point

    C.   The SSID and encryption standard being used

    D.   The wireless technology being used

6. When you get an e-mail that says it came from a different domain than it really came from, this is known as _____.

    A.   A brute force attack

    B.   A DDoS attack

    C.   A man-in-the-middle attack

    D.   A spoofing attack

7. What type of attack is it when an attacker takes over a session between a server and client?

    A.   A DoS attack

    B.   A DDoS attack

    C.   A session hijacking

    D.   A spoofing attack

8. What is the type of attack that works by getting other people to trust the attacker?

    A.   Spoofing

    B.   Man-in-the-middle

    C.   Social engineering

    D.   DoS

9. What is the best way to protect against viruses?

    A.   Use NTFS permissions.

    B.   Use an up-to-date antivirus software.

    C.   Be sure to use strong passwords.

    D.   Do not use e-mail on a system.

10. Which of the following uses TKIP and a preshared key?

    A.   WPA-Personal mode

    B.   WPA-Enterprise mode

    C.   WPA2-Personal mode

    D.   WPA2-Enterprise mode

Lab Exercises

Worksheet 16.1.1: Answer Security Policy Questions

In this activity, you will answer security questions regarding the IT Essentials classroom.

1. List the person(s) responsible for each piece of network equipment that is used in your classroom (for example, routers, switches, and wireless access points).

_____

2. List the person(s) responsible for the computers that are used in your classroom.

_____

3. List the person(s) responsible for assigning permissions to use the network resources.

_____

4. Which Internet websites do you have permission to access?

_____

_____

_____

5. What type of Internet websites are not permitted to be accessed in the classroom?

_____

_____

6. List activities that could damage the network or the computers attached to the network with malware.

_____

7. Should anyone, other than the network administrator, be allowed to attach modems or wireless access points to the network? Please explain why or why not.

_____

_____

Worksheet 16.2.3: Research Firewalls

In this activity, you will use the Internet, a newspaper, or a local store to gather information about hardware and software firewalls.

1. Using the Internet, research two hardware firewalls. Based on your research, complete the table that follows:

Company/ Hardware Name	Website URL	Cost	Subscription Length (Month/Year/Lifetime)	Hardware Features

2. Which hardware firewall would you purchase? List reasons for your selection.

_____

_____

_____

_____

_____